THIS IS THE STORY OF A FAMILY AS TOLD THROUGH FOOD. Judy, the family matriarch, speaks to preserving the traditions she grew up with in China and regional Chinese foodways. Bill, the dad, calls on his experience cooking in his family's Chinese restaurant to explain the techniques behind classic dishes. Daughters Sarah and Kaitlin have your vegetable-forward and easy weeknight recipes covered. Put them all together, and you have the first cookbook from the funny and poignant family behind the hugely popular multigenerational blog, *The Woks of Life*.

You'll find a compendium of go-to, accessible, and essential Chinese recipes, from Pork & Shrimp Siu Mai and Spicy Beef Biang Biang Noodles to Cantonese Pork Belly Fried Rice and Salt-and-Pepper Fried Oyster Mushrooms. Helpful tips and tricks appear throughout, including an elaborate rundown of the Chinese pantry, explanations of essential tools (including the all-important wok), and game-changing Chinese cooking secrets, like how to "velvet" meat to make it extra tender and juicy.

Whether you're new to Chinese cooking or you already dabble in bean paste and chili oil, you'll find inspiration from this chorus of voices and trustworthy recipes that will become a part of your family story, too.

THE WOKS OF LIFE

Recipes to Know and Love
from a Chinese American Family

For the curious and
hungry readers of
The Woks of Life,
our extended family

THE WOKS OF LIFE

Bill, Judy, Sarah & Kaitlin Leung

FOOD PHOTOGRAPHS BY
SARAH LEUNG & KAITLIN LEUNG

LIFESTYLE PHOTOGRAPHS BY
CHRISTINE HAN

Clarkson Potter/Publishers
New York

Contents

Stuck with Each Other

Some say that between your previous life and the next life, you choose your family. Others say that you stay with the same people from lifetime to lifetime—in the same boat, but perhaps in slightly different seats.

In our family, it certainly feels like this isn't our first rodeo. Bill and Judy meet, marry, and have daughters Sarah and Kaitlin—each personality seemingly carved in stone and each more strong willed than the last.

While most people find it easier to forge their own path in the world at least an arm's length from their family, we've found ourselves doing just the opposite. Despite our aforementioned strong-willed personalities, we're together *a lot*, spending inordinate amounts of time deliberating shrimp placement and the correct temperature for chili oil. It's all in the name of *The Woks of Life*, a food blog we started in 2013 to document our family's history through recipes—some from old-world Shanghai, others from a Chinese restaurant kitchen in the Catskills. Many

were inspired by the streets of Flushing, Queens, and countless more were dreamt up in our home kitchen in a New Jersey suburb. Through food, we've preserved collective decades of experience, spanning parents, grandparents, aunts, cousins, and friends.

When someone asks us how we manage to pull it off, you can see in their eyes the mental flash of their own family dynamic, usually followed by a slow head shake of utter disbelief that anyone could take on such an endeavor with their parents, siblings, or kids. Recording your family's heritage and history can be daunting. A few rough edges are inevitable—and trust us, we've had our fair share. But we also choose to work together in the same way that we might have chosen our family in the cosmic "before."

Growing up, Judy would ask Sarah and Kaitlin: "Are you glad you chose us as your parents?" The answer is here, in this book, and also on *The Woks of Life*.

We're all here. For our personal histories, for the web of memories and pathways that we share with so many around the world, and, yes . . . we're here for the food.

How did we end up here?

Our family cares a lot about food. Like, a weird amount. It's hard to say exactly when and why it's gotten to the level that it has, but we'll try to explain.

JUDY

Bill and I both come from immigrant families. He lived with his two sisters and their parents, Cantonese immigrants who came to the US in the 1940s and '50s, in Liberty, New York. Liberty was one of many little upstate towns collectively known as the "Borscht Belt," a popular summer destination for Jewish families from New York City that had its heyday from the 1920s to the 1960s. I lived just a stone's throw away in Monticello, after leaving Shanghai with my family when I was sixteen.

For both Bill and me, food was a life raft that connected our families to where they came from. In Bill's small town, penny pinching was just a way of life for a working family. As for me, back in China, we were downright poor, and money was still tight after we moved to America. Food became an everyday treasure that anchored our days, and we worked to maximize enjoyment and ensure that little went to waste. Nothing felt more like home than an afternoon spent making dozens of dumplings to stash away for future busy weekdays or preparing a special poached chicken for a night of mahjong with friends.

Bill learned to cook from his father and stepfather—both chefs—and his mother, an excellent home cook. Cooking was one of the most common jobs for immigrant Chinese men in those days, so learning how to prepare and enjoy food was a valuable skill. When Bill and I first started dating, we both helped run Sun Hing, his parents' restaurant. Fast-forward through our early days as newlyweds in the late '80s, and along came Sarah and Kaitlin, both before I turned twenty-six. With two American babies and me still improving my English, ready or not, parenthood was in full gear.

SARAH AND KAITLIN

With two parents who take food seriously and know how to enjoy it, dinner at our house has always been an all-hands-on-deck event. Building familiarity in the kitchen began with little tasks here and there—trimming vegetables, taste testing (rather, snagging bits of roast duck before it got to the table), and remembering to make the rice.

Then there were the little lessons we learned along the way, like how to reveal the tender chunks of fillet from a whole steamed fish, the finer points of sandwich construction (i.e., how to not end up with a giant wad of roast beef hanging from your teeth), and how to mix up a bowl of cold noodles with just spaghetti, soy sauce, and sesame oil. "What's for dinner?" was the omnipresent question, and the dinner table was where we always came together.

Paging through cookbooks became our favorite hobby, and on weekends we played chef and sous chef and devoured old *Iron Chef* reruns (the original Japanese version). Soon, we were trying out new recipes for family parties and juggling mixing bowls and roasting pans on Thanksgiving.

Aside from being our favorite hobby, cooking became the medium that moderated the full spectrum of our family's life. When we visited our grandparents, preparing an elaborate dinner was the activity that facilitated the exchange of gossip and questions about how school was going. For every family argument, there was the plate of dumplings to ruminate over. And to break through an icy cold shoulder between sisters, there was the begrudging snack break of instant noodles that made it hard to remember what we were mad about in the first place.

Those years were the build-up to the food fanatics that we now are. Little did we know that the eternal question, "What's for dinner?" would become the only constant after our parents moved halfway across the globe.

BILL

Call it a shock when, in 2011, we suddenly found ourselves at different corners of the world. When a new work assignment came knocking at my company, Judy and I relocated to Beijing. We put our New Jersey house into hibernation, loaded our suitcases with bulk-size jars of peanut butter and two-pound bags of coffee beans (priorities!), and headed east. Kaitlin found herself navigating her freshman year of college solo in Philadelphia, and Sarah was starting her senior year of college in the Hudson Valley.

In China, Judy quickly became our translator, interpreter, and guide. She organized weekend trips to check out Xi'an night markets, old water villages just outside of Shanghai, the Harbin ice festival, and other destinations where we could discover new flavors outside our Shanghainese and Cantonese roots. It wasn't long before we realized how little we had really explored the vast universe of Chinese cuisine.

KAITLIN

Armed with just a microwave and a very small student budget, I hunted for the flavors of my childhood in college cafeterias and Philadelphia's food trucks, all between doing mountains of homework and odd jobs around campus. Suddenly, we didn't have the benefit of a nightly family dinner to stay up to date on our day-to-day comings and goings, let alone what was for dinner.

To solve this problem, we passed pictures of food back and forth via text. There was a quick snapshot of my dorm cafeteria breakfast, and the grainy picture of the all-nighter bowl of instant noodles I'd dolled up with some kimchi. For Sarah, there were perfectly roasted chickens and experiments in pasta. My parents would send close-ups of Friday night dinners out, paper bags filled with shaobing (think cross between a biscuit and a scallion pancake), or a tray of glistening braised pork hocks from a street vendor. Everything as innocuous as a subpar muffin to a container of coveted Chinese New Year leftovers from my grandparents was worth sharing and commenting on.

Summers off were spent in Beijing together. There were strolls through winding hutongs (alleys) and trips to the local market, where farmers sold seasonal vegetables, fruits, pickles, handmade dumpling wrappers, and fresh tofu. It seemed that every time we stepped out the door, we found new things to eat, like hand-pulled Lanzhou noodles with fragrant chili oil, a plate of stir-fried wild greens we'd never seen before, or a batch of beef and tomato dumplings.

SARAH

As a senior in college, I was finally off the school meal plan, with an apartment and a kitchen to cook in. While I craved the food of my childhood more than anything else, I became starkly aware of how little I knew about my parents' cooking when confronted by the a-little-of-this, a-little-of-that "recipes" they relayed to me over the phone. To make my mom's braised pork belly, I was told, "You need soy sauce and wine. Just add it until it looks like enough!" Which soy sauce? What kind of wine? How much would I need for my one pound of pork?

I needed more instructions—clearer recipes. The logical thing to do was to record them somewhere so we could all go back to them again and again, with access to them forever. Kaitlin and I were already avid food blog readers, but we couldn't find any recipes that tasted like home. After graduating from college, demoralized by my job search and unsure of what to do next, I bought a camera and began laying the groundwork for the blog.

It felt obvious that all four of us would contribute to it. Each of us brought knowledge to the table: My dad had the American Chinese takeout recipes down pat, the restaurant secrets, and the Cantonese home-cooking chops. My mom brought recipes from Shanghai and the surrounding region, and a mission to preserve the traditions she grew up with in China. My sister and I came with the desire to learn, a penchant for creating shortcuts and quick recipes, and the ability to draw clarity from our parents' generation's informal cook-by-feel approach.

Our first recipes were for the foods we grew up on, like Red Braised Pork Belly with Eggs (page 189), Blanched Greens with Oyster Sauce (page 232), and Classic Scallion Pancakes (page 70). By the time we ran out of those, I had interviewed for a job in Beijing and moved in with my parents. Inspired by the plethora of good eats across the city, we began tackling dishes we never thought we could make at home, pushing ourselves to figure out a complex dim sum item, little-known technique, or that just-right balance of ingredients.

We published blog posts to update each other as much as our extremely small readership—to share thoughts, stories, and memories associated with each dish. But as our roster of recipes grew, more and more comments came in from readers—the parent of an adopted child from China, someone who was able to re-create a dish from their favorite childhood restaurant, and another family who'd finally found something akin to their grandma's long-since-forgotten congee recipe. It became abundantly clear that we weren't the only ones who wanted to preserve these recipes. A diverse audience was hungry to learn more.

......

Our blog—and this book—reflects on the dishes woven into the fabric of our lives, from generation to generation in our family, and maybe in yours too. Chinese cuisine has almost two hundred years of history in America, and regardless of whether or not you're Chinese, you probably have memories associated with some of these dishes.

We cover a wide range of Chinese recipes, from homey Cantonese classics to the Americanized Chinese food common in many restaurants. There are recipes that bring to mind a mom's or grandma's cooking (together, we can save them from fading into obscurity!), as well as recipes based on travels and research that represent Chinese regional cuisines beyond our roots. Some are all about tradition. Others blend old and new.

We take food seriously. Sometimes comically so, and sometimes to the detriment of a happy and harmonious household. And for some reason, it never gets old. We're always wondering what our next meal will be. Because for us, food is never *just* about the recipe; it's also about how you enjoy it, share it, and pass it on.

A family timeline

1964: Bill is born in Liberty, New York.

1967: Judy is born in Shanghai, China.

1983: Judy's family immigrates to Monticello, New York (a fated 12 miles from Liberty).

That same year, Bill's parents open Sun Hing, the family's Chinese restaurant in New Jersey, while Bill is in college.

1985: Judy's grandmother and Bill's mother (longtime friends) hatch a plan to set up Judy and Bill.

1986: Bill and Judy meet. Judy asks a now-infamous question: "Do you want my number or not?"

1989: Bill and Judy are married. (Despite being nearly swallowed by puffs of '80s satin and lace, Judy makes it out alive.)

1990: Sarah is born.

1992: Kaitlin is born. (Sarah has mixed emotions.)

1997: The family visits China for the first time together. Much food is consumed despite the jet lag.

2008: Fast forward: Sarah heads to college, separating the family for the first time and beginning the eternal conversation: "What did you eat for dinner?"

2011: Bill and Judy temporarily move to Beijing. Sarah and

Kaitlin, both in college, survive with tiny rice cookers, instant noodles, and shelf-stable tofu.

2013: Sarah decides to take postgrad life into her own hands and starts *The Woks of Life*. All four of us climb aboard. Later that year, she

moves to Beijing to join Bill and Judy.

2014: Reunited and it feels so good! Potentially more important: the discovery of the best chili oil ever (page 275), a life-changing moment.

2015: The pace picks up, and recipe content shifts from family favorites to dishes we never thought we could make. A recipe for sesame balls is attempted, frying explosions occur, and it is shelved for the safety of all involved . . .

2016: The blog hits a new traffic milestone: over 1 million pageviews per month!

2019: Sarah begins working on *The Woks of Life* full time. We begin affectionately referring to the blog as "the train that won't stop running."

2020: The most harebrained test of family bonds yet: we decide to write a cookbook, spending day and night testing recipes throughout the pandemic. (Also, we somehow manage to nail that recipe for sesame balls.)

2021: Sarah ties the knot, and her husband, Justin (new family tiebreaker and dishwasher extraordinaire), joins the family at the start of a summer filled with cookbook photo shoots.

2022: The book you're holding in your hands is published!

Who's Who

Without each of our unique perspectives, *The Woks of Life* simply wouldn't be what it is. So, let us introduce ourselves.

BILL / DAD/HUSBAND

I worked in restaurants throughout high school and college, learning techniques and restaurant secrets from my father and then stepfather, both chefs. I also learned to cook from my mother, whose generosity and spirit of sharing I always try to live up to. My mother and stepfather eventually opened a restaurant of their own, and when Judy and I began dating and later started a family, we were there through the stacks of egg rolls and endless orders of beef and broccoli. I aim to bring the same wok smarts from those days into recipes that span Chinese takeout, dim sum, banquet dishes, and Cantonese home cooking.

JUDY / MOM/WIFE

I grew up in Hubei and Shanghai in the midst of the Cultural Revolution, then moved to America at the age of sixteen. Calling my experience a culture shock would be putting it mildly! It took a while for me to grow an appreciation for the foods and flavors of America, though meeting Bill when I was nineteen helped ease the transition. My recipes often reflect my desire to preserve the foods and traditions I grew up with, as well as recipes from other regions of China that I've come to learn and deeply appreciate.

SARAH / DAUGHTER/OLDER SISTER

You could say that *The Woks of Life* was the result of my growing desperation as a jobless recent college graduate who couldn't stomach another career fair or half-baked attempt at my parents' cooking. I'll do anything it takes to recreate a taste memory, but I also love developing recipes with smart workarounds that get you results with less time or effort and are just as good as the old ways (even if my mom disagrees with the shortcut!). I'm all about efficiency and organization, and as Kaitlin says, big sister energy runs through my veins!

KAITLIN / DAUGHTER/YOUNGER SISTER

Born just in time to savor the peak of the '90s (hi, listening to N*SYNC while eating chicken tenders, i.e., my childhood idea of nirvana), some say I'm notorious for being unable to follow a recipe. I call this "freestyling"—sometimes with mixed results—but the upside of cooking by instinct and mad inspiration is that I often stumble on new combinations or ways of doing things. In a family of overachievers, I still do pretty well for myself. The day my chili oil (page 275) became the top result on Google just about made me cry.

Before You Begin . . .

The one hundred recipes in our cookbook are for every generation and, yes, for every ~~wok~~ walk of life. While we fully recognize that we will never have a 100 percent comprehensive review of the vast depths of Chinese cooking, we like to think of ourselves as studious strivers, always aspiring to learn more. We also know from experience that our readers are looking to deepen their knowledge as well.

To that effect, we've built in handy QR codes throughout the book to reference more in-depth techniques and to highlight other useful content on the blog. We hope that you scan them and use them. Also, whenever we mention other content within this book, we've included page numbers for easy reference.

We have also provided serving suggestions in our recipes with the understanding that many are meant to be served with additional dishes and perhaps rice to round things out. An appetizer may serve four as a light starter, or more if you add a couple other starters to serve alongside it. Similarly, a meat dish that uses 12 ounces of meat but feeds four is meant to be enjoyed along with one to two other dishes.

Some recipes, like our Garlic Chive & Shrimp Dumplings (page 35) or Hong Kong Egg Tarts (page 31), require a bit more precision. In those cases we've included metric weight measurements in addition to cup and spoon measures to help you achieve the optimal result. If you prefer cooking entirely with metric, scan the QR code at right for a conversion chart.

Metric Conversions

Our Cookbook Comment Page

As bloggers who constantly interact with our readers, we'd also love to hear from you! Whether you have a cooking question or just want to share your experiences with this book, head to our dedicated cookbook comment page.

Cooking Tools

We aren't pointing out colanders and sheet pans here—
we assume you already have those! Our aim instead is to
list the equipment necessary for Chinese cooking and
to elaborate on how tools you may already have can be
used to make these recipes.

Wok with a Lid

A wok is the most important, versatile tool in a Chinese
kitchen (or any kitchen, in our opinion!). It's crucial for
proper stir-frying, as its thin metal gets wickedly hot—
it's your only chance at achieving that elusive "wok
hei" smoky, seared flavor (see page 23). A wok is also
an ideal vessel for boiling, blanching, steaming, braising, and frying.

GAUGE AND MATERIAL: Look for a 14- to
16-gauge (the former being thicker and more heavy
duty, while the latter is lighter and easier to maneuver) carbon steel spun or hammered wok. Carbon
steel is lightweight, nonstick after seasoning, great
at high temperatures, and long lasting. Avoid nonstick coatings (they can be unsafe at higher temperatures), stainless steel (you'll be scrubbing stuck-on
food 'til the cows come home, though if you already
have one, use it for cooking acidic foods or for
steaming), and cast iron (not terrible, just heavy—
and it takes longer to heat up).

HANDLES, SIZE, AND SHAPE: Make sure your
wok comes with a lid and a long handle (a small
helper handle at the other end is also good). That single long handle makes it a "pow wok," which allows
the cook to grab the wok with one hand and toss food
in the air in that flourish-y fancy chef way (with a
searing-hot flame, it's the stuff wok hei dreams were
made of). We find a wooden handle is ideal for home
cooking, as it's comfortable to use and won't heat up
and burn you when you grab it (like some metal han-

dles). Size-wise, a 14-inch wok is ideal for most home
uses; anything smaller may be too limiting to successfully make some of the recipes in this book. Note
that if you have an electric or induction stove, you'll
need a flat-bottomed wok, and if you have gas, you
have the option of using a round-bottomed wok (our
preference because it's easier to maneuver food over
its smooth, uninterrupted surface) with a wok grate
or ring.

Scan the QR code for our Complete Wok Guide,
from seasoning to care and maintenance.

Wok Grates and Rings

If using a round-bottomed wok, you may want to use a
wok ring that sits on top of your burner and ensures that
the wok stays put while cooking. You can buy stainless-
steel wok rings for less than $10 or get a sturdier cast-
iron option for not much more. You may
also consider a wok grate, which re-
places the grate on your stove
and allows your wok to sit
closer to the burner. Just
make sure it'll fit onto your
stove before buying.

Our
Complete
Wok Guide

Wok Spatula

For most recipes, you can use any run-of-the-mill
wood, bamboo, or metal spoon or spatula you have
lying around, but to level up your stir-frying experience, get a metal wok spatula. Its distinctive shovel-like

shape makes it ideal for scooping and flipping. A thick, sturdy handle and the spatula's curved front edge (contoured to the wok's round, sloping sides) both make it easier to move around large amounts of food. Some wok spatulas come in a set along with a hoak (a Chinese wok ladle), but we rarely use it while stir-frying.

Cast-Iron Pan

A 10-inch cast-iron pan is a great tool to have in any home kitchen. We like it for searing larger pieces of meat and making crispy rice.

Nonstick Pan

For a long time, we rejected nonstick pans. Fearing scratched coatings, we purged them from our cabinets seemingly for good. But while you can absolutely manage without one (we have a trick to properly heat carbon steel and cast iron to make it nonstick; see page 23), we've found some better quality nonstick pans (we like Misen) since "the purge." And truthfully, the convenience and comforting assurance of a nonstick pan make it a great tool to have in your arsenal.

A Few More Key Pots and Pans

We won't wax philosophical about butter warmers, saucepans, and stockpots. Suffice it to say you'll need a few pots and pans of varying sizes—a small one for jobs like making sauces or toasting spices, a medium deep pot for frying (large enough for batch-frying but small enough so you don't have to use a gallon of oil), and a large stockpot for, well, stocks. Or, you know—for when you want to poach a whole Cantonese chicken (see page 146).

Bamboo (or Metal) Steamer

A bamboo steamer consists of multiple stacked bamboo baskets, enabling you to cook multiple things at once with just one wok and burner. The bamboo steamer is also a condensation-free cooking environment, preventing water from dripping onto the food inside (important for buns and dumplings). A standard set comes with two layers and a lid and will set you back about $20, but you can add more layers as needed. If you do a lot of steaming and want something you can easily wash and dry, you can also find stackable metal steamers in Chinese grocery stores and online.

SIZE AND CARE: A 10-inch steamer set is ideal for a 14-inch wok. Never soak your steamer in water or put it in the dishwasher. Bamboo is highly absorbent, and excess moisture will cause mold and mildew to grow. We usually just air-dry it after use, but if it gets messy, quickly scrub it under warm water with mild dish detergent, rinse, and thoroughly air-dry (overnight or longer, depending on the humidity) before storing.

HOW TO USE IT: To use a bamboo steamer, fill your wok with water so it comes ½ inch up the sides of the steamer. The bottom of the steamer must be submerged in water so it doesn't scorch, but the boiling water in the wok should not touch the food inside. While steaming, add more boiling water as needed to maintain this level. (Any added water should be boiling, or the food inside could cook unevenly.) Place a layer of perforated parchment paper, damp cheesecloth, or thin cabbage leaves on the bottom of each rack, then add a single layer of buns or dumplings ½ to 1 inch apart. Stack, cover with the bamboo lid, and steam. You can also fill shallow, heatproof bowls with raw meats, fish, rice, or even cake batter to steam, as long as the lid still fits and there's enough clearance between the dish and the walls of the steamer to allow steam to circulate.

Metal steamers can accommodate much more water, making them a more convenient option for long steaming times. However, condensation will form under the lid and may drip onto the food inside (this is fine for most things, but bad for buns and dumplings). To prevent this, wrap a thin kitchen towel around the lid to absorb excess moisture. Tie the ends securely on top of the lid so they don't droop and potentially come into contact with your heat source.

Metal Steaming Rack

If you don't have space to store a bamboo or tiered metal steamer, a cheap, easy-to-store steaming rack is up to most steaming jobs. Even if you have a bamboo steamer, buy a rack like this for steaming items that don't fit inside it (like a whole fish). Look for a small, circular stainless-steel rack with wire feet or legs. A 2-inch-tall rack is perfect for your wok, allowing you to fill the wok with water and set a heatproof dish on the rack to steam eggs, fish, meat, or vegetables. That said, you don't need a wok to use this type of rack. Any pot with a lid will work,

More on How to Steam Food, Chinese-Style

so long as it can accommodate whatever you're steaming. (Note that metal steaming racks aren't ideal for buns or dumplings, which need more airflow for even cooking and don't do well with dripping or pooling condensation.) You can get racks at varying heights from ½ inch to 3 inches to fit in a range of cooking vessels (this is especially helpful if you're cooking several dishes and your wok is occupied). Don't want to buy one of these either? A couple sturdy bamboo chopsticks across the bottom of your wok can hold a plate (albeit a bit precariously). An empty tuna can gets the job done too.

Plate Grabber

With all the steaming that goes on in Chinese kitchens, a stainless-steel plate grabber is a handy tool to have if you're not confident maneuvering a plate out of a steamer with a kitchen cloth. The whole thing operates like one big claw that grabs onto the rim of the plate on opposite ends, so you can easily lift it up and out while keeping your hands away from hot steam. That said, keep in mind that this tool only works with rimmed dishes and won't work for bowls or shallow dishes with curved sides.

Cleaver (and/or Your Favorite Knife)

The ultimate tool for slicing, dicing, chopping, julienning, scraping, and scooping, Chinese cleavers are the whole package. Rather than a set of knives, each with its own role, many Chinese cooks and chefs use this one cutting tool for everything. But don't go hacking through pork or chicken bones just yet—if that's what you're looking to do, you *will* need a heavy-duty cleaver or you risk chipping the blades of lighter cleavers. In a pinch, we've used our heaviest cleaver to split small pieces of wood into kindling, which should give you an idea of how durable it should be. As for beef bones or large ham bones, spare your cleaver (and your sweat), and leave those to a professional butcher. Anytime you do cut through bone, rinse the meat under cold water afterward to avoid getting bone shards in your final dish.

If you are in the market for a cleaver—heavy or light (or both)—buy something utilitarian from a restaurant-supply store in your local Chinatown. Our cleavers are either family heirlooms, $30 restaurant-supply buys, or sturdy locally made ones we brought back from China in our checked luggage. Avoid fancy German or Japanese cleavers, which can be expensive and are often too delicate for heavy-duty bone cracking. All that said, you don't *need* a cleaver to cook the recipes in this book. Most jobs can be done with whatever knives you're used to cooking with.

Kitchen Shears

A good pair of sharp kitchen shears is essential for trimming fish fins, removing the spiny bits and legs from whole shrimp, dividing poultry, and harvesting things from the garden. Buy a high-quality pair, and it will last for years.

Rice Cooker

Without a doubt, this is the most essential of all electronic cooking tools in a Chinese kitchen, and if you cook a lot of rice, it's the tool that will save you the most headache. Rice cookers these days come in a variety of styles and price points. Some have tons of different settings (for cooking different kinds of rice, porridges, and the like), while others just have an on/off switch—like our favorite, the Tiger JNP Series rice cooker. It's pricier than average, but no other rice cooker in our experience can cook white rice faster—12 to 15 minutes. It only has two options ("Cook" or "Keep Warm"), and that's how we like it.

Digital Scale

A digital scale is always on our kitchen counter. While you don't strictly need one for the recipes in this book, we do include weight measurements in recipes that call for more precision.

Meat/Frying Thermometer

A good instant-read thermometer is particularly important when it comes to getting oil temperatures right for chili oil (page 275) and for deep-frying. If you find a thermometer with a wide temperature range, you can use it for both measuring the internal temperature of a roast chicken and high-temp jobs, like frying. If you have two separate tools for the job (i.e., an old-school analog meat thermometer and

an analog candy thermometer), that's fine too. Just make sure they're calibrated accurately according to the manufacturer's instructions.

Spider/Large Strainer

The Chinese spider is a shallow, bowl-shaped wire strainer with a long bamboo handle. It's great for removing fried foods from hot oil, quickly getting blanched vegetables out of boiling water, or scooping a large batch of wontons directly into hot soup. We like versions that are 7 to 8 inches in diameter—enough to scoop a large volume of food, but not so big that it's hard to maneuver in a regular pot. You can find these at Chinese restaurant-supply stores, Chinese grocery stores, or online.

Fine-Mesh Strainer

A fine-mesh strainer is just as useful as a spider. It removes pesky air bubbles for glassy steamed eggs (see page 165) and smooth Hong Kong Egg Tarts (page 31), and it's also a handy tool for straining stocks, broths, and frying oil (to reuse).

Chinese Rolling Pin

An 11-inch-long and 1-inch-thick Chinese wooden rolling pin (no handles, no taper) is smaller than what you're probably used to, but that's what makes it ideal for nimble jobs like rolling out dumpling wrappers and bao dough.

Bamboo/Wood Chopsticks

If you don't feel super confident in your chopstick skills, you can ignore this one and use whatever utensil you feel will do the job in question. But at our house, chopsticks are the ultimate cooking tool. Tasks like flipping bacon, beating eggs, fishing pickles out of jars, and testing a poached chicken for doneness all employ the humble chopstick. As we mentioned earlier (see page 16), you can even use a pair of chopsticks as a rack for steaming in your wok. (In the immortal words of a gregarious coworker at Bill's first job and occasional dinner guest, "Dang, Bill! You use those sticks for everything!") Go for simple, versatile wooden or bamboo chopsticks that have a little heft to them and tapered ends.

9 Essential Chinese Pantry Ingredients

Cooking Chinese food doesn't need to be daunting. Here are the nine ingredients we count on the most. (For more on other Chinese ingredients used in this book, see Building Out Your Chinese Pantry & Fridge, page 304.)

1. Salt (yán, 盐)

Salt is as essential to the Chinese pantry as it is to any other pantry. We cook almost exclusively with fine-grain sea salt, which has a pure flavor, does not contain additives to prevent clumping (as does table salt), and dissolves and distributes quickly into whatever you're cooking. Use fine-grain sea salt if you want to replicate the recipes in this book as closely as possible to how we executed them in our own kitchen. Chinese cooks generally don't employ coarse or crunchy finishing salts. Regardless of what you use, the first kitchen lesson we were taught was that you can always add but you can't take away!

2. White Pepper (bái hújiāo, 白胡椒)

White pepper is spicier than floral black pepper, and in Chinese cooking it is used nearly exclusively. We keep very finely ground white pepper powder on hand for most applications, so the white pepper flavor distributes more evenly in each recipe. Recipes in this book that call for "white pepper powder" need this fine powdery version, but sometimes we do call for freshly ground white pepper or whole peppercorns.

3. Cooking Oil (yóu, 油)

Your cooking oil will ideally have a high smoke point—such as canola oil (400° to 425°F), light olive oil (425° to 450°F), peanut oil (450°F), or avocado oil (520°F)—to withstand the high temperatures of your wok. You also want an oil with a neutral flavor rather than a strongly flavored one like coconut oil or extra-virgin olive oil. While avocado oil has the highest smoke point, it can be expensive (some also describe its flavor as grassy, but we find it to be mild).

4. Light Soy Sauce (jiàng yóu, 酱油)

Soy sauce is a liquid seasoning and condiment brewed by fermenting soybeans. We have about seven different kinds in our pantry, but the most ubiquitous is Chinese light soy sauce (shēng chōu, 生抽). It is thinner and lighter in color than the familiar (Japanese) Kikkoman you've seen on tables at sushi restaurants and takeout joints. The distinction of "light" differentiates Chinese light soy from Chinese dark soy (next on this list). "Light soy sauce" does not refer to low sodium. General rule of thumb: If it is a Chinese brand of naturally brewed soy and it does not say "dark" on it, it is light soy sauce! The main ingredients in naturally brewed soy sauce should be water, soybeans, salt, and wheat flour. We like Pearl River Bridge soy sauces. If wheat is an issue, some Chinese brands, like Lee Kum Kee, now make gluten-free soy sauce.

5. Dark Soy Sauce (lǎo chōu, 老抽)

Dark soy sauce is thicker and darker than light soy sauce. It is used for flavor but, more important, to darken the color of sauces, fried rice, and noodles. You need only a teaspoon to take a dish from pale to amber brown. It's just as salty as light soy sauce, so be careful not to over-season. You may also see mushroom-flavored dark soy sauce at the Chinese market, which has a bit of extra umami, and can be used interchangeably with regular dark soy sauce.

6. Shaoxing Wine (shàoxīng jiǔ, 绍兴酒)

Shaoxing wine is a type of Chinese rice wine with a dark golden color and a mildly sweet, fragrant aroma. The production process involves fermenting rice, water, and a small amount of wheat (if you are gluten intolerant, substitute a dry cooking sherry). It's a key ingredient in our cooking and will help create that elusive restaurant flavor. We use it in marinades, wonton and dumpling fillings, to deglaze our wok, and to add flavor to stir-fries, sauces, and braises. We buy it in large gallon jugs; if you want something a little more high quality, look for a three-year-aged Shaoxing wine, which will cost only a few dollars more than the standard stuff.

7. Oyster Sauce (háo yóu, 蚝油)

Oyster sauce is pure umami. Bill's father used to say, "Want to make anything taste better? Just add oyster sauce." Made with oyster extracts, it is a dark brown color, with a viscosity and texture similar to ketchup or barbecue sauce. It doesn't lend a strong seafood flavor to dishes; rather, it's an all-purpose seasoning that we regularly add to marinades, sauces, and braises. There are both regular and premium versions—we pay the few extra bucks for the good stuff. There are also gluten-free versions, as well as vegetarian versions made with mushrooms if you have a shellfish allergy or are sticking to a vegetarian/vegan diet.

8. Sesame Oil (zhīmayóu, 芝麻油)

Sesame oil comes in both untoasted and toasted varieties. You can easily tell the difference. Untoasted sesame oil has a light color similar to vegetable oil, while the toasted variety is much darker in color. The difference in flavor is also stark. Raw sesame oil is quite mild, while toasted sesame oil has a very strong nutty flavor. We only call for toasted sesame oil and use it as a flavor agent (not as a cooking oil). Measure it carefully and use in moderation, as it can quickly overpower a dish.

9. Cornstarch (yùmǐ diànfěn, 玉米淀粉)

Cornstarch is an essential thickening, dredging, and binding agent. While we regularly stock potato starch, tapioca starch, mung bean starch, and wheat starch in our pantry, we use cornstarch the most because it's the most versatile and widely available of the bunch. As a thickener, you need to first disperse it in water to create a slurry before adding it to simmering liquid so it seamlessly combines with the other ingredients in your recipe. It also results in more robust, glistening, visually appealing sauces (that aren't as clear/translucent as sauces thickened with root starches like tapioca or potato starch). Cornstarch also works well in batters and crispy coatings, acts as a binder for meat and vegetable fillings, and helps seal in the moisture of meats and seafood before cooking (a process called velveting; see page 22), resulting in tender proteins with a silky texture.

OUR THOUGHTS ON MSG
While monosodium glutamate (wèijīng, 味精), or MSG, is not an essential ingredient, you'll see it occasionally pop up in this book. MSG is synthesized glutamic acid, an amino acid that occurs naturally in many foods, like tomatoes and parmesan cheese. It's the protein that triggers umami, the savory fifth sense. The bias against MSG began in the late 1960s, when the term "Chinese restaurant syndrome" entered the lexicon. MSG's supposed negative side effects have been largely debunked, however, problematizing that term and launching conversations about how both language and food are tied to shifts in cultural attitudes. Let's treat MSG like what it is—another seasoning in your spice cabinet. In this book, we call for it in recipes where it really takes the dish the extra mile. It's always optional, so you can decide whether you'd like to try it in your own cooking.

Key Techniques

Thinly Slicing Meat

Texture is a huge part of the experience of eating Chinese food. Proteins are sliced, chopped, or julienned to get the optimal texture for their intended use. But how do you julienne an unwieldy, irregularly shaped piece of pork shoulder or flank steak? The secret to doing this is to freeze the meat until it's just firm enough to slice, but not so firm that the knife can't cut through it. If the meat is coming out of your freezer and is frozen solid, simply thaw it in the refrigerator until soft enough to slice but still semi-frozen in the middle. Always slice meat against the grain for the best texture and tenderness.

In China, ground meat is usually made at home. Hand chopping a piece of pork shoulder or de-boned chicken thigh allows you to control the ratios of meat and fat, grind size, and texture. Scan the QR code on this page to check out this technique, and apply it to any recipe that calls for ground meat.

Velveting Meat

Velveting is a Chinese marinating technique that ensures tender, juicy results after cooking meats either in a hot wok or boiling water. If you've ever wondered how Chinese restaurants achieve such silky slices of meat, this is the secret.

A mix of oil and cornstarch locks in moisture and gives proteins that signature velvety texture. Beyond that, you can add moisture to the meat itself by adding water and mixing until the meat has absorbed the liquid. You can also add liquid seasonings like rice wine, oyster sauce, soy sauce, and/or sesame oil.

For beef, baking soda acts as an optional additional tenderizer. Don't go overboard, though! If you add too much baking soda or let the beef sit in it too long, it will result in an off flavor and rubbery texture. (Some techniques call for more baking soda, which is then rinsed off the beef. For ease, we're using a smaller amount and skipping the rinsing step.)

You will see this technique throughout this book, with adjustments according to the needs of each recipe. However, here are our general guidelines:

FOR 1 POUND OF CHICKEN OR PORK

2 to 3 tablespoons water

2 teaspoons cornstarch

2 teaspoons neutral oil

2 teaspoons oyster sauce or light soy sauce

How to Make Ground Meat

FOR 1 POUND OF BEEF

2 to 3 tablespoons water

2 teaspoons cornstarch

2 teaspoons neutral oil

2 teaspoons oyster sauce or light soy sauce

¼ teaspoon baking soda

Slice, cube, or julienne the meat. Add the water, cornstarch, oil, oyster sauce (or light soy sauce), and baking soda (if velveting a tougher cut of beef). Mix with your hands until the meat absorbs the liquid. Marinate for 30 minutes at room temperature before cooking.

Perfectly Tender Meats for Stir-Fries

Another trick for tender proteins is a simple one that most people don't know about: Meats in stir-fries are often precooked 75 to 80 percent of the way through before being removed from the wok. Then, other ingredients are cooked before returning the meat (and any juices) to the wok to finish cooking. This preserves the tenderness and juiciness of the meat and ensures it doesn't get overdone.

How to Prevent Food from Sticking to Your Wok

We've all dealt with terrible messes from food sticking to a pan or wok—even a seasoned wok. This usually happens when cooking meat, seafood, tofu, and eggs, as well as starchy ingredients like rice or noodles. But one Chinese kitchen mantra is the key to preventing this kitchen calamity: rè guō xià yóu (热锅下油).

This basically means, when cooking one of these "sticky" ingredients, preheat your wok thoroughly (usually until it just begins to smoke) BEFORE adding oil. That's it. Just that one simple step, and you'll have a surface nonstick enough for even delicate pieces of tofu to roll around like kids on a slip 'n slide. This method also works with seasoned cast-iron and other carbon-steel pans. Since there are other factors that dictate whether or not a wok needs preheating, we will specify in each recipe when preheating is needed.

Four Tips for Achieving Wok Hei

Wok hei is a complex charred, savory aroma and flavor that you get in stir-fries cooked very quickly at extremely high heat. It's an art in and of itself to consistently achieve wok hei.

It's important to note, however, that you're not trying for wok hei in every dish you cook in your wok. Saucier stir-fries, pan-fried foods, and braises are not wok hei dishes. But a dry stir-fried noodle dish like Chicken Chow Fun (page 108) or Leafy Greens, Four Ways (page 236) are recipes that truly sing with wok hei!

Preheat your wok properly before cooking:

In most cases (though not all), the wok should be lightly smoking before you begin cooking. That's how you know it's hot enough.

Use high heat the whole time:

Keeping the heat high for most of the stir-frying process will give you your best chance at wok hei. To do this without burning or overcooking your dish, it's best to prepare all the elements of the dish before you turn on the stove. At such high temperatures, cooking times at each step of a recipe are often measured in seconds rather than minutes.

Cook in small batches:

This depends on the size of your wok, but if you have a 14-inch wok for home use, cooking in smaller batches can help compensate for the fact that you don't have the roaring heat of commercial stoves. Cooking a smaller volume of food means the wok won't cool down as much or as quickly. For maximum chances of wok hei, divide the recipe in half, keeping your wok no more than one-third full. Most important, do not double recipes where wok hei is important.

Reheat the sides of the wok halfway through cooking:

The wok will cool down as you add more ingredients. To reheat the sides of the wok, pile all the ingredients in the center. The concentration of moisture in the middle of the wok will prevent the food from burning as the sides are given a chance to heat up again. Then you can rapidly stir the food around the superheated sides to generate wok hei.

Dim Sum

Dim sum outings have always been a cherished tradition in our family. Every Sunday after Thanksgiving, or after paying our respects to departed loved ones during Qingming (Tomb Sweeping Day) in early spring, we head to a dim sum brunch with aunts, uncles, and cousins. As a kid, most of my requests were funneled through a Cantonese-speaking parent. (My chances of being bilingual went out the window when my kindergarten teacher told my parents to speak only English at home—the '90s were a different time.) But when it came to elusive items—like my favorite Taro Puffs (page 41)—the language barrier didn't stop me from hopping out of my seat to chase them down. Before our blog, we never thought we could make our own dim sum at home. But through rigorous experimentation and much taste-testing, we've cracked the code on many of our favorites. We've aimed to make these recipes as clear and simple as possible, while preserving the sheer magic of great dim sum. SARAH

广式烧卖 guǎng shì shāomai

Pork & Shrimp Siu Mai

SARAH Make a batch of these classic Cantonese-style siu mai, and they'll transport you to your favorite dim sum restaurant. The hallmark of quality siu mai is a well-emulsified pork and shrimp filling that has some "snap" when you bite into it. To achieve this, the old-school way is to whip the filling using chopsticks in one direction for a long time (like, halfway through an episode of *Jeopardy!*). It occurred to me that an electric mixer could do the job just as well—and faster too! (This technique also works for other dumpling and bao fillings.) The finishing touch? Instead of the recognizable (but hard-to-find) bright orange fish roe on the top, we use finely minced carrots for a pop of color.

Makes 24 siu mai

FOR THE FILLING

3 small or 1 to 2 large dried shiitake mushrooms

½ cup hot water

8 ounces peeled and deveined shrimp (any size)

1 teaspoon plus 1 tablespoon sugar

⅛ teaspoon baking soda

2 tablespoons water

1 pound ground pork

1 tablespoon cornstarch

1 tablespoon Shaoxing wine

1 teaspoon fine sea salt

¼ teaspoon white pepper powder

1 tablespoon neutral oil

1 tablespoon oyster sauce

½ teaspoon toasted sesame oil

FOR ASSEMBLING THE SIU MAI

24 very thin yellow Hong Kong–style round dumpling wrappers or thin yellow square wonton wrappers

2 tablespoons very finely minced carrot

Ultimate Chili Oil (page 275) or chili garlic sauce, for serving

MAKE THE FILLING: Soak the shiitake mushrooms in the hot water for 2 hours (or overnight) until fully rehydrated. Squeeze any excess water out of the mushrooms. Trim away any tough stems, and very finely chop the mushrooms—you should have about ¼ cup.

Add the shrimp to a medium bowl, and toss them with 1 teaspoon of the sugar, the baking soda, and the 2 tablespoons water. Set aside for 15 minutes, then rinse the shrimp in a colander under running water until the water runs clear. Drain.

Meanwhile, to the bowl of a stand mixer fitted with the paddle attachment (or just a large bowl, if mixing by hand), add the ground pork, the remaining tablespoon sugar, the cornstarch, Shaoxing wine, salt, and white pepper. Mix on medium-low speed for 5 minutes, or until the mixture resembles a paste that sticks to the sides of the bowl. (Alternatively, mix vigorously in one direction with a pair of chopsticks by hand for 10 to 15 minutes until you get the same result.)

Scrape down the sides of the bowl, add the shrimp, and beat on low speed for 2 minutes. Increase the speed to medium and beat until the shrimp is well incorporated into the pork, another 2 minutes. (If mixing by hand, roughly chop the shrimp, add them to the pork, and mix in one direction for 10 minutes.)

Add the chopped mushrooms, the neutral oil, oyster sauce, and sesame oil. Mix on medium speed for 1 minute (or by hand for 2 to 3 minutes).

ASSEMBLE THE SIU MAI: Line a bamboo steamer with perforated parchment paper, damp cheesecloth, or thin cabbage leaves. Take one wrapper and place a tablespoon of filling in the middle. Squeeze the sides of the wrapper up around the edges of the filling to create an open-topped pocket. Use a butter knife to continue filling the wrapper until it's stuffed to the top with filling, and then scrape the top flat. (Each siu mai should weigh

(RECIPE CONTINUES)

about 35g.) If using square wrappers, fold over any excess wrapper and squeeze the wrappers to the sides of the siu mai.

Continue until you've assembled all the siu mai, transferring them to the lined steamer basket as you go, placed 1 inch apart. (Place any siu mai that don't fit in the steamer on a parchment-lined plate or sheet pan to cook in later batches or freeze; see Make Ahead.) Top the center of each siu mai with a small amount of the minced carrot.

COOK THE SIU MAI: Fill a wok with enough water to submerge the bottom rim of your bamboo steamer by ½ inch (you may need to add more boiling water during steaming to keep the water at this level). Bring the water to a simmer over medium-high heat. Place the covered steamer in the wok and steam each batch over medium heat for 9 minutes. Serve with the chili oil.

MAKE AHEAD

Place the assembled siu mai ½ inch apart on a parchment-lined sheet pan. Cover tightly with plastic wrap (or use a clean plastic grocery bag) and freeze overnight. Once frozen, transfer the siu mai to an airtight container. Cook the frozen siu mai directly (without thawing first). Steam for 11 minutes.

迷你叉烧包 mínǐ chāshāo bāo

Mini Char Siu Bao

For many people, char siu bao (BBQ pork buns) are a must-have indulgence, with their undeniably delicious sweet-savory filling. While you might stop by a Chinese bakery for a full-size bun, minis are a popular pick at dim sum houses because you can still get your fix while leaving room for other tasty morsels. Be sure to have these with a cup of Chinese red tea to cut the richness of the pork—and to give you a fighting chance against an impending food coma. These are also fantastic at a party, in the little ones' lunch boxes, or as an afternoon snack.

Makes 32 mini buns

FOR THE DOUGH

1 recipe Milk Bread (page 284), ingredients mixed, ready for first proofing

FOR THE FILLING

2 tablespoons neutral oil

½ cup finely chopped shallot or onion

2 tablespoons sugar

2 tablespoons oyster sauce

2 teaspoons light soy sauce

1½ teaspoons toasted sesame oil

1 teaspoon dark soy sauce

2 tablespoons all-purpose flour, plus more for shaping and rolling

¾ cup low-sodium chicken stock

2 cups finely diced Char Siu Roast Pork (page 173), cut no larger than ¼ inch

FOR FINISHING THE BUNS

Egg wash: 1 large egg, lightly beaten with **1 tablespoon water**

Sugar water: 1½ tablespoons sugar dissolved in **1½ tablespoons boiling water**

PROOF THE DOUGH: Following the instructions on page 284, set the dough to complete its first proofing (1 to 2 hours, or until the dough doubles in size).

MAKE THE FILLING: Meanwhile, heat the neutral oil in a wok over medium heat. Add the shallot and stir-fry for 2 minutes. Stir in the sugar, oyster sauce, light soy sauce, sesame oil, and dark soy sauce. Bring the mixture to a simmer, then whisk in the 2 tablespoons flour, followed by the chicken stock. Reduce the heat to medium-low and cook, stirring constantly for 2 to 3 minutes, until thickened. Stir in the char siu and continue to cook until the filling is thick and gooey, with no liquid remaining.

Turn off the heat and transfer the filling to a large plate or container. Set aside to cool to room temperature, then cover and refrigerate for at least 1 hour. (You can also make the filling up to 1 day in advance of proofing the dough and assembling the buns.)

SHAPE AND FILL THE BUNS: Line two baking sheets with parchment paper. Punch the air out of the proofed dough and knead for 5 minutes. Transfer the dough to a lightly floured surface and shape it into a long 24-inch tube.

Cut the tube in half crosswise, then into fourths, then into fourths again to make 32 equal-size pieces. (For greater accuracy, weigh the entire dough ball, divide the weight by 32, and then cut and weigh the individual pieces to match that weight.)

To shape the buns, briefly knead the dough balls to punch out any air bubbles and make them smooth. Use a Chinese rolling pin to roll each ball into a 3½-inch circle, with the center slightly thicker than the edges. (While assembling the buns, be sure to keep your hands clean. Any grease from the filling on your fingers will make it very difficult to seal the buns.)

(RECIPE CONTINUES)

Add a scant tablespoon of filling to each dough circle and crimp it closed, making sure it's tightly sealed. Lay the buns seam side down on the prepared baking sheets, spaced about 3 inches apart. Cover the buns with clean towels and allow to rise at room temperature for 1 hour.

BAKE THE BUNS AND SERVE: Arrange two racks in the upper and lower thirds of the oven, and preheat the oven to 350°F.

Brush the buns with the egg wash, then bake for 12 to 15 minutes, until golden brown. Remove the buns from the oven and immediately brush them with the sugar water to give them a nice shine. Let cool and enjoy!

(These buns are best eaten fresh, but you can store the baked buns in an airtight container in the refrigerator for 4 to 5 days, or in the freezer for up to 1 month. To enjoy again, reheat in the microwave for 30 seconds; thaw beforehand if they're frozen.)

WHY FLOUR OVER CORNSTARCH?
You may have noticed that we use flour to thicken the char siu bao filling rather than our usual thickening agent of choice, cornstarch. In this case, the flour gives more body and heft to the filling, helping it hold together better as you assemble the bao and during baking.

港式蛋挞 gǎng shì dàntà
Hong Kong Egg Tarts
(Dan Tat)

SARAH The first time I tried a warm, fresh-from-the-oven egg tart, I was at a work lunch on my first day at a new job in Beijing. I grew up with these tarts as a room-temperature snack (they never seemed to be piping hot at dim sum). On that day in Beijing, the second the server put the tarts on the table, I focused my attention away from small talk and onto the glassy custard in front of me. The warm, melt-in your-mouth pastry disappeared the second I took a bite. Unbeknownst to my new colleagues, I was having a moment, wondering where this "real" egg tart had been all my life. Now, when I'm craving that same blissful experience, I make this recipe. Weigh the ingredients accurately here for the best results!

Makes 18 tarts

1¾ cups (245g) **all-purpose flour,** plus more for rolling

⅛ teaspoon **fine sea salt**

¾ cup (1½ sticks; 170g) **unsalted butter,** slightly softened but still cold, cut into ½-inch cubes

3 tablespoons **cold water**

1 cup **hot water**

½ cup (100g) **sugar**

3 large **eggs,** at room temperature

½ cup **evaporated milk,** at room temperature

1 teaspoon **vanilla extract**

MAKE THE PASTRY: In a bowl, combine the 1¾ cups flour and the salt. Add the butter cubes and, working quickly, break them up roughly using a pastry cutter or a fork and your fingers until the mixture resembles coarse crumbs with some pea-size lumps remaining. (Do not do this in a food processor, as it's very easy to grind the butter too small and end up with a crumbly shortbread-like texture in the final tarts rather than flaky pastry.)

Add the cold water and bring the dough together with your hands. The dough will seem crumbly and dry—that's how it should be. Don't be tempted to add more water. Just squeeze it together with your hands; by continually pressing it together, it will eventually form a rough disc of dough. Wrap the dough tightly in plastic wrap or place in a reusable bag and refrigerate for 20 minutes.

On a lightly floured surface, roll out the dough into a 6 by 15-inch rectangle, moving quickly to avoid overworking it. With the short side of the rectangle facing you, fold the rectangle into thirds, like a business letter, folding the top third of the rectangle over the middle third and then folding the bottom third over that. Give the dough a quarter-turn (left or right) and repeat this rolling and folding step once more. Rewrap the dough and refrigerate for 1 hour.

MAKE THE FILLING: Add the hot water to a medium bowl, whisk in the sugar to dissolve, and set aside to cool to room temperature.

In a large bowl, whisk together the eggs, evaporated milk, and vanilla. Then thoroughly whisk in the sugar water. Pour the filling through a fine-mesh strainer into a large measuring cup or pitcher (something with a pour spout). You should have about 2½ cups of custard filling. Refrigerate the filling while you roll out the dough.

ASSEMBLE AND BAKE: Position an oven rack in the lower third of the oven, then preheat the oven to 375°F. Have ready 9 ungreased mini egg tart pans (2¾ inches in diameter) or a nonstick standard muffin pan. Since

(RECIPE CONTINUES)

each batch will bake in the lower third of the oven, you'll have to bake the tarts in two batches of 9 tarts each.

On a lightly floured work surface, roll out the dough to an even ⅛-inch thickness. The dough will puff up as it bakes, so the thinner you make the dough at this stage, the more room you'll have for the custard.

Use a 4-inch round cutter to cut out as many circles as possible (cut them close together to minimize scraps). Use a thin metal spatula or bench scraper to transfer each dough circle to a mini tart pan (or the cup of a muffin pan). Press the dough into the pans, leaving a lip of dough flared out over the top of the cups (the tart shells will shrink as they bake, so you want ample clearance).

If necessary, reroll the dough scraps and cut out more circles until you have 9 tart shells. (If you have 9 more mini tart pans or another muffin pan, you can prepare the remaining 9 tart shells and refrigerate them until the first batch finishes baking. If not, wrap any remaining dough back up in plastic or your reusable bag, and return it to the refrigerator. Assemble the second batch of tart shells after the first batch is baked and cooled.)

Divide half of the custard filling among the 9 tart shells, filling the cups about ⅛ inch from the top.

Immediately (and carefully) transfer the tart pans to the oven, reduce the oven heat to 350°F, and bake for 26 to 29 minutes, until the filling is just set (if a toothpick can stand up in a tart on its own, it's done).

Cool the tarts for at least 10 minutes before removing them from the pans and enjoying. Repeat with the second batch of tart shells.

Store any leftovers in an airtight container in the refrigerator for up to 3 days; reheat in the toaster oven before enjoying.

韭菜鲜虾水晶饺 *jiǔcài xiān xiā shuǐjīng jiǎo*

Garlic Chive & Shrimp Dumplings

These dumplings feature a tasty filling of garlic chives and shrimp encased in a chewy translucent wrapper, perfect when paired with chili garlic sauce or fragrant chili oil. To achieve the correct appearance and texture in the wrapper (yes, they're homemade!), you'll need three kinds of starch. The tapioca starch gives the wrappers a shiny, translucent look, while the wheat starch and cornstarch improve the dough structure and texture. Cornstarch is readily available in grocery stores, but you may need to venture to your local Chinese market for the wheat starch and tapioca starch. Weighing the starches will yield the most accurate results, but if you must use a measuring cup, measure by spooning the starches into the cup (in addition to any tablespoons) and leveling off the top, or you may end up with dry dough.

Makes 18 dumplings

FOR THE WRAPPERS

¾ cup plus 2 tablespoons (100g) wheat starch

¾ cup (95g) tapioca starch

3 tablespoons (20g) cornstarch, plus more for kneading

1¼ cups water

2 teaspoons neutral oil

FOR THE FILLING

8 ounces peeled and deveined shrimp (any size)

1 cup very finely chopped Chinese garlic chives (flat leaves, stems with unopened flower buds, or both)

½ cup very finely chopped water chestnuts or jícama

2 tablespoons cornstarch

1 tablespoon neutral oil

1 tablespoon oyster sauce

1 tablespoon Shaoxing wine

1 teaspoon toasted sesame oil

¾ teaspoon fine sea salt

½ teaspoon sugar

¼ teaspoon white pepper powder

FOR ASSEMBLY, COOKING, AND SERVING

Cornstarch, for kneading and rolling

4 tablespoons neutral oil

⅔ cup water, for steaming

Ultimate Chili Oil (page 275) or chili garlic sauce, for serving

MAKE THE DOUGH FOR THE WRAPPERS: In a large bowl, combine the wheat starch, tapioca starch, and 3 tablespoons cornstarch, mixing them with a fork or whisk.

Measure out exactly 1¼ cups of water and pour it into a deep medium saucepan along with the neutral oil. Cover and bring to a boil. Watch it closely—the second it comes to a rolling boil, remove it from the heat. (If you let it boil too long, you'll lose liquid to evaporation, and the water-to-starch ratio will be wrong.)

Immediately add about one-third of the starch mixture to the just-boiled water in the saucepan. Using the blunt end of a Chinese wooden rolling pin (without handles), a wooden spoon, or a rubber spatula, mix the starch into the water quickly and vigorously for 1 minute. The starch will begin to clump, with some of the mixture transparent and some of it in opaque lumps. This is normal!

Add another third of the starch mixture and mix it for 1 minute; the mixture will thicken to more of a paste-like consistency. Finally, add the rest of the starch and mix for 2 more minutes to bring it together into a shaggy dough. It won't be smooth or cohesive yet, and it will look dry, with some starch still not mixed in. Cover tightly with the saucepan lid and rest the dough for 5 minutes to allow the starch to further absorb moisture.

(RECIPE CONTINUES)

Lightly dust a clean, dry work surface with some cornstarch, and set a small bowl of additional cornstarch next to your work surface. Uncover the pot and begin pounding the dough with the end of the rolling pin, the wooden spoon, or rubber spatula, folding the dough over as you do so, until it becomes smooth and opaque, about 3 minutes. When the dough begins to stick to the rolling pin as you pound it, lightly dust your hands with cornstarch and knead the dough by hand on the work surface until it is smooth, 1 to 2 minutes. The dough should now be smooth, pliable, and elastic (if you pull on it, it should stretch).

Use your hands to roll the dough into a log about 1½ inches thick and 15 inches long, dusting the work surface lightly with additional cornstarch as needed to prevent sticking.

Divide the dough log in half crosswise, and then divide each half into 9 equal pieces. If you're doing this by eye,

score each log half into 9 sections before you slice so the pieces are as even as possible. (For greater accuracy, weigh the dough prior to rolling and cutting, and divide that number by 18; each piece should be about 25g.)

Dust the work surface with cornstarch again, and arrange the dough pieces with space between them so they don't touch. Cover with a large overturned bowl while you make the filling.

MAKE THE FILLING: In the bowl of a stand mixer fitted with the paddle attachment, add the shrimp and beat on low speed for 1 minute. (If you don't have a mixer, roughly chop the shrimp, then add to a bowl and beat vigorously with a pair of chopsticks for 2 minutes.)

Add the chives, water chestnuts, cornstarch, neutral oil, oyster sauce, Shaoxing wine, sesame oil, salt, sugar, and white pepper. Beat on low speed for 1 minute, until the

MAKE AHEAD
The assembled dumplings can be refrigerated for up to 24 hours before cooking. You can also freeze the dumplings after cooking; thaw them overnight in the fridge, then pan-fry and steam as instructed in the recipe.

mixture resembles a sticky, cohesive paste. (If mixing by hand, beat vigorously in one direction for 2 minutes.)

ASSEMBLE THE DUMPLINGS: Coat a rolling pin lightly with cornstarch and roll each piece of dough into a 4-inch circle, keeping the remaining dough pieces covered so they don't dry out.

Add 1 heaping tablespoon of the filling to the middle of each dough circle (or weigh the total filling, then divide that number by 18, for about 25g filling per wrapper). Pleat the edges of the wrapper in a circle around the filling. Hold the pleats and lift the dumpling up so the filling drops below the pleats you just made and squeeze the pleats together to seal the top. Turn the dumplings seam side down and gently flatten each with the palm of your hand, so they look like small hockey pucks. Place the filled dumplings on a plate and repeat until you've used all the filling and wrappers.

COOK THE DUMPLINGS: Heat a 10-inch nonstick pan (one that has a lid) over medium heat. When the pan is hot, add 2 tablespoons of the neutral oil and place about half the dumplings in the pan seam side down, spacing them about 1 inch apart. Fry for 30 seconds to 1 minute, until the bottoms form a bright white crust.

Pour in ⅓ cup of the water (oil may splatter when the water is added, so use the lid as a shield), and immediately cover the pan with the lid. Steam the dumplings for about 6 to 7 minutes, until the water has evaporated, the dumplings are cooked through and translucent, and the bottoms are crisp. Use a spatula or chopsticks to transfer the dumplings to a plate. Repeat with the second batch, using the remaining 2 tablespoons oil and ⅓ cup water.

Serve the dumplings with the chili oil or chili garlic sauce.

萝卜糕 luóbo gāo

Lo Bak Go Radish Cake

BILL I've sampled many versions of lo bak go and come to the conclusion that nothing compares to our homemade recipe, which is packed with dried shrimp, mushrooms, and Chinese cured sausage. For whatever reason, these cakes are often translated as "turnip cakes," even though they're made with radish and not turnip. The most important thing here is to select a daikon radish (lo bak) that is heavy and plump, an indication that it hasn't been sitting around for too long. Also make sure to budget enough time to let the cake set after steaming (about 1 hour), before pan-frying. That said, you don't have to fry and eat this turnip cake all in one sitting. Slice and pan-fry a couple slices whenever you like for a quick breakfast or snack!

Serves 12

FOR THE SHRIMP, MUSHROOM, AND SAUSAGE MIXTURE

1½ tablespoons dried shrimp

3 large or 5 medium dried shiitake mushrooms

2 tablespoons neutral oil

⅓ cup finely chopped Chinese cured pork sausage (about 2 ounces or 1 to 2 links) or Chinese cured pork belly

1 scallion, white and green parts finely chopped

FOR THE RADISH MIXTURE

1½ cups water, or more as needed

20 ounces daikon radish, grated (about 5 cups)

¾ teaspoon fine sea salt

½ teaspoon sugar

½ teaspoon toasted sesame oil

¼ teaspoon white pepper powder

FOR THE RICE FLOUR MIXTURE

1¼ cups (155g) rice flour

1 tablespoon cornstarch

½ to 1½ cups water

FOR STEAMING, PAN-FRYING, AND SERVING

Neutral oil, for greasing loaf pan and pan-frying

Oyster sauce, chili garlic sauce, or Ultimate Chili Oil (page 275), for serving

MAKE THE SHRIMP, MUSHROOM, AND SAUSAGE MIXTURE: In a small bowl, cover the dried shrimp with water and soak for 2 hours, then finely chop them. In a separate small bowl, soak the mushrooms in hot water for 2 hours, until rehydrated. Remove any tough stems from the mushrooms, and roughly chop them.

Heat a wok over medium heat. Add the neutral oil, reconstituted shrimp and shiitake mushrooms, and the sausage. Cook for 3 minutes. Stir in the scallion and cook for another 30 seconds. Transfer to a bowl.

MAKE THE RADISH MIXTURE: Add the 1½ cups water and the grated daikon to the wok. Bring to a low simmer over medium heat. Reduce the heat to medium-low and gather the radish in the center of the wok—away from the sides—so it doesn't brown. Cook until the radish is tender and slightly translucent, about 10 minutes. Stir occasionally for even cooking, but always bring the radish back to the middle of the wok to prevent browning. Add up to 1 additional cup of water as needed, depending on the water content of the radish. You should end up with about 1 cup of standing liquid. Turn off the heat and stir in the salt, sugar, sesame oil, and white pepper. Leave the mixture in the wok.

MAKE THE RICE FLOUR MIXTURE: To a medium bowl, add the rice flour and cornstarch. Add ½ to 1½ cups water (if you like a denser lo bak go, use ½ cup; if you like a more tender, almost pudding-like lo bak go, add all the water). Stir until well combined.

(RECIPE CONTINUES)

COMBINE THE MIXTURES: Pour the rice flour mixture into the wok with the radish mixture (the heat should still be off), and add the shrimp, mushrooms, and sausage. Use your wok spatula to mix everything thoroughly; the consistency should resemble thick pancake batter. If the batter is thinner than that, stir over low heat for 15 to 30 seconds, breaking up any clumps that may form, until the mixture resembles a uniform thick and smooth batter.

STEAM THE CAKE, PAN-FRY, AND SERVE: Brush a 9 by 5-inch loaf pan liberally with neutral oil. Pour in the batter and shake the pan to spread it to an even thickness. Place a 2-inch-tall metal steaming rack in the bottom of a clean wok (or any pot with a lid that will accommodate the loaf pan) and fill with enough water to come up to about 1 inch below the rack.

Bring the water to a simmer over medium-high heat, then place the loaf pan on the rack. Cover tightly with the wok lid and steam over medium-high heat for 50 minutes, until the cake is cooked through, with a slight sheen to it. (Due to the long steaming time, you may need to replenish the wok with more boiling water, so peek at the water level occasionally—preferably without letting too much steam out of the wok.)

Remove the loaf pan from the wok. Let the cake set and cool for at least 1 hour at room temperature. Loosen the sides of the loaf pan with a knife or spatula and turn the cake out onto a cutting board (it should come out easily). Use a sharp knife dipped in water to slice the cake into however many ½-inch-thick slices you'd like.

Add 1 to 2 tablespoons neutral oil to a nonstick or seasoned cast-iron pan over medium to medium-high heat. Fry the slices until golden and crispy, about 6 minutes per side. Serve with the oyster sauce on the side!

MAKE AHEAD
After steaming the loaf and allowing it to set at room temperature, refrigerate it for up to 1 week and slice and fry as you like. You can also freeze it for up to 1 month. Just defrost it overnight in the refrigerator before slicing and frying.

芋角 yù jiǎo

Taro Puffs *(Wu Gok)*

BILL   For Sarah and Kaitlin, wu gok have always been the ultimate prize at dim sum. It's hard to decide which is the best part—the flaky and delicate wisps of golden-fried taro on the outside or the juicy pork and shrimp filling. When Sarah, Kaitlin, and their cousins spot wu gok on a dim sum cart, they launch into *Mission Impossible* mode, tracking the cart's trajectory and shoving the dim sum stamp card into the hands of the cousin physically closest to it, shouting, "Get two!" The chosen cousin then weaves through the Sunday brunch crowd to handpick the best-looking puffs from the bemused auntie pushing the coveted cart.

Overkill? Maybe. But wu gok are an increasingly rare sight, as making them requires precision in mixing the taro dough and frying the puffs at the proper temperature. We share everything you need to make them here. You need large, football-size taro (not the small fist-size ones) for this recipe, and both the filling and taro dough must be chilled overnight before shaping the puffs. Finally, don't be tempted to cut down on the lard—that would be like cutting the butter in a croissant recipe—you just don't do it!

Makes 12 puffs

FOR THE FILLING

2 medium dried shiitake mushrooms

½ cup hot water

2 ounces peeled and deveined shrimp (any size)

1 tablespoon oyster sauce

2 teaspoons cornstarch

¼ teaspoon toasted sesame oil

⅛ teaspoon fine sea salt

⅛ teaspoon sugar

⅛ teaspoon white pepper powder

2 teaspoons finely chopped fresh cilantro (optional)

1 tablespoon neutral oil

2 ounces boneless pork shoulder or butt, finely minced (about ¼ cup) or ground pork

1 large garlic clove, finely minced

1 tablespoon finely chopped shallot

2 teaspoons Shaoxing wine

FOR THE TARO DOUGH

1 pound (450g) large taro root

2½ cups water

⅔ cup (80g) wheat starch

6 tablespoons (80g) pork lard

2 teaspoons sugar

¾ teaspoon fine sea salt

½ teaspoon five-spice powder

⅛ teaspoon baking soda

TO FINISH THE PUFFS

Neutral oil, for shaping and frying

How to Make Lard to Use in Your Cooking

MAKE THE FILLING: In a small bowl, soak the mushrooms in the hot water for 2 hours (or overnight), until rehydrated. Reserve ⅓ cup of the mushroom-soaking water, leaving behind any sediment at the bottom of the bowl. Remove any tough stems from the mushrooms. Finely chop the mushrooms and the shrimp.

In a medium bowl, combine the reserved mushroom-soaking water, the oyster sauce, cornstarch, sesame oil, salt, sugar, white pepper, and cilantro (if using).

Heat the 1 tablespoon of neutral oil in a wok over medium-high heat. Add the pork, using a spatula to break it up, and cook just until it turns color (do not brown it), about 30 seconds. Add the mushrooms, shrimp, garlic, and shallot, and stir-fry for 30 seconds. Pour the Shaoxing wine around the perimeter of the wok. Stir the cornstarch mixture to re-incorporate the cornstarch, which may have settled to the bottom of the bowl, and add to the wok. Cook until the filling thickens

(RECIPE CONTINUES)

and there is no standing liquid, about 1 minute. Transfer to a plate and chill overnight in the refrigerator.

MAKE THE TARO DOUGH: Trim both ends of the taro, then stand the taro upright and use a sharp knife to carefully slice away the brown outer skin. Cut the peeled taro into ¾- to 1-inch chunks (you'll have about 3 cups, but make sure you weigh it at 1 pound/450g for accuracy).

In a medium pot, add the taro chunks and 2½ cups water. Bring to a boil, then simmer for 8 to 9 minutes, until the taro is fork-tender. Use a slotted spoon to transfer the taro to a large bowl, reserving the taro-cooking water in the pot. Use a potato masher or ricer to mash the taro just until smooth. Don't overwork the taro, or it will have a gummy consistency.

Add ½ cup of the reserved taro-cooking water (it should still be warm) to a small pot and stir in the wheat starch.

Whisk until the starch and water are completely combined, with no lumps. Place the pot over low heat and use a rubber spatula or wooden spoon to stir vigorously until the wheat starch thickens into a smooth, stiff paste, 30 to 60 seconds. Remove from the heat.

Use a stiff rubber or bamboo/wood spatula to scrape the paste into the bowl with the taro. Mix in the lard, sugar, salt, five-spice powder, and baking soda, then mash until everything is well incorporated and there are no visible wheat starch or taro lumps in the dough. If the dough crumbles in your hand, add 1 to 2 teaspoons more of the reserved taro-cooking water until it becomes more pliable. Let cool to room temperature, then cover tightly with plastic wrap and refrigerate overnight to let the dough firm up.

SHAPE THE PUFFS: Line a sheet pan with parchment paper. Divide the dough into 12 equal pieces (55g to 60g each). With oiled hands, roll each piece into a ball and place on the prepared sheet pan. Set 3 taro balls aside and refrigerate the rest to ensure the lard in the dough stays cold while you work with the remainder.

Shape each of the 3 balls into a small cup about 1 inch deep, with the edges thinner than the middle. Add about 1 tablespoon of the filling (13g to 14g) to each cup and use a spoon to lightly compress the filling and remove any air pockets (avoid touching the filling with your fingers, or you may stain the taro balls). Pinch the dough closed around the filling and use your palms to form the dough into an oval, like an egg. Place the ovals back onto the sheet pan in the refrigerator and fill and shape the remaining puffs in batches of 3. Work quickly so the dough and filling remain cold as you assemble. Rest the filled ovals, uncovered, at room temperature for 1 hour.

FRY THE PUFFS: Line a plate with paper towels. Heat 3 inches of neutral oil in a medium pot until it reaches 325°F on an instant-read thermometer. (Note: The oil temperature is very important! If the oil isn't hot enough, the outer crust may not form, causing the puff to flake apart. If the oil is too hot, the taro puffs will not form their signature wispy webbing.) Use a slotted spoon to slowly lower 2 or 3 taro puffs into the oil, one at a time. The temperature will drop when you add them, so increase the heat as needed to maintain a temperature of at least 325°F. Use the slotted spoon to gently nudge the puffs

to ensure they don't stick to the pot or each other. Fry them undisturbed for 3 to 4 minutes, until a wispy webbing has formed around each puff and the color is a deep golden brown. Carefully lift each puff out with the slotted spoon, letting excess oil drain off, then transfer to the plate to drain completely. Fry the remaining puffs in batches.

To serve, cut the taro puffs in half with kitchen shears, like they do at dim sum restaurants, so they can cool more quickly. (This also makes sharing easier!)

TIP! STRETCH FRYING OIL
What do you do with used frying oil? You can minimize it in the first place by using smaller, deeper pots for frying. This can halve the amount of oil you need and still get everything cooked in smaller batches. (We've built this into almost all of our recipes.) After frying, strain the oil through a fine-mesh strainer, cover, and refrigerate. You can use the oil for miscellaneous cooking until it's gone. In fact, the taste of "cooked oil" will add flavor to your food. If the oil starts to smell, smokes heavily when heated, or develops foam or solids on the surface, it's time to get rid of it. Pour it into a nonrecyclable container and throw it away right before garbage day so it doesn't hang around too long.

MAKE AHEAD
To prepare these in advance, freeze the filled taro ovals on a parchment-lined tray until solid (covered with plastic wrap or a clean plastic grocery bag), then transfer them to an airtight container for up to 3 months. The night before you'd like to cook them, arrange them on a parchment paper–lined tray to defrost overnight in the refrigerator. Let the taro puffs come to room temperature (about 1 hour) before frying.

菌菇素春卷 jūn gū sù chūnjuǎn

Vegetable & Mushroom Spring Rolls

Made with a meaty blend of shiitake mushrooms, enoki mushrooms, and bamboo shoots, these crispy spring rolls have so much flavor that you might not even notice or care that they're vegetarian. We especially love the enoki mushrooms, which add a nice crunch and moisture to the filling. Make a big batch and keep them in the freezer—it's an absolute treat to take a few out and fry them up whenever a craving hits. They're perfect with rice vinegar for dipping.

Makes 25 spring rolls

FOR THE FILLING

2 ounces dried shiitake mushrooms (about 20 medium)

3 cups hot water

1 tablespoon cornstarch

7 ounces fresh enoki mushrooms

3 tablespoons neutral oil

1 tablespoon finely julienned fresh ginger

2⅔ cups finely julienned carrot (about 8 ounces)

¾ cup thinly sliced shallots (from 3 to 4 medium)

8 ounces canned bamboo shoots, julienned (about 2 cups; see Tip, page 47)

2 tablespoons Shaoxing wine

2 tablespoons light soy sauce

1 tablespoon oyster sauce or vegetarian oyster sauce

½ teaspoon white pepper powder

½ teaspoon toasted sesame oil

Fine sea salt

FOR ASSEMBLY, FRYING, AND SERVING

1 teaspoon cornstarch

2 tablespoons boiling water

1 (12-ounce) package spring roll wrappers (25 sheets)

Neutral oil, for frying

Rice vinegar, for serving (ideally, Shanghai rice vinegar)

MAKE THE FILLING: Soak the shiitake mushrooms in the hot water for 2 hours (or overnight), until fully rehydrated. Drain, reserving the mushroom-soaking water. Squeeze out any excess water, remove any tough stems, and thinly slice the mushrooms.

Add 2 tablespoons of the mushroom-soaking water to a small dish with the cornstarch to make a slurry. (Save the remaining mushroom-soaking liquid.)

Trim off about 1 inch of the root ends of the enoki mushrooms, then wash, drain, and separate the large bunches into thinner strands.

With a wok over medium heat, add the neutral oil. Cook the ginger for 30 seconds, until caramelized on the edges. Add the carrots and shallots, and stir-fry for 2 minutes, until the oil turns an orange color from the carrots and the shallots absorb some of that orange hue.

Add the sliced shiitakes and the bamboo shoots. Increase the heat to high and cook for 8 to 10 minutes, stirring occasionally, until any liquid released from the vegetables has cooked off completely.

Reduce the heat to medium and add the Shaoxing wine, light soy sauce, oyster sauce, white pepper, and sesame oil. Stir to combine. Add the enoki mushrooms and 1 cup of the reserved mushroom-soaking water (leaving behind any sediment at the bottom of the bowl). Increase the heat to high and cook for 2 minutes, until the enoki mushrooms are cooked through and there is still some visible sauce in the wok. Add salt to taste.

(RECIPE CONTINUES)

Stir the cornstarch slurry again to fully combine, then pour the slurry into the center of the mixture. Immediately turn off the heat, and with the residual heat, stir and mix everything well. The mixture should be wet, but there should be no standing liquid. (If there is still standing liquid, continue cooking over medium-low heat to reduce it.)

Transfer the filling to a bowl and let cool completely (to expedite, transfer to the refrigerator).

ASSEMBLE THE SPRING ROLLS: Prepare another slurry, this time by mixing 1 teaspoon cornstarch with 2 tablespoons boiling water. Line a sheet pan with parchment paper.

Place a spring roll wrapper on a flat, clean work surface, with one corner pointing toward you (it should look like a diamond). Place about 2 heaping tablespoons of the filling 2 inches from the corner closest to you. (For accuracy, you can weigh the filling and divide that total by 25 to get an exact filling weight for each spring roll.)

Roll the corner over the filling once and gently press down on both sides of the filling to flatten the spring roll wrapper and squeeze out any air bubbles. Next, fold both the left and right sides of the wrapper toward the center. Continue rolling the spring roll into a tight cigar. When you're about 2 inches from the opposite corner of the wrapper, stir the cornstarch slurry with your finger, then gently brush it on the edges of the wrapper (like an envelope seal) and finish rolling. (Using egg wash can create stains on the wrapper after frying, which is why we use cornstarch slurry.) Place the spring roll seam side down on the prepared sheet pan. Repeat until you've assembled all the spring rolls. The spring rolls must be either fried or frozen within 1 hour of assembly (see Freezing Spring Rolls).

FRY THE SPRING ROLLS: Place a wire cooling rack on a sheet pan or line a plate with paper towels. Fill a small pot (which requires less oil) with 2 to 3 inches of the neutral oil—just enough to submerge the spring rolls when frying. Heat the oil slowly over medium heat until it reaches 350°F on an instant-read thermometer. (Or dip a bamboo or wooden chopstick into the hot oil. The oil is ready when small bubbles form around

See How We Wrap Spring Rolls

the chopstick.) Fry the spring rolls in small batches of 4 to 5 at a time. Use chopsticks or a slotted spoon to turn the spring rolls a few times during the frying process, and fry until golden brown, about 5 minutes. If you notice the oil temperature dropping, increase the heat under the pot. If the wrappers begin to form bubbles on their surface, the oil is too hot; turn off the heat until the oil cools to 350°F. Transfer the fried spring rolls to the wire rack or plate to drain. Serve with rice vinegar for dipping.

TIP! Canned bamboo shoots can sometimes have a unique aroma that you may not be a fan of. Soak the shoots overnight and rinse thoroughly in a colander to neutralize it.

FREEZING SPRING ROLLS
Place uncooked spring rolls on a sheet pan lined with parchment paper. Cover tightly with plastic wrap (or use a clean plastic grocery bag) and freeze overnight. When frozen solid, transfer them to a freezer bag or container and store for up to 3 months. When you're ready to fry them, transfer them directly from the freezer to the fryer. Do not thaw them beforehand.

From top, left to right: With my mother and older sisters in the kitchen where I grew up; my grandfather at the helm of a lunch buffet in the Catskills; my biological father cooking at Singer's, a Chinese/American deli and restaurant on Main Street in Liberty, NY; my stepfather (the grandfather Sarah and Kaitlin grew up knowing) with his legendary Thanksgiving turkey, which we still make every year to this day; my stepfather manning the main wok station at our family-owned restaurant, Sun Hing.

Cooking in the Catskills

BILL

I COME FROM a long line of cooks. My grandfather became a chef when he arrived in America, and my father served the Chinese side of the menu at Singer's Restaurant in our town of Liberty, New York. Singer's was smack-dab in the middle of the Borscht Belt (a.k.a. "The Jewish Alps"), a Catskills resort area that Jewish New Yorkers escaped to during the hot and sticky months of summer. Later, my stepfather worked at one of the area's biggest resorts—Grossinger's Catskill Resort Hotel—as a roast cook in its glamourous 1,300-seat dining room. He then became head chef at the Holiday Inn, a hoppin' destination with a live band that played until 2 a.m. on Fridays and Saturdays (my high school music teacher moonlighted as the band leader). My mother was also a remarkable home cook, and I remember hanging around her in the kitchen, standing on a chair to watch her churn out dishes like pork bone soup, shrimp stir-fries, and homey plates of steamed chicken and mushrooms.

Growing up, my favorite time was always Chinese New Year, when both my parents were in the kitchen together, cooking all the classics for the holiday, like nian gao (sweet rice cakes). Mom was deliberate and fastidious, tasting often to make sure everything she cooked was perfect. Each night of the week leading up to the new year, she'd sit on a small bench in the kitchen in front of a large batch of rice flour and water, pouring in hot brown sugar syrup and skillfully mixing the batter with her hands until it was smooth as silk. The resulting cakes were shared as gifts for family and friends, ready to be sliced and pan-fried until crisp on the outside and chewy and sweet on the inside.

We'd sometimes play hooky, taking the day off from work and school to be with family—and, yes, cook more food! We'd begin by cooking up a lo han jai (Buddha's Delight) and frying a big batch of colorful

and crispy shrimp chips. Over the course of the day, more elaborate and intricate dishes came together, like Poached "White Cut" Chicken (page 145), pan-fried whole fish, and Cantonese Roast Pork Belly (page 180)—these three items were always put out along with burning incense as an invitation to our ancestors to celebrate with us.

In addition to the Lunar New Year, we had other food-centric celebrations like the Dragonboat Festival (duānwǔ jié, in Mandarin), when we'd make zòngzi (see page 53)—sticky rice bundles wrapped in bamboo leaves. Then there were the mahjong nights when my mother invited other Chinese families in the area for a huge, homemade meal (people raved about her ketchup shrimp), making sure everyone had a good time regardless of whether they won or lost.

Sadly, my father died when I was in third grade, leaving behind my mom, me, and my two older sisters. Even though I was so young, I still remember my biological father cooking at home, as well as the precious few times I was allowed to step into the Singer's

kitchen for a short workday visit. When my mother married my stepfather, he carried on our connection with the kitchen. Though he was my stepfather, we rarely referred to him as such. He was a loving presence in my and my sisters' later years, and after he became the head chef in charge of the Holiday Inn's Chinese-Polynesian-American restaurant, he became instrumental in my kitchen education.

During the summer before my junior year of college, I started out as a busboy at the Holiday Inn on weeknights and weekends, funding my fishing hobby and the mini-bikes and snowmobiles that occupied my time. I mostly cleared tables and served as a runner, and my only responsibility that came close to cooking was making the Caesar salad dressing. As my college planning began, however, I needed to stockpile tuition money, so I moved into the kitchen, working twelve-hour days, chopping onions, washing vegetables, and assembling egg roll after egg roll for popular pupu platters. Regular tasks included peeling fifteen pounds of shrimp for the dinner service and marinating bus

Opposite: Carrying on kitchen lessons I learned from my parents while cooking dinner for Judy, Sarah, and Kaitlin.
Left: Reminiscing about old times with a childhood buddy at Revonah Hill, a swimming hole and old summer hangout spot from our grade school days.

boxes filled with spareribs and char siu. As I gained more experience, I made my way from the prep table to roasting chickens for "chicken flamingo" (there was nothing "flamingo" about it—it was just half a roast chicken) and cooking at the wok. My stepfather taught me how to flawlessly reproduce the same dishes day after day (the hallmark of a great chef), and gave me invaluable kitchen lessons, like how to thicken a sauce until it's glossy, double-frying pupu platter items until perfectly crispy, and breaking down whole chickens and big cuts of beef and pork.

By the late '70s and early '80s, the popularity of those Catskills resorts was winding down, and Grossinger's closed in 1986, just as I was finishing college in Rochester. It marked the end of the Catskills resort industry that had supported generations of my family. The last time I saw Grossinger's—not too long ago—it was an abandoned ruin, with the once luxurious pool overgrown with weeds and covered in graffiti. When those resorts shut down, countless jobs were lost and local businesses suffered, including Chinese restaurants.

But the silver lining was that all those long hours had paid off. My stepfather always said that I earned more than a paycheck. The knowledge I acquired was the real money in my pocket. Although we eventually left the Catskills (my parents went on to open their own restaurant in New Jersey), I'll never forget those early days: New Year's with my family, mahjong parties, and tasty weeknight meals. To this day, I thank my mother for teaching me about what good food tastes like and how to coax it out of a home kitchen; and I thank my father for the professional kitchen lessons I still use every day.

Although those who taught me—and the places where I learned—are now just warm memories, I like to think that I'm keeping those recipes, techniques, and traditions alive when I share them with Sarah and Kaitlin, and with everyone who visits *The Woks of Life*.

广式肉粽 guǎng shì ròu zòng

Bill's Mother's Cantonese Zongzi

JUDY Zongzi (or zung, in Cantonese) consist of glutinous rice with sweet or savory fillings wrapped in bamboo leaves or reed leaves. They are commonly served around the time of the Dragonboat Festival (in late spring or early summer), and every family has their own recipe. This is our version, and it's bursting with treasures: salted duck egg yolks (available in vacuum-sealed packages in Chinese grocery stores), pork belly, Chinese sausage, and peanuts (we use raw ones, which you can also find in Chinese groceries). It's a take on Bill's mother's recipe with mung beans, a traditional Hakka Chinese addition. It may be time-consuming to make these (start one to two days ahead of serving), but your efforts will be rewarded with happy faces and stomachs. If you're short on time, scan the QR code to learn how to cook zongzi in an Instant Pot pressure cooker.

Makes 14 zongzi

36 to 40 dried bamboo leaves or reed leaves (2 to 3 leaves per zongzi)

4 cups uncooked short-grain glutinous rice (also called sweet rice or sticky rice)

⅔ cup raw shelled skinless peanuts

1 pound boneless pork belly

¼ cup light soy sauce

2 tablespoons Shaoxing wine

1 tablespoon fine sea salt, plus more for serving

1 teaspoon five-spice powder

1 teaspoon sugar

½ teaspoon white pepper powder

1½ cups split mung beans

3 links Chinese cured pork sausage (preferably thicker links weighing about 2 ounces each)

14 salted duck egg yolks

DO THE NIGHT BEFORE: The evening before you plan to assemble the zongzi, add the bamboo leaves to a large bowl and submerge them in cool water, weighting them down with another heavy bowl. To another large bowl, add the glutinous rice and cover with 2 inches of water. In a medium bowl, submerge the raw peanuts in water as well. Soak the leaves, rice, and peanuts overnight.

Cut the pork belly into 14 equal pieces (1 piece per zongzi) and place in a large bowl. Add 2 tablespoons of the light soy sauce, the Shaoxing wine, 1 teaspoon of the salt, the five-spice powder, sugar, and white pepper. Mix well. Cover the bowl with an overturned plate and refrigerate overnight.

DO THE NEXT DAY: Place the split mung beans in a medium bowl, cover with 2 inches of water, and let soak for 1 hour.

Meanwhile, drain the soaked leaves and rinse each leaf well on both sides. Use kitchen shears to trim 1 inch from the base of each leaf. (The bottom ends are too tough for folding.) Place the leaves in a clean bowl of water.

Using a fine-mesh strainer, drain the soaked rice. Place it back in the bowl and stir in the remaining 2 tablespoons light soy sauce and 1½ teaspoons of the salt.

Drain the soaked peanuts. Drain the mung beans and mix them with the remaining ½ teaspoon salt. Slice the sausages into 14 roughly equal pieces.

How to Cook Zongzi in an Instant Pot

(RECIPE CONTINUES)

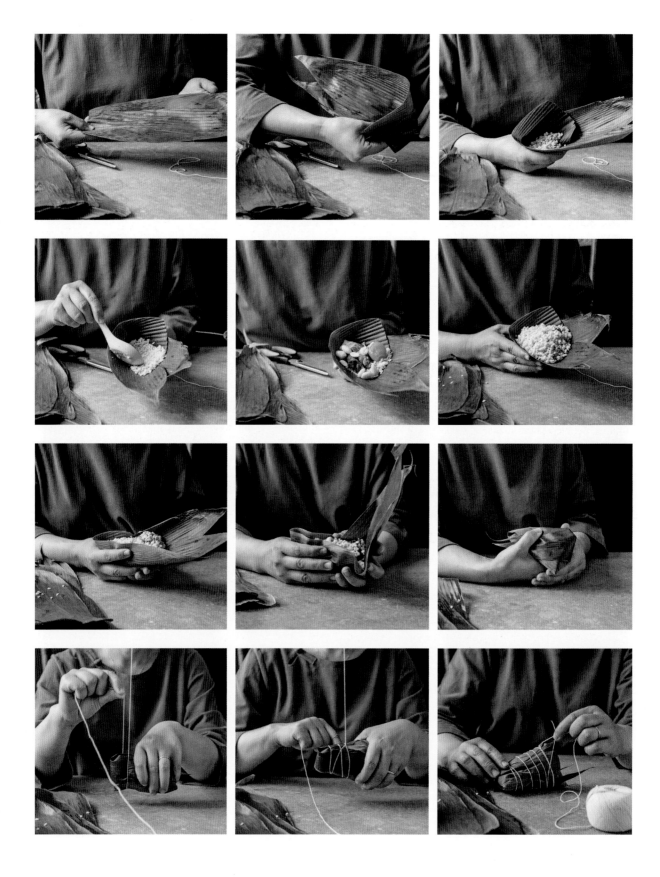

WRAP THE ZONGZI: Position 2 of the soaked leaves vertically so they are parallel to each other but overlapping by about two-thirds of their width (you can use a third leaf if the leaves are smaller than average). Keeping the leaves pressed together, roll the base of the leaves into a wide cone.

Add a scoop of mung beans to the bottom of the cone. Next, add a thin layer of rice to the cone, spreading it so it extends about 3 inches up the leaves from the mung beans. Top with a piece each of pork belly, sausage, and salted egg yolk, then add a sprinkling of peanuts. Cover with more glutinous rice and mung beans to fill any air pockets, bringing the filling to just below the rim of the cone.

Fold the long end of the leaves down to cover the opening of the cone, using the hand that is holding the zongzi to gently press the two sides of the zongzi together. Use both hands to fold the long end of the leaves down over the sides to create a tight seal. Tie the zongzi securely with kitchen string. (It's best to tie one end of the twine to an anchor point or kitchen fixture, like your kitchen sink, because you will only have one hand to tie the zongzi—your other hand will be holding the zongzi. (Most home zongzi makers use their teeth to anchor one end of the twine.) The zongzi should be tied tightly enough to stay firmly sealed, but not so tight that there's no room for the rice to expand as it cooks. Repeat to make the remaining zongzi. If any leaves rip during the wrapping process, you'll need to discard the ripped leaf and start over, or wrap a new leaf over the open seam. That's why we call for more leaves than are technically needed.

COOK THE ZONGZI: Nestle the zongzi neatly in a large stockpot, packing them tightly and avoiding large gaps. Fill the pot with water up to about 3 inches below the pot's rim (you'll need a lot of water for the lengthy cooking time).

Place the stockpot over high heat and bring to a boil. When the water boils, reduce the heat to medium-low, cover, and simmer for 5 hours. The water should remain at a low simmer—constantly moving, but with no large bubbles. Check the pot periodically to make sure the zongzi are always submerged. If you need to adjust the water level, add only boiling water (do not add cold water).

After 5 hours, open a zongzi and see how you like the texture. The filling should be sticky and homogenous. Simmer for up to 1 hour longer, if desired. Serve with salt to taste.

MAKE AHEAD
Freeze the cooked zongzi in resealable bags or an airtight container for up to 3 months. To reheat, place the zongzi in a pot (no need to thaw beforehand) and add enough water to cover. Cover and bring the water to a boil. Lower the heat to a simmer and cook for 30 minutes.

咖喱鸡角 gālí jī jiǎo
Chicken Curry Puffs

When Chinese bakeries and dim sum houses whip up curry puffs, they make the filling both sweet and savory. Here, we're using ground chicken, stirred into a smooth curry sauce punctuated by plenty of caramelized onions. These have a pleasant balance of salt, spice, and sugar, making them perfect for an appetizer, afternoon snack, or even breakfast with a cup of tea. These puffs taste best made with our homemade puff pastry, but you can also use store-bought.

Makes 18 puffs

FOR THE FILLING

1 tablespoon neutral oil

12 ounces ground chicken or turkey

1 cup diced yellow onion (about 1 small onion)

1 large garlic clove, minced

¾ cup plus 3 tablespoons water

1 tablespoon Madras curry powder

1½ teaspoons sugar

¾ teaspoon fine sea salt

¼ teaspoon ground black pepper

¼ teaspoon ground cumin

¼ teaspoon turmeric powder

1 tablespoon cornstarch

FOR ASSEMBLY, BAKING, AND SERVING

Homemade Rough Puff Pastry (page 59), or 1 (17-ounce) package frozen puff pastry

1 large egg, lightly beaten

1 large egg yolk, lightly beaten

Black or white untoasted sesame seeds, for topping

MAKE THE FILLING: Heat the oil in a large skillet over medium-high heat. Add the chicken and cook until it turns color, about 5 minutes. Add the onion and garlic, and cook until the onion is translucent, about 4 minutes. Add ¾ cup of the water, the curry powder, sugar, salt, black pepper, cumin, and turmeric. Stir and cook for 2 minutes to let the flavors meld.

In a small bowl, stir together the cornstarch and the remaining 3 tablespoons water, then add to the chicken mixture, stir, and simmer until thickened. You'll know it's ready when there's no pooling liquid. Transfer the filling mixture to a medium bowl and let cool. You will have about 1¾ cups of filling.

ASSEMBLE THE PUFFS: If your puff pastry is frozen, let it defrost at room temperature for 35 to 40 minutes. Line two baking sheets with parchment paper.

If using rough puff pastry, unfold it carefully to ensure there are no rips or tears. Cut it into 2 equal rectangles and put one half back in the refrigerator while you make the first batch of curry puffs. (If using store-bought pastry, you'll already have 2 equal sheets. Take one of them out and leave the other in the fridge.) With a rolling pin, lightly roll the pastry into a 12-inch square. Then cut the square into nine 3-inch squares.

Spoon about 1½ tablespoons of filling into the center of each square. Brush 2 adjoining edges with the beaten whole egg. Fold the square diagonally to form a triangle, pressing the edges together, then crimp the edges with a fork. Transfer the triangle to the prepared baking sheet and continue until you've assembled 9 puffs. Refrigerate this first batch to chill for up to 1 hour while you repeat these steps with the remaining sheet of puff pastry. Transfer the second batch of puffs to the refrigerator to chill for at least 15 minutes.

(RECIPE CONTINUES)

BAKE THE PUFFS: Position two racks in the upper and lower thirds of the oven, then preheat to 425°F.

Brush the puffs with the beaten egg yolk and sprinkle with the sesame seeds. Transfer the puffs to the oven and immediately reduce the oven temperature to 400°F.

Bake for 14 to 16 minutes, rotating the pans halfway through, until the puffs are golden brown. Let them cool for 5 minutes before enjoying.

MAKE AHEAD
The puffs can be frozen, unbaked, for up to 3 months. No need to thaw before baking. Reheat any leftovers in the toaster oven until crisp.

HOMEMADE
ROUGH PUFF PASTRY

Makes 2 pastry sheets

1½ cups (210g) all-purpose flour, plus more for rolling
¼ teaspoon fine sea salt
15 tablespoons (210g) unsalted butter, very cold
7 to 8 tablespoons ice water, as needed

In a large bowl, whisk together the 1½ cups flour and the salt. Use a box grater to grate the cold butter on top of the flour (or use the grating attachment on a food processor). Mix in the butter pieces with a fork and your fingers until the mixture resembles coarse crumbs with some pea-size lumps remaining. Add the ice water 1 tablespoon at a time, mixing and pressing the dough with a rubber spatula until it comes together. Use your hands to press the dough into a disc, wrap the disc tightly in plastic wrap, and refrigerate for 30 minutes.

Unwrap the chilled dough (save the plastic; you'll reuse it several times). On a lightly floured surface, use a floured rolling pin to roll out the dough into a 6 by 15-inch rectangle, keeping the edges and corners straight. With the short side of the rectangle facing you, fold the rectangle into thirds, like a business letter, folding the top third of the rectangle over the middle third, and then folding the bottom third on top. Wrap tightly in plastic wrap and chill for 30 minutes.

On a lightly floured surface, roll out the dough once again into a 6 by 15-inch rectangle, and then fold it into thirds once more. Rotate the dough 90 degrees and repeat, rolling the dough out again into a 6 by 15-inch rectangle and folding it again into thirds. Wrap and chill for another 30 minutes.

Repeat the above step once more. Then wrap the dough one final time and refrigerate for at least 1½ hours. (You can also make the pastry to this point and then transfer it to the freezer for up to 3 months.) It's now ready to use.

Starters

For our family, the start of a meal is just as important as the main event. Any dinner guest at our house knows that before the meal even begins, I make sure we shower them with a spread of pan-fried dumplings and maybe a charcuterie board, in case they still feel peckish. In this chapter, you'll find American treats like Crab Rangoon (page 78), but you'll also find Chinese liáng cài, or cold starters. These dishes are often just as coveted as the hot dishes served later in the meal, providing a mix of flavors and textures to whet the appetite. I often turn to easy cold dishes like "Sour Spicy" Napa Cabbage Salad (page 71) or Fast Sizzled Cucumber Salad (page 73) to round out a meal; these also make great leftovers for the next day's breakfast with a bowl of hot rice, pao fan (see page 65), or congee. **JUDY**

葱油饼 *cōng yóubǐng*

Classic Scallion Pancakes

JUDY The scallion pancakes of my childhood were small, crispy discs cooked by street vendors on a large round griddle—perfect for holding in one hand and eating on the go. In my middle-school years, I spent afternoons wandering the narrow streets of Shanghai with my friends, and whenever our after-school adventures led us near a scallion pancake vendor, we couldn't resist that alluring scallion oil aroma. Even though one pancake cost only a handful of pennies, I rarely had money to spare, and more than once my friends chipped in so I wasn't left out of the fun. It was one of my greatest simple pleasures, and I'm forever grateful for their thoughtfulness and friendship. Here, I've recreated that classic scallion pancake, just as I remember it.

Makes 8 small pancakes

1½ cups (210g) all-purpose flour, plus more as needed

½ cup boiling water

2 to 3 tablespoons cold water

Neutral oil, for shaping dough and cooking

1 teaspoon fine sea salt

1 cup finely chopped scallions (from about 4 scallions), white and green parts, patted dry before chopping

In the bowl of a stand mixer fitted with the dough hook, add the 1½ cups flour. With the mixer on low speed, slowly stream in the boiling water. Periodically stop the mixer and use a rubber spatula to push the flour toward the center of the bowl, until the dough hook has worked in all the flour.

When a shaggy dough has formed, gradually add the cold water, 1 tablespoon at a time, just until the dough lifts off the sides of the bowl. Give the dough about 1 minute to absorb the liquid after each addition of water.

Transfer the dough to a clean surface and knead by hand for 5 minutes, until soft and smooth. If the dough is sticky or tacky, add more flour, 1 tablespoon at a time, until the dough smooths out.

Divide the dough into 8 equal pieces and form each piece into a smooth ball. Brush the dough balls with a little oil to prevent them from drying out, then cover them with an overturned bowl. Let rest at room temperature for 45 to 60 minutes.

To test if the dough is properly relaxed, use your palm to flatten a dough ball. If the dough stays flat and doesn't bounce back, it's ready to be rolled. (Be patient because relaxed dough will be easier to work with and yield a softer pancake.) Brush a clean work surface and a rolling pin lightly with oil. Transfer a dough ball to the oiled surface and roll it out into a thin 4 by 9-inch rectangle. Brush it with a thin layer of oil and sprinkle it evenly with a pinch of salt (about ⅛ teaspoon) and 2 tablespoons of the chopped scallions. Roll the pancake lengthwise into a tight, long cigar with the seam side up.

Press the seam closed so no scallion bits are poking out. Roll the tube up into a spiral—like a snail shell—to form a disc. Tuck the loose ends under the disc, then brush the top with some oil and repeat these steps with the remaining 7 dough balls, oiling the work surface and rolling pin as needed.

Finally, roll each disc into a pancake 4 to 5 inches in diameter. (A 4-inch pancake will be thicker and chewier; a 5-inch pancake will be flatter and crispier.)

Heat a large cast-iron pan or nonstick pan over medium heat. (If using cast iron, preheat until it just starts to smoke; if using a nonstick pan, simply heat it until hot.) Add 2 to 3 tablespoons oil, or enough to coat the bottom of the pan in a generous layer (to get even coloring and crispy results.) Add 2 pancakes at a time to the pan, and cook each side for 3 to 4 minutes, until they're an even golden brown. Repeat with the remaining three batches of pancakes. (Don't be tempted to rush the process; higher heat levels will burn the pancakes before the dough cooks through!)

MAKE AHEAD
Place the rolled, uncooked pancakes between layers of parchment paper, and transfer to a resealable plastic bag. Freeze for up to 3 months. When you're ready to cook, simply follow the cooking steps in the recipe. There's no need to thaw the pancakes before cooking.

雪菜毛豆炒香干 *xuě cài máodòu chǎo xiānggān*

Edamame, Tofu & Pickled Mustard Greens
Stir-Fry

This dish has been in our rotation for as long as we can remember. Edamame beans get blistered with cubes of dòufu gān (pressed tofu), chili, ginger, garlic, and pickled mustard greens—ingredients we always have on hand in the freezer, fridge, or pantry. It's often served as a starter, but as a filling source of protein, this stir-fry can also be the only dish you put on the table. For large gatherings, this is super fast to make (in under 10 minutes!), as well as an easy dish to serve with plain rice, scooped over noodle soup, or with a quick pot of pao fan (boiled leftover rice; see How to Make Pao Fan).

Serves 4

FOR THE SEASONING MIXTURE

2 tablespoons water

4 teaspoons Shaoxing wine

1½ teaspoons light soy sauce

¾ teaspoon sugar

½ teaspoon fine sea salt

½ teaspoon toasted sesame oil

¼ teaspoon white pepper powder

FOR THE REST OF THE DISH

2 tablespoons neutral oil

1⅔ cups frozen shelled edamame (soybeans; about 10 ounces), rinsed in hot water to thaw

1 large (⅛-inch thick) slice fresh ginger

3 dried red chilies, seeded and sliced into small pieces

¾ cup finely chopped pickled mustard greens (xuě cài, 雪菜; also sometimes "potherb cabbage"; about 5 ounces)

2 teaspoons minced garlic (about 2 cloves)

8 ounces spiced or plain pressed tofu (dòufu gān, 豆腐干), cut into ¼- to ½-inch cubes

MAKE THE SEASONING MIXTURE: In a small bowl, combine the water, Shaoxing wine, light soy sauce, sugar, salt, sesame oil, and white pepper.

STIR-FRY THE EDAMAME: Heat a wok over medium-high heat until it just begins to smoke. Add 1 tablespoon of the neutral oil, along with the edamame. Stir-fry for 2 to 3 minutes, until tender and lightly blistered. Periodically spread the edamame in a single layer, so all the beans cook evenly. Transfer to a plate.

ASSEMBLE THE DISH: Reduce the heat to medium, then add the remaining tablespoon neutral oil. Add the ginger and cook for 30 seconds, until the ginger is fragrant and lightly browned at the edges. Add the chilies, followed by the pickled mustard greens. Stir-fry for 1 minute, then add the garlic. Stir to combine.

Add the tofu and stir-fry for 1 minute. Stir in the edamame and add the prepared seasoning mixture. Stir-fry for another 2 minutes. Serve.

HOW TO MAKE PAO FAN
In a medium pot, add leftover cooked white rice along with enough water to submerge it. Bring to a simmer over medium heat, and cook for about 10 minutes, or until it reaches your desired consistency (less time for thinner pao fan and longer for a thicker consistency). If it gets too thick, stir in a little more water.

From top, left to right: My parents back in Hubei; a family dinner in Shanghai's famous Yu Garden while on our first family trip to China; Sarah and Kaitlin discovering just how good a fresh piece of fried dough from a street vendor can taste (they also tried sugar cane for the first time, which is what you see in the cart next to them); enjoying dim sum in Shenzhen; eating giant river snails in Zhangjiajie, Hunan.

Memories of Morsels Past

JUDY

I SPENT MY early childhood in Hubei, a province in central China, where my parents met and married, just after China's Great Leap Forward (1958-62). Both originally from Shanghai, they had gone to Hubei when they were called upon—as educated young people—to help rural villages industrialize the nation's agriculture. Although I would eventually move to America and be introduced to peanut butter, restaurant meals, and food blogging, I grew up with very different food memories than those of my daughters.

During the Great Leap Forward, the government had ordered the establishment of People's Communes, where everyone ate in communal canteens. These canteens survived into my childhood (they lasted into the early 1980s), and for some meals (usually lunch), we ate dàguōfàn, or "big wok meals," at the village cafeteria. I would grab an enameled metal bowl from home and walk with it to the cafeteria a few minutes away, where the cook would scoop whatever was available that day into my bowl. My favorites were braised eggplant and the steamed pork with broken rice they served during festivals and holidays.

Though I was very young, I still remember how the rare appearance of meat at the dinner table could make my family happy for days. A memorable treasure was the whole salted pig head we'd bring back from biennial trips to visit relatives in Shanghai. The pig head hung discreetly in the kitchen, away from prying eyes, and we'd slice off a little piece for a special meal every once in a while, trying our best to make it last and not flinching when we had to fight off flies. It was perhaps the most precious item in our small one-room home.

Mealtimes weren't necessarily a sit-down affair. There was no such thing as a dining-room table. We ate meals on a low table outside, while standing in doorways, or on the go. I would often take my bowl of

Left: Me and my best friend on a school spring outing.
Above: A more recent trip to Shanghai in 2011; when in Shanghai, we can never resist the sight of fried dough (luckily, there's never a shortage of it!).
Opposite: Me and Bill enjoying a street food market in Beijing. I never thought I'd have a chance to live in China again, but when Bill was offered a temporary work assignment there, we jumped at the opportunity!

rice and go for a walk around the neighborhood, visiting friends and seeing what there was to eat in other houses, taking just a morsel or two for a little variety. One of my favorite "bites" was a taste of our neighbors' pickled chilies, so vibrant and tasty with my plain rice.

While I always had food to eat, my parents were worried that I wasn't getting the nutrition I needed in my growing years, as we relied mostly on rice and seasonal vegetables. When I was in fifth grade, they sent me to live with my paternal grandmother in Shanghai, where meat and seafood were more available. At the time, I resented being sent away from my parents, even if it did bring relief from stressful pig-head maintenance. But I had to admit that food in the big city did offer more variety. My grandmother would wake up before daybreak—around 4:30 a.m.—to get in line at the market for the chance to buy fresh fish or a slab of pork belly for special guests. Despite her diligence, she often had to settle for meat and produce that were less

than fresh—or buy other ingredients entirely if they were sold out.

By the time she'd return, I would just be waking up to our neighbors' loud chatter. Our home was tucked within a maze of alleyways—rows of houses where multiple generations of families lived together. It wasn't unusual for seven or eight families to share one house, with one family per room. There were no secrets in our building, or any building for that matter. The single-layer wood-panel walls meant that everyone knew everyone else's business.

In the mornings, the grandmothers would gather in the communal kitchen to begin preparing the day's meals, swapping stories of shopping conquests and defeats from their morning market trips. Some were overjoyed with what they'd managed to get their hands on—like pork bones for soup, or particularly fresh fish—while others cursed someone who'd cut the line. The fun part was seeing what everyone else was

eating and sharing cooking tips in the common area, where each family's coal-burning stove was lined up next to the stone sink we all shared. Squawking old ladies returning from the market, splashes of water reverberating off of enamel wash basins, cleavers hitting cutting boards, the rapid whoosh of a palm leaf fan reviving old coals, and the chatter that ensued as spatulas clanged against woks were the soundtrack of my mornings in Shanghai.

Against all odds, my food repertoire expanded. While I missed our neighbors' pickled chilies in my village in Hubei, in Shanghai I reveled in the rich stickiness of my grandmother's red braised pork belly (page 189), every bowl of wonton soup (see page 257), and my first bite of a juicy soup dumpling. In Hubei, I'd never eaten seafood, but in Shanghai, I got to enjoy steamed yellow croakers and meaty pan-fried belt fish. I've since traveled to China many times to revisit my favorites with Bill and the girls, and I've shared those recipes on the blog and in this book.

But there's something particularly special about my memories from those days. Even when I manage to find a stall on one of the few quiet streets left in the shadows of Shanghai's skyscrapers, they don't quite match the tastes of my childhood. Though many of those meals were far from perfect, nothing will ever compare with them. When I think about it, I'm reminded of an old Chinese saying: wù yǐ xī wéi guì (物以稀为贵), What is rare becomes precious.

凉拌酸辣白菜

liángbàn suān là báicài

"Sour Spicy" Napa Cabbage Salad

When you're sitting down to a heavy meal of Sichuan dishes (like our Mapo Tofu on page 250 or Kung Pao Chicken on page 150), this "sour spicy" salad brings a welcome and refreshing contrast. The star ingredient is napa cabbage, an excellent blank canvas for the tart, lightly sweet, and spicy dressing. This salad is best prepared right before serving for optimal crunch and flavor.

Serves 4

12 ounces napa cabbage

2 scallions, white and green parts julienned

1½ teaspoons Ultimate Chili Oil (page 275), or to taste

1 teaspoon grated garlic (from 1 large clove)

1 teaspoon light soy sauce

1 teaspoon rice vinegar

1 teaspoon toasted sesame oil

¾ teaspoon sugar

¼ teaspoon ground Sichuan peppercorns

Fine sea salt

Break the napa cabbage into individual leaves and wash them, then shake off any excess water. Slice the leaves crosswise into ¼-inch-wide strips. Use a salad spinner to thoroughly dry the shredded leaves.

In a large bowl, mix the napa cabbage with the scallions, chili oil, garlic, light soy sauce, rice vinegar, sesame oil, sugar, ground Sichuan peppercorns, and salt to taste. Toss thoroughly, until all the cabbage is evenly coated. Serve immediately.

响油黄瓜 xiǎng yóu huángguā

Fast Sizzled
Cucumber Salad

When the hot, humid days of summer hit, our smashed cucumber salad is one of the most popular recipes on the blog. This version has a slightly more "pickled" flavor from a couple good spoonfuls of rice vinegar. It also boasts an easy shortcut for the perfect amount of freshly toasted chili oil, which is ideal if you haven't yet committed to making your own (see page 275) or if your stash is running low. Just be sure to let the oil cool adequately before tossing it with the cucumbers. You're aiming for cool and crunchy, with a slight sour pucker that goes great as a starter or side with richer dishes.

Serves 4

3 large garlic cloves, minced

2 to 3 teaspoons Sichuan chili flakes

2 teaspoons toasted sesame seeds

¼ teaspoon ground Sichuan peppercorns

¼ cup neutral oil

1½ pounds seedless English cucumbers (about 2 medium)

2 tablespoons rice vinegar

¾ teaspoon sugar

½ teaspoon fine sea salt, or to taste

To a small heatproof bowl, add the garlic, as much of the chili flakes as desired, the sesame seeds, and ground Sichuan peppercorns.

In a small saucepan, heat the oil over medium heat until shimmering. Turn off the heat and pour the oil over the garlic and spice mixture (it should sizzle!), using a rubber spatula to scrape all the oil from the saucepan into the bowl. Let cool (to expedite, transfer to the refrigerator).

Trim the ends of the cucumbers and cut the cucumbers into pieces about 2 inches long and ½ inch thick.

Add the cucumbers to a medium bowl, then add the rice vinegar, sugar, salt, and the cooled oil mixture. Toss to combine and serve.

凉拌双丝 liángbàn shuāng sī

Shredded Potato & Carrot Salad

We first had this refreshingly light and crunchy salad in China. While we tend to think of potatoes as either mashed, roasted, or fried, the script is flipped here. The potatoes are shredded, soaked to remove some of their starch, and then blanched. The result is a crunchier texture similar to jícama, but with the mellowness and satisfaction we all crave from potatoes. You'll see potatoes prepared this way in China often, for both cold dishes like this one and for stir-fries. They're a perfect companion to the sweet and crunchy carrots.

Serves 4

1 large russet potato (10 to 12 ounces)

1 medium carrot, julienned

1 long hot green pepper or Anaheim pepper, seeded and julienned

3 tablespoons neutral oil

1½ tablespoons whole Sichuan peppercorns

1 tablespoon minced garlic (from about 3 cloves)

1 tablespoon light soy sauce

2 teaspoons rice vinegar

1 to 2 teaspoons Ultimate Chili Oil (page 275)

¾ teaspoon sugar

½ teaspoon fine sea salt, or to taste

¼ cup finely chopped fresh cilantro leaves and stems

Peel and rinse the potato, then cut off a thin slice on one of its long sides to make a stable flat surface. Position the potato on your cutting board so it's resting on the flat side and carefully cut it into very thin slices, keeping the slices overlapping in a neat line. Then cut the potato slices into long, thin matchsticks. (You could also use a mandolin for this job.)

Transfer the matchsticks to a large bowl of cold water and let soak for 10 minutes. Drain and then soak again in fresh water for another 10 minutes. (This process removes excess starch to give the potatoes a crisp texture after cooking.)

Meanwhile, bring a medium pot of water to a boil. Also prepare a large bowl of ice water. When the water comes to a boil, add the potato and carrot. Simmer for 2 minutes. Add the pepper and simmer for another 30 seconds. Use a strainer to transfer the vegetables to the ice water to stop the cooking process.

Heat the neutral oil in a wok over medium-low heat. Add the Sichuan peppercorns and allow them to infuse the oil for 10 minutes. You should see small bubbles forming around the peppercorns, and they will darken in color slightly, but should not burn.

Add the minced garlic to a small heatproof bowl. Pour the hot oil through a strainer on top of the garlic—the garlic will sizzle and smell fragrant. Stir in the light soy sauce, rice vinegar, chili oil, sugar, and salt.

Thoroughly drain the vegetables (you don't want any residual water diluting the dressing), then add the vegetables to a large bowl. Add the cilantro, then pour in the sauce and toss until thoroughly combined. Serve immediately (or make up to 1 day in advance and serve at room temperature).

老上海土豆沙拉
lǎo shànghǎi tǔdòu shālā

"Old Shanghai" Potato Salad

JUDY This Shanghai-style potato salad—a true relic of old Shanghai—is an example of Haipai cuisine, a mash-up of various Western cooking influences developed in Shanghai in the early twentieth century, when the city was already a hub of international business and culture. Haipai is slang for "foreign," but it was also shorthand for a fashionable, international lifestyle. Dining at restaurants that served steaks, coffee, and European-style pastries and cakes? *Very* haipai (and very expensive). This salad is the closest we ever got to haipai. It's based on a Russian-style Olivier salad, which is a mayonnaise-based potato salad with assorted vegetables, a protein (usually ham, chicken, or Russian red kolbasa sausage, known in Chinese as hóngcháng), and apples. When I was growing up in China, it was served on the eve of every Spring Festival (Lunar New Year).

Serves 4

1 pound russet potatoes, scrubbed (3 medium or 2 large)

⅓ cup small-diced carrot

⅓ cup frozen peas

½ cup peeled and small-diced apple (any variety)

½ cup small-diced ham

½ teaspoon fine sea salt, plus more to taste

¼ cup mayonnaise

2 tablespoons whole milk

2 teaspoons white vinegar

½ teaspoon sugar

Add the whole potatoes to a medium pot and cover with water. Place over high heat, cover, and bring to a boil. Reduce the heat to medium-low and simmer until the potatoes are fork-tender, 15 to 20 minutes for medium potatoes and 25 to 30 minutes for large potatoes. Prepare a bowl of ice water, then use a slotted spoon to transfer the cooked potatoes to the ice bath (you'll need the cooking water again in the next step).

Bring the pot of potato-cooking water to a boil once again. Add the carrot and cook for 1 minute. Add the peas and cook for an additional 20 to 30 seconds, until the peas are bright green. Remove the carrot and peas using a strainer, and transfer to the ice bath also. Pour the potatoes, carrot, and peas through a colander to drain thoroughly. Let cool.

Peel the potatoes, then dice them into ½-inch cubes. Place the potatoes, carrots, and peas in a large bowl and add the apple and ham. Season with a pinch of salt and toss to distribute.

In a small bowl, whisk together the mayonnaise, milk, vinegar, sugar, and the ½ teaspoon salt to make the dressing. Add the dressing to the potato mixture and toss until thoroughly combined. Check the seasoning and add salt to taste, if needed. Serve cold or at room temperature.

蛋黄丁，土豆烧酥切小块，青豆（碗豆）烧酥，红肠丁 罐头浸果
冰砖一块（冰淇淋）以上几样事面准备好待用。
    蛋黄 放入碗内，用d线拌器搅顺时针续拌边敷拌边加色拉油
（加色拉油是青面续拌稠3再拈）拌到需要量时 倒入以上准备好的
料田拌均，（拌好的 色拉田加夹盐,如觉得太稠可加入少量醋）
冰砖去拌好以后 放入再拌.

THE SECRET "SAUCE"

This is my aunt's handwritten recipe for this salad, and it contains a secret hack from Shanghai's older generation. Her version calls for vanilla ice cream, added 1 tablespoon at a time, until the potato salad reaches the right creaminess and balanced flavor. Vanilla ice cream in potato salad might sound crazy, but it was a common, very haipai addition. —JUDY

炸蟹角 zhà xiè jiǎo

Crab Rangoon

This luxurious homemade crab rangoon has real crab, white cheddar cheese, plenty of scallions, and a touch of spicy Dijon mustard (a surprisingly effective stand-in for Chinese hot mustard). The bright red dipping sauce is sweetened with pineapple juice and sharpened with white vinegar. As these little rangoons emerge from the frying oil, we all find ourselves eagerly waiting for them to cool so we can devour them one after another.

Makes 24 crab rangoons

FOR THE DIPPING SAUCE

1 teaspoon neutral oil

1 teaspoon minced garlic

½ teaspoon minced ginger

3 tablespoons tomato ketchup

3 tablespoons pineapple juice

1 tablespoon white vinegar

2 to 3 teaspoons sugar

⅛ teaspoon fine sea salt

FOR THE WONTONS

4 ounces cream cheese

2 ounces crab meat (either lump or claw), picked through to remove stray bits of shell

¼ cup shredded white cheddar cheese or other melting cheese

2 tablespoons chopped scallion, white and green parts

1 teaspoon minced garlic

½ teaspoon Dijon mustard

⅛ teaspoon white pepper powder

24 wonton wrappers, preferably Shanghai style

1 large egg, beaten

Neutral oil, for frying

MAKE THE DIPPING SAUCE: In a saucepan over medium heat, add the oil, garlic, and ginger. Cook for 30 to 60 seconds, just until fragrant. Stir in the ketchup and cook for 30 seconds. Add the pineapple juice, vinegar, sugar to taste, and salt. Bring to a simmer, then remove from the heat and let cool.

MAKE THE FILLING AND ASSEMBLE: In a medium bowl, combine the cream cheese, crab, cheddar cheese, scallions, garlic, Dijon mustard, and white pepper.

Place 1 teaspoon of filling in the center of a wonton wrapper. Brush a thin layer of the beaten egg on the wrapper around the crab filling, all the way to the edges. Avoid getting egg on the other side of the wrapper. Fold the wrapper diagonally into a triangle, sealing it tightly around the filling. Add another dab of egg on both sides of the mound of filling, then fold the two points inward to form a three-pointed shape (reminiscent of a Chinese gold ingot or lotus flower), making sure the wrapper is firmly sealed around the filling.

FRY THE WONTONS AND SERVE: Fill a small, deep pot with 3 inches of oil and place over medium-high heat until the oil temperature reaches 400°F.

Fry the wontons in small batches of 4 or 5, for just under 2 minutes per batch, flipping them once halfway through, until golden. (Frying them longer may cause the wontons to burst open.) Serve with the dipping sauce.

MAKE AHEAD
Place the crab rangoons about ½ inch apart on a parchment-lined sheet pan. Cover and freeze overnight, transfer to a resealable bag, and store in the freezer for up to 3 months. No need to thaw them before frying. Alternatively, freeze the wontons after frying and reheat in a 375°F oven or toaster oven for 10 minutes. Bonus, you can also freeze the sauce and reinvigorate it with a quick reheat in the microwave!

凉拌香干 liángbàn xiānggān
Liangban Pressed Tofu

JUDY Before Bill and I had someone to help us care for Sarah and Kaitlin after school, I would rush home to New Jersey from my job in Manhattan to pick up the girls on time from their after-school program. When we got home, my number-one priority was getting dinner on the table. If there were no leftovers to fall back on, I would turn to this liángbàn (cold tossed) pressed tofu, which I always had on hand because it doesn't need any cooking. I would ask one of the girls to put the rice on and prepare this quick recipe. With some veggies and maybe a can of fried dace fish with black beans (the Chinese equivalent of grabbing a can of tuna), dinner was on the table fast.

With your knife blade parallel to the cutting board, slice each block of pressed tofu horizontally so you have thinner rectangles, ¼ to ½ inch thick. Then slice the rectangles into strips as thin as you can manage.

To a medium bowl, add the tofu, as much of the garlic as desired, the cilantro, chili oil, salt (taste the pressed tofu first to avoid over-salting), black vinegar (if using), sesame oil, sugar, and white pepper. Toss together until thoroughly combined.

Serve immediately at room temperature or prepare up to 48 hours in advance and then serve chilled if you find yourself short on time!

Serves 4

8 ounces spiced or plain pressed tofu (dòufu gān, 豆腐干)

1 or 2 large garlic cloves, minced

1 tablespoon finely chopped fresh cilantro leaves and stems

1 teaspoon Ultimate Chili Oil (page 275)

½ teaspoon fine sea salt, or to taste

½ teaspoon Chinese black vinegar, or to taste (optional)

½ teaspoon toasted sesame oil

¼ teaspoon sugar

¼ teaspoon white pepper powder

猪肉香菇白菜饺子 zhūròu xiānggū báicài jiǎozi

Pork, Mushroom & Cabbage Dumplings

SARAH

Kaitlin and I learned to make these from our Pópo, our maternal grand-mother. I remember us sitting around a big bowl of filling, chatting in broken English (her) and small attempts at Chinese (us), while pleating wrappers over the course of an afternoon. Whenever our grandparents came to visit, we would make four or five trays' worth to freeze for the weeks and months ahead. Over the years, Pópo would proudly note, "Waaahh!"—my dumplings were getting better than hers! My grandpa (Gōnggong) would pass by our oper-ation, stopping to offer a raspy grunt of appreciation before ambling off for his afternoon nap. This filling is one of my favorites: a combination of pork, mush-rooms, napa cabbage, and ginger (you can also substi-tute ground dark-meat chicken for the pork). Whatever you do, grab your family or a few friends, and have a good, long chat while you assemble these dumplings.

Makes about 72 (6 dozen) dumplings

FOR THE FILLING

10 medium dried shiitake mushrooms

2 cups hot water

1 pound napa cabbage

1 teaspoon fine sea salt

1 tablespoon neutral oil

1 pound ground pork

¼ cup Shaoxing wine

2½ tablespoons light soy sauce

1 tablespoon minced fresh ginger

2 teaspoons sugar

2 teaspoons toasted sesame oil

½ teaspoon white pepper powder

FOR ASSEMBLY AND SERVING

2 (14-ounce) packages round Shanghai-style dumpling wrappers (about 40 wrappers per package, depending on the brand) or Homemade Dumpling Wrappers (see page 86)

Ultimate Chili Oil (page 275) and/or Ultimate Dipping Sauce (page 276), for serving

MAKE THE FILLING: Place the mushrooms in a medium bowl and cover with the hot water. Soak for 2 hours (or overnight), until fully rehydrated. Reserve ½ cup of the soaking liquid (leaving behind any sediment at the bottom of the bowl). Trim and discard any tough stems from the mushrooms, then finely chop them.

Slice the cabbage leaves lengthwise into thin strips, then finely chop them crosswise. Place in a large bowl and stir in the salt. Set aside for 30 minutes (no more!) to allow the salt to draw the water out of the cabbage.

Heat the neutral oil in a wok or large pan over medium heat. Add the mushrooms and cook, stirring occasionally, for about 5 minutes, until they are softened and just beginning to crisp around the edges. Let the mushrooms cool.

To a large bowl, add the pork, Shaoxing wine, light soy sauce, ginger, sugar, sesame oil, and white pepper. Add the ½ cup mushroom-soaking water and stir vigorously with a pair of chopsticks or a wooden spoon for 10 to 15 minutes, until it forms a cohesive paste. (Alternatively, stir with a rubber spatula until the pork absorbs most of the liquid, then mix in the bowl of a stand mixer fitted with the paddle attachment on low speed for 7 minutes.)

(RECIPE CONTINUES)

MAKE AHEAD
To freeze the dumplings for future cooking, cover the sheet pans of assembled dumplings with plastic wrap (or use a clean plastic grocery bag). Put the sheets in the freezer overnight. Transfer the frozen raw dumplings to freezer bags and store for up to 3 months.

Squeeze the napa cabbage dry, then add to the bowl with the pork along with the mushrooms. Stir for another 2 to 3 minutes, until the cabbage and mushrooms are incorporated into the filling.

ASSEMBLE THE DUMPLINGS: Line two sheet pans with parchment paper. If using store-bought wrappers, have a bowl of water nearby. Holding a dumpling wrapper in your hand, dampen the edges with some water. If using homemade dumpling wrappers, you do not need the water to seal them. You will, however, have to roll out each wrapper just before filling (see instructions on page 86).

Put 1 scant tablespoon of filling in the middle of the wrapper and fold the circle in half, then pinch

4 Ways to Fold a Dumpling

the wrapper together at one end. Make pleats on one side of the wrapper, sealing the dumpling as you go, until you reach the other end. Press the pleats together and use a little more water, if necessary, behind the pleats to make sure the dumpling is completely sealed.

Place the dumpling on a sheet pan, then repeat with the remaining wrappers and filling, ensuring the dumplings are not touching each other on the sheet pan. After assembly, the dumplings must be immediately cooked or frozen (see Make Ahead).

COOK THE DUMPLINGS AND SERVE: To cook the dumplings, you can boil, steam, or pan-fry them, depending on your preference. See opposite for instructions on each. Serve with the chili oil and/or dipping sauce.

How to Cook
Dumplings

Learn how to cook your dumplings according to your
desired texture, from slippery boiled dumplings to
al dente steamed dumplings and crispy pan-fried ones.
If cooking frozen dumplings, there is no need to thaw
them before using any of these three methods.

Boiling

Bring a large pot of water to a boil. Drop the dumplings in (no more than 20 at a time for a large pot of water), stirring them gently as you do so to prevent sticking. Bring the water back up to a boil, then add ¼ cup cold water to cool it back down. Continue cooking the dumplings this way for 6 to 8 minutes, or for 1 to 2 more minutes after they rise to the surface. (Periodically adding ¼ cup cold water whenever the water returns to a boil prevents the wrappers from becoming starchy and overcooked.)

Steaming

Line a bamboo steamer with perforated parchment paper, damp cheesecloth, or thin cabbage leaves. Place the dumplings in the steamer basket ½ to 1 inch apart. Fill the wok with enough water to come ½ inch up the sides of the steamer. Bring the water to a simmer over medium-high heat. Place the covered steamer in the wok and steam the dumplings for 8 minutes (or 10 minutes for frozen dumplings).

Pan-frying

Heat a large cast-iron or nonstick skillet over medium heat. Add 1 to 2 tablespoons of neutral oil to coat the pan, then add the dumplings, spaced about ½ inch apart. Fry until the bottoms of the dumplings are lightly golden. Add ½ cup water to the pan, then cover immediately with a tight-fitting lid. Reduce the heat to medium-low and steam-fry for 6 to 7 minutes for fresh dumplings or 8 to 9 minutes for frozen dumplings, checking once toward the end of the cooking time and adding additional water if needed. Uncover, increase the heat to medium, and continue cooking until the water has completely evaporated and the bottoms of the dumplings are crispy and golden, about 3 more minutes.

HOMEMADE DUMPLING WRAPPERS

Can't find dumpling wrappers? You can make your own with just flour and water. These homemade wrappers are self-sealing and do not require water to moisten them. It is best to fill each wrapper immediately after rolling it out.

Makes about 72 (6 dozen) wrappers

4 cups (560g) all-purpose flour, plus more for rolling
1⅓ cups tepid water

In a large bowl, add the 4 cups flour and gradually stir in the water to form a dough. Knead for about 10 minutes, until smooth. If the dough is sticking to the sides of the bowl, add additional flour, 1 tablespoon at a time. (Alternatively, place the flour in the bowl of a stand mixer fitted with the dough hook. Add the water and mix on low speed until smooth.) Cover the dough with an overturned bowl and let rest for 1 hour.

Divide the dough into 4 equal pieces. Take one piece to work with and keep the remaining pieces under an overturned bowl to prevent them from drying out. Divide the quarter of dough into 18 equal pieces (use a digital scale to make them exactly the same size, about 12g each). Cover the pieces with a damp towel.

On a lightly floured surface, take one small piece of dough and form it into a round ball. Flatten it with the palm of your hand. With a floured Chinese rolling pin, roll the dough into a circle 3½ inches in diameter, turning the circle a quarter-turn left or right with each roll to keep it even. Fill the wrapper and assemble the dumpling according to the instructions on page 84. Repeat, rolling out each wrapper just before filling it, until you've used all the remaining dough.

EXTRA DUMPLING WRAPPERS?
So your dumpling filling is gone, and you're left with extra wrappers. Don't throw them away!

○ **FREEZE THEM.** Put any leftover store-bought wrappers in a plastic freezer bag, squeeze the air out of it, and freeze for up to 3 monvths. If freezing homemade wrappers, dust both sides of each wrapper with flour and place between sheets of parchment paper before freezing. Thaw the frozen wrappers in the refrigerator before using.

○ **TURN THEM INTO A SHORTCUT SCALLION PANCAKE.** Brush leftover wrappers lightly with neutral oil, sprinkle with salt and chopped scallion, then layer them on top of each other (4 to 7 layers), with the top layer kept dry. Use a rolling pin to roll the stack into a larger circle, however thick or thin you prefer. Pan-fry until golden brown.

红油抄手 *hóng yóu chāoshǒu*
Chili Oil Wontons

KAITLIN Sarah and I grew up mostly on Cantonese and Shanghainese dishes, so the first time we ate deliciously spicy, Sichuan peppercorn–tingly Sichuan food, we were immediately obsessed. These wontons are a fiery bowl of perfection that takes advantage of the sweet flavor of cooked garlic, the spicy zing of raw garlic, and the richness of pork. If you like, substitute my mom's pork and shrimp filling from her Shanghai Street-Stall Wonton Soup (page 257). After assembling, we like to cook half the wontons and freeze the other half, which is why the dipping sauce makes enough for 15 of the 30 total wontons. If you want to cook all the wontons right away, just double the sauce!

Makes 30 wontons and sauce for 15 wontons

FOR THE WONTONS

8 ounces napa cabbage

¾ teaspoon fine sea salt

8 ounces fatty ground pork (70% lean) or ground dark-meat chicken

2 tablespoons water, plus more for sealing the wontons

1 tablespoon neutral oil

1 tablespoon toasted sesame oil

1 tablespoon Shaoxing wine

2 teaspoons light soy sauce

1½ teaspoons grated fresh ginger

½ teaspoon sugar

¼ teaspoon white pepper powder

30 wonton wrappers, preferably Shanghai style

FOR THE SAUCE

4 large garlic cloves, minced

1½ teaspoons sugar

1 teaspoon ground Sichuan peppercorns

1 tablespoon neutral oil

⅓ cup Ultimate Chili Oil (page 275; about 70% oil, 30% flakes)

2½ tablespoons light soy sauce, or to taste

1 teaspoon toasted sesame oil

Toasted sesame seeds

2 scallions, white and green parts finely chopped

2 tablespoons finely chopped fresh cilantro leaves and stems (optional)

MAKE THE WONTON FILLING: Slice the cabbage leaves lengthwise into thin strips, then finely chop them crosswise. Place in a large bowl and stir in the salt. Set aside for 30 minutes (no more!) to allow the salt to draw the water out of the cabbage.

To a large bowl, add the pork, 2 tablespoons water, the neutral oil, sesame oil, Shaoxing wine, light soy sauce, ginger, sugar, and white pepper. Stir vigorously with a pair of chopsticks for about 10 minutes, until the filling has emulsified into a paste-like consistency. (You can also use a stand mixer fitted with the paddle attachment and beat on low speed for 5 minutes.)

Squeeze the excess water out of the cabbage with your hands, then add the cabbage to the pork. Stir thoroughly to incorporate.

ASSEMBLE THE WONTONS: Line a sheet pan with parchment paper. Prepare a small bowl of water. With a wonton wrapper in the center of your palm, dab the outer edges of the square with water. To the center, add 1 scant tablespoon of the filling. Fold the wonton wrapper in half into a rectangle and press the edges together. Put a dab of water on one of the bottom corners (the filling side, not the seam side). Bring the two bottom corners together and, using the wetted corner to seal the wonton, press the corners together.

Place the wonton on the sheet pan. (If desired, boil and taste a few wontons before assembling the rest; see Tip on page 88.) Repeat with the remaining wrappers and

3 Ways to Fold a Wonton

(RECIPE CONTINUES)

filling, ensuring that the finished wontons are not touching each other on the sheet pan. Within 1 hour of assembly, you must either cook the wontons or transfer them to the freezer. In this recipe, we're cooking half of the wontons right away and freezing the other half. To freeze: Cover the sheet pan of wontons with plastic wrap (or use a clean plastic grocery bag) and freeze overnight; when frozen solid, transfer the wontons to freezer bags to store for up to 3 months.

PREPARE THE SAUCE: In a large, wide heatproof bowl (big enough to later toss the wontons in), arrange half the garlic, the sugar, and ground Sichuan peppercorns in small piles directly next to each other. In a small saucepan, heat the neutral oil over medium-high heat until it shimmers. Use a rubber spatula to scrape all the oil out of the pan and onto the garlic and seasonings (it will sizzle!). Stir in the chili oil, light soy sauce, sesame oil, and remaining garlic until combined.

COOK THE WONTONS AND SERVE: Bring a large pot of water to a boil. Stir the boiling water in a circle to keep it moving slowly (this will prevent the wontons from sticking to the bottom of the pot). Add 15 wontons (or all 30 if you made a double batch of sauce) and simmer for 4 to 5 minutes (5 to 6 minutes, if frozen), or until the wontons float—an indication that the filling inside has mostly cooked through. During cooking, anytime the water comes back up to a vigorous boil, add ¼ cup cold water to cool down the pot. (This periodic addition of cold water prevents the wrappers from overcooking before the filling is cooked through.) Once the wontons are floating, cook them for 1 additional minute, then use a spider strainer or slotted spoon to lift them out of the water, allowing any excess water to drain off. Transfer the wontons to your bowl of sauce.

Gently toss the wontons in the sauce, then sprinkle with the toasted sesame seeds, scallions, and cilantro (if using).

TIP! WONTON TASTE TEST

We always cook one or two wontons to taste the seasonings before we assemble the rest. We might add a little more Shaoxing wine (for depth), water (for juiciness), salt, or soy sauce. Whenever you're making wontons, keep in mind that the filling should be well seasoned, but not to the point that the wontons are overly salted when tossed in the sauce or added to a bowl of soup.

纯素夫妻肺片 chún sù fūqī fèi piàn

Vegan "Fuqi Feipian"

At our favorite Sichuan spots, fūqī fèi piàn is the dish that hits the table first. Made of sliced honeycomb tripe and beef heart and tongue, or sometimes beef shank, it's a cold appetizer dressed in a sauce that combines the spicy and mouth-numbing flavors Sichuan cuisine is known for. For this vegan version, though, you can skip the trip to the butcher counter. Made with bean curd sticks (also called dried bean threads or yuba), seitan (wheat gluten), and king oyster mushrooms, believe us when we say it's just as delicious as the original, with the same crunch from chopped peanuts and Chinese celery, and varied textures that mimic the mix of offal. If you don't need to keep the recipe vegan, you can use regular oyster sauce instead of the vegetarian oyster sauce.

Serves 4

1 ounce dried bean threads (yuba), soaked for 2 hours until softened

4 ounces fresh or thawed frozen wheat gluten (seitan) or 1.75 ounces dried, soaked for 2 hours until softened

1 tablespoon neutral oil

4 ounces fresh king oyster mushrooms (1 or 2 mushrooms), thinly sliced

2 medium garlic cloves, minced

3 tablespoons Ultimate Chili Oil (page 275)

1 tablespoon hot water

2 teaspoons toasted sesame seeds

1 teaspoon ground Sichuan peppercorns

2 teaspoons vegetarian oyster sauce or oyster sauce (if not keeping vegan)

1 teaspoon light soy sauce

1 teaspoon Chinese black vinegar

½ teaspoon sugar

¼ teaspoon fine sea salt

¼ teaspoon toasted sesame oil

2 tablespoons finely chopped celery (ideally, Chinese variety)

1 tablespoon chopped roasted peanuts

1 tablespoon finely chopped fresh cilantro leaves and stems

Cut the rehydrated bean threads in half lengthwise, then cut them into 2-inch lengths. Thinly slice the seitan, so you have thin strips that are similar in size and shape to the bean threads.

Place the bean threads and seitan in a shallow heatproof bowl. Place a 2-inch-tall metal steaming rack in the bottom of a wok (or any pot with a lid that will accommodate your heatproof dish) and fill it with enough water to come to about 1 inch below the rack. (You can also use a bamboo steamer if your dish fits in it with enough clearance for the steam to rise around the dish; fill your wok with enough water to come ½ inch up the sides of the steamer. You may need to add more boiling water to the wok during steaming to maintain this water level.) Bring the water to a simmer over medium-high heat. Place the dish on the steaming rack or in the steamer, cover, and steam over medium-high heat for 12 minutes.

Heat a large skillet or cast-iron pan over medium heat. Add the neutral oil, spreading it evenly in the pan, then add the oyster mushroom slices in one layer and fry until lightly golden on both sides, 6 to 7 minutes per side.

To a large bowl, add the garlic, chili oil, hot water, sesame seeds, ground Sichuan peppercorns, vegetarian oyster sauce, light soy sauce, black vinegar, sugar, salt, and sesame oil. Add the bean threads and seitan, along with the mushrooms. Stir in the celery, peanuts, and cilantro, and toss until everything is evenly coated. Serve at room temperature.

八宝辣酱 bā bǎo làjiàng

Eight Treasures Spicy Relish

BILL This hearty mixture of eight "treasures" (in this case, pork, peanuts, peppers, bamboo shoots, carrots, baby corn, water chestnuts, and tofu) can be served as a starter, as a side dish, or as a quick snack with a bowl of rice or pao fan (see page 65). While I was raised by a family of great cooks, we always bought our bā bǎo làjiàng in a can rather than making it ourselves. Then Judy came along with her '80s perm and no-nonsense attitude ("So, do you want my number or not?"), and she didn't even recognize my version. The one she grew up with was spicier and drier. We still fight about it to this day, though she's warmed to this recipe, which recreates the nostalgic flavor of the relish I shared with my parents and sisters as a kid—with a few adjustments that make it even better.

Serves 6

FOR THE PORK

6 ounces boneless pork shoulder or butt, cut into ¼-inch cubes

1 tablespoon water

1 teaspoon oyster sauce

1 teaspoon Shaoxing wine

½ teaspoon cornstarch

½ teaspoon neutral oil

FOR THE REST OF THE DISH

¼ cup peanut oil or neutral oil

¾ cup raw shelled peanuts

¾ cup diced red Anaheim pepper or red bell pepper

¼ cup spicy bean sauce

1 teaspoon minced fresh ginger

3 large garlic cloves, finely chopped

2 tablespoons finely chopped shallot

¾ cup diced canned bamboo shoot halves (in ¼-inch cubes)

¾ cup diced carrot (in ¼-inch cubes)

¾ cup diced canned baby corn (in ¼-inch cubes)

¾ cup diced spiced or plain pressed tofu (dòufu gān, 豆腐干; in ¼-inch cubes)

¾ cup diced water chestnuts (in ¼-inch cubes)

1 tablespoon hoisin sauce or sweet bean sauce

1 tablespoon oyster sauce

2 teaspoons sugar

1 teaspoon toasted sesame oil

½ teaspoon fine sea salt, or to taste

½ teaspoon white pepper powder

3 cups low-sodium chicken or pork stock

2 teaspoons cornstarch

1 tablespoon water

MARINATE THE PORK: In a medium bowl, combine the pork, water, oyster sauce, Shaoxing wine, cornstarch, and neutral oil. Marinate at room temperature for 20 minutes.

COMBINE AND COOK: Heat a wok over medium-low heat and add 3 tablespoons of the peanut oil. Add the peanuts and stir-fry continuously for 5 minutes, until the peanuts begin to turn golden brown. Add the red pepper and stir-fry for 1 to 2 minutes, then stir in the spicy bean sauce and cook for 1 more minute.

Use your wok spatula to clear a space in the center of the wok (move the peanuts and peppers off to the side), and add the remaining tablespoon peanut oil, the seasoned pork, and the ginger. Stir-fry in the center of the wok until the pork turns opaque, about 1 to 2 minutes. Then stir the pork together with the peanuts and peppers.

Add the garlic and shallot and cook for 2 minutes, stirring often. Increase the heat to medium-high and add the bamboo shoots, carrots, baby corn, tofu, water

chestnuts, hoisin sauce, oyster sauce, sugar, sesame oil, salt, and white pepper. Stir-fry until everything is uniformly combined.

Add the stock and bring to a boil. Reduce the heat to low and simmer, uncovered, for 30 to 40 minutes, stirring occasionally, until the liquid has reduced to about 1 cup.

Combine the cornstarch with 1 tablespoon of water to make a slurry, then gradually add it to the wok while stirring, and continue to cook until the sauce is reduced to your liking. (I like some sauce in my Eight Treasures, and Judy likes hers cooked until there is no standing liquid.) Serve hot or at room temperature. Store in an airtight container in the refrigerator for up to 5 days.

Noodles

Noodles are always there for us. It doesn't matter how many things are going on or what's in our fridge; at any point, we can scrape together a bowl of noodles. (And we're willing to bet you can too!) A bowlful can be as simple or as complex as you like—all you need is a great sauce, steaming broth, or a jumble of whatever protein and vegetables are on hand. There's something about the unstoppable momentum of slurping up noodles that brings relief when I'm going through trying times (or just need some comfort food). Even in the dead of summer, I'll never say no to a piping hot bowl of noodle soup. These are just some of the noodle dishes we've come to rely on—not just a symbol of long life but also a literal lifeline. **SARAH**

担担面，简易版 dàndàn miàn, jiǎnyì bǎn

Shortcut Dan Dan Noodles

We love dan dan noodles, but even for us, making them can feel like a lot of prep. Most of the work is in the sauce, which requires a batch of unsalted chili oil infused with various spices. This glorious shortcut, which counts on a pre-mixed sauce that you can keep in the fridge (for up to 6 months!), requires just a little advanced planning. It's as close to instant gratification as you can get when it comes to a good bowl of home-made dan dan. The addition of concentrated chicken bouillon brings the sauce to life when it hits hot, freshly boiled noodles, but if you'd like to make this vegetarian, omit the bouillon and the pork. As for the noodles, opt for a slightly thicker, fresh Shanghai-style noodle, which balances out this (admittedly saltier) sauce. Whether you're eating these solo on the couch or feeding a crowd, we've included the accompanying noodle ingredients in quantities for a single serving, so you can multiply them as needed!

Makes about 2¼ cups of sauce (enough for 18 servings)

FOR THE SHORTCUT DAN DAN SAUCE

1½ cups Ultimate Chili Oil (page 275), without optional salt

⅓ cup light soy sauce

1 tablespoon sugar

2 tablespoons Chinese sesame paste

5 teaspoons dark soy sauce

4 teaspoons chicken bouillon paste

1 teaspoon ground Sichuan peppercorns (ideally, freshly ground)

¼ teaspoon five-spice powder

FOR EACH SERVING OF NOODLES (MULTIPLY AS NEEDED)

3 to 4 ounces ground pork or chicken

1 teaspoon Shaoxing wine

¼ teaspoon cornstarch

1 tablespoon neutral oil

2 medium garlic cloves, minced

2 tablespoons Sichuan preserved vegetables (suì mǐ yá cài, 碎米芽菜)

5 ounces fresh white wheat noodles or 2.5 ounces dried white wheat noodles

1 handful of fresh spinach leaves

2 tablespoons Shortcut Dan Dan Sauce

MAKE THE SAUCE: In a sterilized airtight glass jar (large enough to hold 2¼ cups of sauce), mix the chili oil, light soy sauce, sugar, sesame paste, dark soy sauce, chicken bouillon paste, ground Sichuan peppercorns, and five-spice powder. Stir with a clean spoon until thoroughly combined, then close with a tight-fitting lid. Store in the refrigerator for up to 6 months. Be sure to use only clean utensils when handling and stir thoroughly prior to each use.

ASSEMBLE AND SERVE: Marinate the ground pork with the Shaoxing wine and cornstarch for 15 minutes. Meanwhile, bring a large pot of water to a boil.

Heat a wok over high heat. When the wok is just beginning to smoke, add the neutral oil. Add the seasoned pork and brown it, stirring often, until crispy and golden, about 1 to 2 minutes. Add the garlic and Sichuan preserved vegetables and cook for 1 minute to take the raw edge off the garlic.

Cook the noodles according to the package instructions. Add the spinach to the noodles in the last 30 seconds of cooking. (Be sure to boil the noodles after you cook the pork. You don't want the noodles sitting around, or they'll clump.)

Drain the noodles and spinach and divide them among your intended number of serving bowls. Top each bowl with the sauce and the pork mixture. Serve immediately, stirring the noodles in the bowls to combine the ingredients. (If needed, add a spoonful or two of the noodle-cooking water to loosen the noodles and sauce.)

新兴捞面 xīnxīng lāo miàn

Happy Family Lo Mein

BILL Everyone has their favorite lo mein, but this Happy Family version marries them all in a single satisfying dish with slices of velveted chicken and beef, roast pork, fresh shrimp, and juicy chunks of lobster. With every possible taste request accounted for, it's no wonder how the dish got its name. This was one of the chef's specials at Sun Hing, my parents' Chinese restaurant in New Jersey. You may have seen "Happy Family" stir-fries before, but by adding noodles (which symbolize long life), the promise in the name is all but assured! Though Sun Hing has been closed for decades, with this lo mein in the wok, the memories come flooding back.

Serves 4

FOR THE CHICKEN

2 ounces boneless, skinless chicken breast, thinly sliced

1½ teaspoons water

½ teaspoon neutral oil

½ teaspoon oyster sauce

¼ teaspoon cornstarch

FOR THE BEEF

2 ounces boneless beef flank steak, thinly sliced against the grain

1½ teaspoons water

½ teaspoon neutral oil

½ teaspoon oyster sauce

¼ teaspoon cornstarch

Pinch of baking soda

FOR THE SAUCE

½ cup low-sodium chicken stock

1 tablespoon oyster sauce

1 tablespoon Shaoxing wine

1 tablespoon light soy sauce

1 teaspoon dark soy sauce

½ teaspoon sugar

½ teaspoon toasted sesame oil

¼ teaspoon white pepper powder

FOR THE REST OF THE DISH

10 ounces cooked or uncooked lo mein noodles or 5 ounces dried spaghetti cooked 1 minute past al dente and rinsed (see Note on page 99)

4 to 6 jumbo or extra-jumbo shrimp, peeled, deveined, and butterflied

1½ cups broccoli florets (about 3 ounces)

¼ cup thinly sliced carrot (on the diagonal)

¼ cup sliced bamboo shoots

⅔ cup sliced fresh mushrooms (such as shiitake, cremini, or button)

¼ cup sliced water chestnuts

2 tablespoons neutral oil, plus more for oiling the noodles

½ teaspoon minced fresh ginger

2 medium garlic cloves, finely chopped

2½ cups sliced napa cabbage (about 5 ounces; in 1½ by 2-inch pieces)

1½ tablespoons Shaoxing wine

½ cup fresh snow peas, ends trimmed (about 2 ounces)

2 ounces Char Siu Roast Pork (page 173) or ham, sliced

2 ounces cooked lobster meat, cut into bite-size chunks (or additional shrimp)

1 scallion, split in half lengthwise and cut into 1-inch pieces

PREPARE THE CHICKEN: In a medium bowl, combine the chicken with the water, neutral oil, oyster sauce, and cornstarch. Mix until the chicken has absorbed all the liquid. Set aside to marinate for 30 minutes.

PREPARE THE BEEF: In a medium bowl, combine the beef with the water, neutral oil, oyster sauce, cornstarch, and baking soda. Set aside to marinate for 30 minutes.

TIP! SHORTCUT TO LOBSTER

Most seafood counters and shops that sell live lobsters can also cook them for you on-site (or may even sell pre-cooked lobster meat). A 1½-pound lobster yields about 5 ounces of cooked meat.

MAKE THE SAUCE: In a medium bowl, combine the chicken stock, oyster sauce, Shaoxing wine, light soy sauce, dark soy sauce, sugar, sesame oil, and white pepper.

PREPARE THE NOODLES: If using precooked noodles, dip them in a bowl of hot tap water to loosen them and rinse off any surface starch. Shake off the excess water. If using uncooked noodles, follow the package instructions to boil the noodles, then rinse them in cool water and drain thoroughly. To prevent your noodles from sticking, toss them in a little bit of neutral oil after they have drained.

PRECOOK THE SHRIMP, VEGETABLES, AND MEAT: Fill a wok about halfway with water and bring to a boil. Add the shrimp and cook for 30 seconds, until they just turn color. Use a strainer or slotted spoon to remove them from the wok to a plate.

Bring the water in the wok back to a boil and add the broccoli and carrot. Cook for 30 seconds, then add the bamboo shoots, mushrooms, and water chestnuts. Continue cooking for another 30 seconds, then strain the vegetables from the wok, drain thoroughly, and set aside.

Rinse the wok and set it over high heat to dry completely. When the wok is smoking lightly, add 1 tablespoon of the neutral oil around the perimeter. Add the beef and chicken and sear together for 30 seconds on each side until just cooked through, then remove from the wok.

ASSEMBLE THE DISH: Add the remaining tablespoon neutral oil to the wok along with the ginger. Cook for 10 seconds, just until the ginger begins to release its fragrance. Add the garlic and napa cabbage, and stir-fry for 20 to 30 seconds, until the cabbage is slightly wilted. Add the Shaoxing wine around the perimeter of the wok and stir for another 15 seconds.

Add the cooked noodles, cooked vegetables, shrimp, chicken, and beef. Then add the snow peas, char siu pork, and lobster, and pour the sauce over everything in the wok. Keep the heat at its highest setting and stir-fry for 2 to 3 minutes, mixing all the ingredients thoroughly, until everything is heated through and most of the liquid has cooked off. (If the noodles get a little dry and starchy during cooking, add a tablespoon of water to loosen them.)

Add the scallion and stir until just wilted, 10 to 15 seconds. Serve immediately.

A NOTE ON LO MEIN NOODLES
You can find lo mein noodles either precooked or uncooked. Both must be rinsed and drained thoroughly to remove excess surface starch, or your lo mein will be sticky. If using uncooked noodles, cook them according to the package instructions before rinsing and draining. If you can't find lo mein noodles, using regular spaghetti works in a pinch. Just cook the spaghetti a little past al dente, so the texture is closer to a soft lo mein noodle.

台湾牛肉面 táiwān niúròu miàn

Taiwanese Beef Noodle Soup

The broth for this beef noodle soup is perfectly balanced—spicy from the bean sauce, warm and fragrant from spices like star anise and cloves, and harmonized with sweet tomato and onion. The beef shanks should be tender, but not falling apart, while any tendon-y bits should be soft and gelatinous (good for your skin and joints, as the Chinese grandmas say). If you'd rather not make your own spice sachet, or lǔ bāo (卤包), use the commercially prepared ones you can find in Chinese markets. They go into the hot liquid just like a teabag. We recommend using two sachets for this quantity of liquid, but be sure to check any instructions that come with the store-bought packets regarding the volume of water required.

We find that we rarely finish this pot of soup in one sitting, which is just as well, because it tastes even better the next day and is also freezer-friendly. So while the soup serves eight, we've provided noodle and topping quantities for one serving, so you can multiply as needed and save any leftover soup for later.

Serves 8

FOR THE SOUP

3 pounds boneless beef shank, cut into 2-inch chunks

2 tablespoons neutral oil

6 large garlic cloves, smashed

3 scallions, white parts separated from the green parts

1 large yellow onion, cut into wedges

1 large knob of fresh ginger (2 inches by 1 inch), smashed

1 large ripe tomato, cut into wedges

4 dried red chilies, torn in half

1 tablespoon tomato paste

2 tablespoons spicy bean sauce

1 tablespoon sugar

½ cup Shaoxing wine

½ cup light soy sauce

3 tablespoons dark soy sauce

11 cups water

FOR EACH SERVING OF NOODLES (MULTIPLY AS NEEDED)

5 ounces fresh white wheat noodles or 2.5 ounces dried white wheat noodles

1 handful of leafy greens (such as Shanghai bok choy, spinach, or choy sum)

3 tablespoons chopped pickled mustard greens (xuě cài, 雪菜; also sometimes "potherb cabbage")

2 tablespoons chopped fresh cilantro

1 tablespoon chopped scallion, white and green parts

FOR THE SPICE SACHET

6 whole cloves

2 star anise

1 Chinese cassia cinnamon stick, about 2 inches long

1 teaspoon coriander seeds

1 teaspoon fennel seeds

½ teaspoon cumin seeds

½ teaspoon whole white peppercorns

PREPARE THE SPICE SACHET: Gather the whole cloves, star anise, cinnamon stick, coriander seeds, fennel seeds, cumin seeds, and white peppercorns in a piece of cheesecloth and tie tightly. (Alternatively, place the spices in a coffee filter and fold to close. Place that packet into another coffee filter and tie with kitchen string.) You may also skip this step and use 2 store-bought sachets of Chinese braising spices.

(RECIPE CONTINUES)

MAKE THE BROTH: Rinse the beef with cold water, then add to a stockpot and cover with fresh water. Bring to a boil over high heat, then remove from the heat. Drain and rinse the beef to eliminate any foam or other impurities.

Wash the pot and dry it thoroughly, then set it over medium-high heat. Add the oil, followed by the garlic, the white parts of the scallions, the onion, and the ginger. Cook for 2 to 3 minutes, until everything is lightly blistered and golden. Add the tomato, chilies, tomato paste, and spicy bean sauce. Let everything caramelize for 1 to 2 minutes. Add the beef to the pot again, along with the sugar. Add the Shaoxing wine to deglaze the pot, stirring up any browned bits from the bottom. Next, add the light soy sauce, dark soy sauce, and the green parts of the scallions.

Add 1 cup of the water to the pot, along with the spices you prepared earlier. Bring to a boil, reduce the heat to medium, cover, and braise for 20 minutes to allow the beef to absorb the flavors of the wine, soy sauce, and spices. Uncover and add the remaining 10 cups water. Increase the heat to high to bring the mixture to a boil, then immediately reduce the heat to medium-low, cover again, and simmer for 90 minutes.

COOK THE NOODLES AND SERVE: Bring a large pot of water to a boil and cook the noodles according to the package directions, multiplying the quantities needed by the desired number of servings. During the last minute of cooking time, drop the leafy greens into the pot and blanch.

Portion the noodles and greens among the bowls, and ladle some of the broth on top (ladle it through a fine-mesh strainer for cleaner broth). Spoon 3 or 4 chunks of beef into each serving, and sprinkle on the pickled mustard greens, cilantro, and scallion. Serve immediately. (If you have leftovers, cool and transfer to airtight containers. Refrigerate and consume within 4 days or freeze the broth and beef together for up to 3 months.)

TIP! ABOUT PICKLED MUSTARD GREENS
In this beef noodle soup, the pickled mustard greens (xuě cài, 雪菜) are a must-have. If you buy the seasoned variety, use them straight from the package. If you buy them unseasoned, chop them and sauté with a little neutral oil, a few chopped dried red chilies, and a pinch of sugar.

麻辣牛肉扯面 málà niúròu chě miàn

Spicy Beef
Biang Biang Noodles

Biang biang noodles earned their name from the surprisingly loud sound made when the dough is slapped against a counter as it's stretched. The strip of dough is then ripped in half to make these thick noodles, a mainstay of western Chinese cuisine. They've become incredibly popular in New York City, and the credit for that goes directly to Xi'an Famous Foods. Owners Jason Wang and his dad, David, were once generous enough to show us their noodle-making secrets (they also have an excellent cookbook). This is our version of biang biang noodles, made with beef. You can make the noodle dough up to one day in advance; just make sure to keep it tightly wrapped in the refrigerator to keep it moist.

Serves 4

FOR THE NOODLE DOUGH

3 cups (420g) bread flour or all-purpose flour

½ teaspoon fine sea salt

1 cup water

Neutral oil, for brushing

FOR THE BEEF

1½ tablespoons neutral oil

1¼ pounds boneless beef shank, patted dry and cut into 1-inch chunks

1 tablespoon tomato paste

2 scallions, cut into 2-inch lengths

4 (⅛-inch-thick) slices fresh ginger

1 large garlic clove, sliced

1 star anise

1 tablespoon spicy bean sauce

4 cups water

2 tablespoons Shaoxing wine

1 tablespoon light soy sauce

½ teaspoon sugar

2 teaspoons ground Sichuan peppercorns (optional)

FOR ASSEMBLING THE DISH

2 cups cabbage (in big bite-size pieces)

2 to 3 tablespoons Ultimate Chili Oil (page 275)

2 teaspoons light soy sauce

1½ teaspoons Chinese black vinegar

½ teaspoon sugar

1 scallion, white and green parts chopped

2 tablespoons roughly chopped fresh cilantro

MAKE THE NOODLE DOUGH: In the bowl of a stand mixer fitted with the dough hook or a large bowl, add the flour and salt. With the mixer on the lowest speed (or mixing by hand), slowly stream in the water. A shaggy dough should form after about 1 minute. Knead on low speed (or by hand) for 10 minutes, until smooth. If needed, stop the mixer to press the dough together. Knead the dough by hand into a ball, cover with an overturned bowl, and let it rest for 30 minutes.

Divide the dough into 8 pieces and knead each piece into a smooth ball. Roll each ball into an oval roughly 2½ inches wide and 4 inches long. Lay the ovals on a clean, oiled surface so they're next to each other but not touching and brush the tops lightly with neutral oil. Place a piece of plastic wrap on top of the dough pieces, so that the plastic makes direct contact with the oiled dough. Rest the dough for 2 hours.

MAKE THE BEEF: Meanwhile, in a large pot or Dutch oven, heat the neutral oil over medium-high heat until it shimmers. Add the beef and sear until browned on all sides, about 4 to 5 minutes. Reduce the heat to medium and stir in the tomato paste until it coats the beef. Cook for 1 minute, then add the scallions, ginger, garlic, star anise, and spicy bean sauce, and cook, stirring, for another minute.

(RECIPE CONTINUES)

Add the water, Shaoxing wine, light soy sauce, and sugar and bring to a boil. Lower the heat to medium, cover, and cook at a rapid simmer for 45 minutes. Uncover the pot and simmer over medium-low heat for another 45 minutes, stirring occasionally. The beef is done when it is fork-tender and the sauce has reduced to about 1½ cups. (If the liquid has reduced too much, add additional water.) Stir in the ground Sichuan peppercorns (if using), cover, and turn off the heat.

STRETCH AND RIP THE NOODLES: Line a sheet pan with parchment paper. Starting with one piece of dough, score it lengthwise down the middle using a paring knife, cutting as deep as possible without going all the way through. This creates a seam that acts as a guide for ripping the noodle after stretching. Lift the dough off the work surface. (If lifting it up makes it uneven, use a rolling pin to flatten the oval to an even thickness.) Hold one end of the dough in each hand, and, starting in the center, begin stretching the dough into a long strip, 20 to 24 inches long. Don't be afraid to revisit thicker sections of the noodle to stretch and even them out.

The next step is how this noodle got its name. Holding the noodle at both ends, slap it repeatedly on the counter in an up-and-down motion while stretching the dough further, until the noodle is 24 to 30 inches long. Open up the seam at the center of the noodle, where you made the score mark, and rip the noodle apart. Lay the noodles on the prepared sheet pan. Repeat this process with the rest of the dough. (If you run out of space, just add another layer of parchment and set more noodles on top.) Cover the noodles with a clean kitchen towel so they don't dry out.

ASSEMBLE THE DISH: Bring a large pot of water to a boil. Add the cabbage and the noodles, stirring them around the pot so they don't stick to each other or to the bottom of the pot. Boil for 2 minutes, until the cabbage is tender and the noodles are al dente. Drain well to remove excess water, then transfer the noodles and cabbage to a large serving bowl. Ladle the beef and sauce over the noodles and cabbage. Top with chili oil, light soy sauce, Chinese black vinegar, sugar, scallion, and cilantro. Toss to combine and serve.

干炒鸡河 gàn chǎo jī hé

Chicken Chow Fun

When ordering noodles at Sunday dim sum brunches, we (along with aunts, uncles, and cousins) reliably split into two factions: team flat noodle vs. team fried noodle. This dish is a prime example of something team flat noodle might lobby for: slippery, chewy wide rice noodles cooked "dry" (without a gravy-like sauce), with plenty of wok hei. The classic beef version is called gon chow gnau ho and is one of the most popular recipes on our blog, but for those who prefer chicken, this chow fun is a tasty alternative. Smoky wok hei is crucial to this dish; to get it, crank up the heat as high as possible to preheat your wok until smoking, and then add the oil. This creates a nonstick effect on the surface of your wok (see page 23).

Serves 4

FOR VELVETING THE CHICKEN

8 ounces boneless, skinless chicken breast, thinly sliced against the grain

1 tablespoon water

1 teaspoon cornstarch

1 teaspoon neutral oil

2 teaspoons oyster sauce

½ teaspoon light soy sauce

FOR THE SAUCE

1 tablespoon oyster sauce

1 tablespoon light soy sauce

2 teaspoons dark soy sauce

½ teaspoon MSG (optional)

½ teaspoon sugar

½ teaspoon toasted sesame oil

¼ teaspoon white pepper powder

FOR THE REST OF THE DISH

1 pound fresh wide rice noodles, either pre-cut or in sheets, or 8 ounces dried wide rice noodles

3 tablespoons neutral oil, plus 1 teaspoon if using dried noodles

3 (⅛-inch-thick) slices fresh ginger

1 medium garlic clove, chopped

4 scallions, white and green parts separated, halved lengthwise, and cut into 3-inch pieces

2 tablespoons Shaoxing wine

6 ounces fresh mung bean sprouts

VELVET THE CHICKEN: Combine the chicken, water, cornstarch, neutral oil, oyster sauce, and light soy sauce. Use your hands to massage the chicken until it has absorbed the marinade. Marinate at room temperature for 30 minutes.

MAKE THE SAUCE: In a small bowl, combine the oyster sauce, light soy sauce, dark soy sauce, MSG (if using), sugar, sesame oil, and white pepper.

COOK THE NOODLES: If you have the noodles that came in sheets, slice them so they're about 1 inch wide. (Cut them right before cooking so they don't have a chance to stick together.) If using dried noodles, boil them according to package instructions, or until al dente. Rinse with cool water, drain, and toss with 1 teaspoon of the neutral oil.

ASSEMBLE THE DISH: Heat a wok over high heat until smoking. Then add 1½ tablespoons of the neutral oil to coat. Add the chicken in one layer and sear for 1 minute on each side, until lightly browned around the edges and about 90 percent done. Remove from the wok and set aside.

With the wok still on high heat, add the remaining 1½ tablespoons oil. Add the ginger, garlic, and the white parts of the scallions. Cook for 15 to 20 seconds, until fragrant. Spread the rice noodles evenly in the wok and stir-fry for about 15 seconds. Add the Shaoxing wine around the perimeter of the wok.

Next, add the sauce and the seared chicken. Stir-fry everything together for 2 to 3 minutes, until the noodles are heated through. Use your wok spatula to scrape the bottom of the wok to prevent sticking and lift the noodles in an upward motion to coat them evenly with the sauce.

Add the bean sprouts and green parts of the scallions. Stir-fry for 1 minute, until the bean sprouts and the scallions are just wilted. Serve immediately.

TIP! Some refrigerated fresh rice noodles can be very stiff and stuck together, even after slicing. If that's the case, you'll need to dip the noodles in hot or boiling water to soften them up right before adding them to the wok to stir-fry.

上海冷面 shànghǎi lěng miàn

Shanghai Cold Noodles

JUDY / During Shanghai's sultry summers, city dwellers reach for these cold noodles for a bit of relief. We Shanghainese like choosing from a large assortment of toppings (see Tip). As for sauces, we include three separate bases: a soy sauce base, a vinegar base, and a nutty sesame base. You need all three to mix up the perfect bowl of noodles, but the proportions can be customized to your liking. Fresh, *thin* noodles are your best bet for this dish, as they take on the delicate sauces better. The other secret for a pleasing chew is to steam the noodles before boiling to lock in the starch and minimize water absorption. If dried noodles are all you have on hand, skip the steaming step and simply boil the noodles until al dente.

Serves 2

FOR THE SOY SAUCE BASE

½ teaspoon sugar

3 tablespoons hot water

1½ tablespoons light soy sauce

FOR THE VINEGAR BASE

½ teaspoon sugar

4 teaspoons rice vinegar (ideally, Shanghai rice vinegar)

FOR THE SESAME BASE

3 tablespoons Chinese sesame paste or creamy peanut butter

2 teaspoons toasted sesame oil

¼ teaspoon fine sea salt

5 to 6 tablespoons hot water

FOR 2 SERVINGS OF NOODLES

8 ounces fresh, thin wheat noodles

1 teaspoon toasted sesame oil

1 scallion, white and green parts finely chopped

MAKE THE THREE SAUCE BASES: Make the *soy sauce base* by dissolving the sugar in the hot water. Then stir in the light soy sauce. Make the *vinegar base* by dissolving the sugar in the rice vinegar. For the *sesame base*, mix the sesame paste, sesame oil, and salt, then gradually add the hot water, 1 tablespoon at a time, mixing well after each addition until the sauce drips off a spoon in a smooth stream.

PREPARE THE NOODLES: Line a bamboo steamer with perforated parchment paper or damp cheesecloth. Fill your wok with enough water to come ½ inch up the sides of the steamer and bring to a boil. Spread the noodles evenly across one level of the bamboo steamer. (If you don't have one, you can place the noodles on a heatproof plate on a metal steaming rack or on two sturdy bamboo chopsticks set across the bottom of the wok.) Cover and steam over high heat—6 minutes for thinner noodles, or up to 8 minutes for thicker noodles.

Meanwhile, bring a medium pot of water to a boil. Transfer the steamed noodles to the boiling water and cook for 20 to 60 seconds (depending on the thickness), until cooked through but still al dente. Immediately drain the noodles and transfer them to a large plate. Toss the noodles with the sesame oil, using chopsticks or two forks to lift them high off the plate to cool them down quickly. The finished noodles should be at room temperature and in individual strands.

ASSEMBLE THE DISH: Divide the noodles into 2 bowls and allow each person to top with each of the three prepared sauce bases to taste. Garnish with the scallion and enjoy.

TIP! FUN NOODLE TOPPINGS
Eight Treasures Spicy Relish (page 93), Hand-Shredded Chicken (page 158), Fast Sizzled Cucumber Salad (page 73), Shredded Potato & Carrot Salad (page 74), and Salt & Pepper Pork Chops (page 185)

牛肉炒面 niúròu chǎomiàn
Beef Pan-Fried Noodles

In the aforementioned noodle battle (see Chicken Chow Fun, page 108), this is the contender from team fried noodles. Thin Hong Kong–style egg noodles are pan-fried into a crispy golden disc, then topped with beef, vegetables, and a velvety brown sauce. As you toss it all together at the table, you get the crunch from the noodles and vegetables, and the tenderness of the gravy-soaked noodles and beef. Ultimately, in the great noodle wars of Sunday dim sum, we'd inevitably appease both sides, because food is our family's most reliable love language. Despite having just downed our fair share of dim sum, we always manage to save some space for a top layer of delicious carbs.

Serves 4

FOR THE BEEF AND MARINADE

8 ounces boneless beef flank steak, thinly sliced into 2½-inch-long pieces

2 tablespoons water

1 tablespoon oyster sauce

2 teaspoons cornstarch

1 teaspoon neutral oil

⅛ teaspoon baking soda

FOR THE REST OF THE DISH

10 ounces fresh Hong Kong–style egg noodles for pan-frying or 6 ounces dried

1 cup low-sodium beef or chicken stock, heated

1½ tablespoons light soy sauce

1 tablespoon oyster sauce

1 teaspoon sugar

1 teaspoon toasted sesame oil

¼ teaspoon white pepper powder

4½ tablespoons neutral oil

½ teaspoon finely julienned fresh ginger

1 cup sliced fresh mushrooms (such as shiitake, oyster, cremini, or button)

¼ cup sliced carrot

2 medium garlic cloves, finely chopped

1 tablespoon Shaoxing wine

5 ounces fresh Chinese broccoli, ends trimmed, cut on an angle into 3-inch pieces (3 to 4 cups)

1 tablespoon cornstarch

2 tablespoons water

MARINATE THE BEEF: In a medium bowl, combine the beef, water, oyster sauce, cornstarch, neutral oil, and baking soda. Mix until the beef has absorbed the marinade and marinate for 30 minutes to 1 hour.

PARBOIL THE NOODLES: Meanwhile, bring a large pot of water to a boil. Add the noodles and ease them apart with tongs or chopsticks. Boil for 1 minute for fresh noodles or 1 to 2 minutes for dried noodles, just until softened. Do not overcook! Drain, rinse with cold water, and set aside in a colander to air-dry for 10 to 15 minutes.

MIX THE SAUCE: In a medium bowl, combine the hot stock, light soy sauce, oyster sauce, sugar, sesame oil, and white pepper.

PAN-FRY THE NOODLES: Heat a wok over high heat until it's just starting to smoke, then add 2 tablespoons of the neutral oil, swirling it around to coat the sides. Reduce the heat to medium and spread the noodles in the wok in an even layer. Fry for 3 minutes, then add ½ tablespoon of the neutral oil around the perimeter of the wok. Continue cooking for another 2 minutes, until the noodles are golden brown and crispy on the bottom. Be patient and check the noodles often, adjusting the heat as needed to prevent burning. If you like them very crispy, cook them longer over lower heat.

Slide a wok spatula on one side of the noodles and another broad spatula on the other side, and flip the noodles over in one big piece. Add another ½ tablespoon neutral oil around the perimeter of the wok. Fry the noodles on the other side for another 3 to 5 minutes, until golden brown. Transfer the noodles to a shallow bowl or rimmed plate.

SEAR THE BEEF: Reheat the wok until just smoking and add another tablespoon of the neutral oil. Sear the beef for 1 minute on each side, until browned. Turn off the heat and remove the beef from the wok.

ASSEMBLE THE DISH: Over medium heat, add the remaining ½ tablespoon neutral oil along with the ginger. After 5 to 10 seconds, stir in the mushrooms, carrot, and garlic. Then add the Shaoxing wine to deglaze the wok, stirring to loosen the browned bits on the bottom. Add the Chinese broccoli and stir-fry for another minute, then add the sauce mixture and the seared beef, and stir for 30 seconds until everything is combined.

Quickly combine the cornstarch and water to make a slurry and add about two-thirds of it to the wok, stirring to thicken the sauce. Continue to add the slurry until the sauce thickens enough to coat a spoon (or until it's your desired consistency). Simmer for another 30 seconds. Pour the entire mixture over the noodles and serve immediately.

懒人素拌面 lǎn rén sù bàn miàn
Lazy Veggie Noodles

KAITLIN My personal brand of cooking is what I like to call "lazy girl" cooking. I generally try to avoid fiddly steps and ingredients, and I'm the kitchen slacker in the family who checks everyone with a skeptical "Will people actually do that? I wouldn't do that!" Much to my dismay, I've come to realize that the price of preserving traditional Chinese cooking often includes fiddly steps and ingredients. Sometimes, though, my laziness in the kitchen is the mother of invention, as it is with these "lazy noodles." You can make this with any kind of noodle (spaghetti works surprisingly well!), any leafy greens, and any type of mushroom you like. This is a perfect starter recipe for anyone looking for a surefire shortcut on a busy weeknight (or, you know, every night).

Serves 4 to 6

1 pound dried noodles, such as spaghetti or any Chinese wheat noodle

3 tablespoons neutral oil

1 pound fresh mushrooms (such as shiitake, oyster, cremini, or button)

½ teaspoon fine sea salt

¼ teaspoon freshly ground white pepper or black pepper

3 large garlic cloves, thinly sliced

4 cups baby spinach or any tender leafy green of your choice

¼ cup light soy sauce

1 tablespoon Ultimate Chili Oil (page 275), or to taste

1 tablespoon honey

1 tablespoon dark soy sauce

2 teaspoons toasted sesame oil

2 tablespoons unsalted butter

Bring a large pot of water to a boil over high heat, add the noodles, and cook according to the package instructions. Drain the noodles and add to a large bowl.

Meanwhile, heat a large skillet over medium-high heat and add the neutral oil. Add the mushrooms, sprinkle with the salt and pepper, and cook for 10 minutes, stirring periodically, until the mushrooms are browned and slightly crispy.

Add the garlic to the mushrooms and cook for 1 minute. Add the spinach and stir until just wilted, about 30 seconds. Add the skillet ingredients to the bowl of noodles, along with the light soy sauce, chili oil, honey, dark soy sauce, sesame oil, and butter. Toss to combine and serve!

过桥米线 guò qiáo mǐxiàn

Crossing the Bridge Noodles

The cuisine of Yunnan (a province south of Sichuan and north of Vietnam, Laos, and Myanmar) has yet to become well known in the West. While it's acclaimed for its complex flavors, this is one of the region's most approachable (and famous!) dishes using a Yunnan staple: rice noodles, or mǐxiàn. The base is usually a chicken and pork stock, and popular toppings include sliced meats, quail eggs, mushrooms, leafy greens, tofu skin, and Chinese chives. Everything is cut small or paper-thin, and just before enjoying, you tip all the ingredients into the hot soup.

The story goes that a woman would take lunch to her husband, a scholar studying for imperial exams on a small island. But by the time she crossed the bridge to the island, the soup was cold and the noodles soggy. So she cleverly loaded a pot with boiling broth slicked with a layer of fat to insulate the soup. The noodles and other ingredients she kept separate, and when she arrived, they mixed everything together for a fresh, warm meal.

Serves 4

3 (⅛-inch-thick) slices fresh ginger

2½ quarts Chicken & Pork Stock (page 268)

2 tablespoons lard or rendered chicken, goose, or duck fat

1½ cups bean sprouts (about 6 ounces)

⅓ cup frozen corn kernels

¼ cup dried wood ear mushrooms, soaked in hot water for 2 hours and roughly chopped

8 ounces boneless beef ribeye steak, sliced paper-thin against the grain, or thinly shaved fatty beef for hot pot

12 ounces dried mixian (rice noodles about the thickness of spaghetti)

4 ounces tender leafy greens (such as pea tips or choy sum), leaves only

2 ounces fresh enoki or seafood mushrooms, ends trimmed, separated into small bunches (or individual stems if using seafood mushrooms)

3 ounces fresh tofu skin, cut into 3-inch-long strands

⅓ cup tender garlic chives, cut into 2-inch lengths

2 ounces dry-cured ham (such as country ham), steamed for 10 minutes and thinly sliced into small rectangles

Fine sea salt

Ultimate Chili Oil (page 275), for serving (optional)

In a medium pot, add the ginger, stock, and lard. Bring to a boil over high heat, then cover and reduce the heat to low. Simmer for 20 minutes.

Bring a large pot of water to a boil over high heat. Blanch the bean sprouts for 15 seconds, then remove with a strainer. Do the same with the corn. Cook the wood ear mushrooms for 3 minutes, then remove. Bring the water back to a boil and blanch the beef for 20 to 30 seconds, then remove. Return the water to a boil and cook the noodles according to the package instructions. Drain and rinse with cold water.

Divide the noodles among four small bowls. Place the bean sprouts, corn, wood ear mushrooms, and beef in separate small bowls. Do the same with the greens, enoki mushrooms, tofu skin, garlic chives, and ham.

Taste the broth for seasoning and add salt, if needed. Bring it back to a rolling boil. To serve, pour the boiling broth into four large soup bowls at the table. Then allow each person to immediately add their noodles and toppings (each person gets one-fourth of each). Mix and enjoy with additional salt and/or chili oil oil (if using).

Homestyle Mushroom Mei Fun

As we consciously try to eat less meat, we have come to really appreciate vegetarian recipes like this noodle dish, made with both fresh and dried mushrooms that pack a hearty umami punch. We enjoy meatless lunches or dinners a few times a week, and this homestyle stir-fried mei fun is on our table often.

Serves 4

10 to 12 small to medium dried shiitake mushrooms

2 cups hot water

1½ tablespoons oyster sauce or vegetarian oyster sauce

1 tablespoon hoisin sauce

1 tablespoon light soy sauce

2 teaspoons dark soy sauce or mushroom-flavored dark soy sauce

1 teaspoon toasted sesame oil

½ teaspoon sugar

¼ teaspoon fine sea salt

¼ teaspoon white pepper powder

3 tablespoons neutral oil

½ teaspoon minced fresh ginger

3 medium garlic cloves, chopped

2 or 3 scallions, white and green parts separated, split lengthwise, and sliced at an angle into 2-inch pieces

4 cups fresh oyster mushrooms, torn into bite-size pieces (about 6 ounces)

1 small carrot, julienned

2 tablespoons Shaoxing wine

3 cups baby bok choy, leaves separated (about 7 ounces)

8 ounces dried rice vermicelli noodles, soaked in water per the package instructions or until softened, drained

1 cup snow peas or snap peas, ends trimmed (about 3 ounces)

Ultimate Chili Oil (page 275), for serving (optional)

Soak the shiitake mushrooms in the hot water for 2 hours (or overnight), until rehydrated. Squeeze any excess water from the mushrooms, reserving the soaking water. Trim off any tough stems, then thinly slice the mushrooms. Pour ½ cup of the mushroom-soaking liquid into a medium bowl, avoiding any sediment, and discard the rest. To the mushroom-soaking water, add the oyster sauce, hoisin sauce, light soy sauce, dark soy sauce, sesame oil, sugar, salt, and white pepper.

Heat a wok over high heat until it's lightly smoking. Add 1 tablespoon of the neutral oil, along with the shiitakes. Reduce the heat to medium and stir-fry for 1 to 2 minutes, until fragrant.

Add the remaining 2 tablespoons neutral oil to the wok, along with the ginger, garlic, and scallion whites. Cook for 30 seconds, then add the oyster mushrooms and carrot. Increase the heat to high, and stir-fry for 2 minutes.

Pour the Shaoxing wine around the perimeter of the wok. Continue stir-frying over high heat for another 2 to 3 minutes, until the mushrooms begin to caramelize and there is no visible liquid.

Still over high heat, add the bok choy and stir-fry for 30 seconds, just until the leaves begin to wilt. Add the noodles and stir-fry for 1 to 2 minutes, scooping the noodles up from the bottom of the wok to prevent sticking, until they're warmed through.

Pour the sauce mixture evenly over the noodles and add the snow peas. Use an upward scooping motion to stir-fry everything for 2 to 3 minutes, until the noodles are evenly coated in sauce and the vegetables are crisp-tender. Add the scallion greens and mix for 30 seconds, until wilted. Taste and adjust seasoning, if necessary. Serve with the chili oil (if using).

Rice

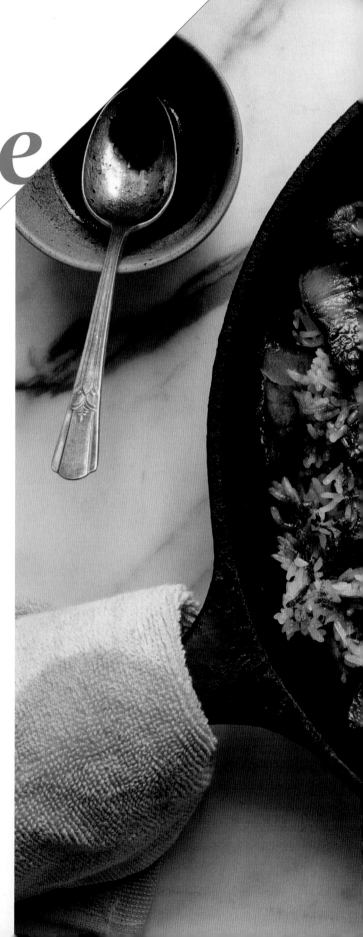

Sarah and I learned how to make rice by the time we were old enough to reach the edge of the kitchen counter, using our index fingers instead of a measuring cup to measure the ratio of rice to water. When we were growing up, every delicious flavor and texture was comfortingly supported by a steaming bowl of rice. Rice can round out flavors, mellow them, act as a palate cleanser, and even become an incredible meal in its own right. In this chapter, we feature rice in its many forms, whether it's made into congee, used as a base for soaking up a silky sauce, stir-fried in the form of rice cakes, or crisped into a soul-warming layer studded with Chinese cured sausage and pork belly. Ultimately, rice is the supporting player for many of the recipes in this book. To this day, I always make a little too much rice—just to make sure there's enough for seconds. **KAITLIN**

铁板煲仔饭 tiě bǎn bāo zǐ fàn

Hong Kong-Style Crispy Rice Skillet

This dish is traditionally made in a clay pot with Cantonese cured meats like lap cheong (cured pork sausage), gon cheong (duck liver sausage), and lap yuk (cured pork belly) nestled in a bed of rice and drizzled with a sweet, seasoned soy sauce right before serving. Many believe the real prize is the thin layer of crispy rice at the bottom of the pot, but it can be difficult to achieve consistently at home, especially if you've never cooked in a clay pot before or don't have one. The pot's relatively small footprint also means the amount of crispy rice can be disappointingly limited. This version uses a cast-iron skillet (or a nonstick pan) for more surface area to crisp up the rice, so you don't have to fight for a piece of it!

Serves 4

FOR THE RICE

1½ cups uncooked long-grain white rice (preferably jasmine)

1⅔ cups water, plus more for soaking the rice

5 teaspoons neutral oil

½ teaspoon fine sea salt

2 ounces (1 to 2 links) Chinese cured pork sausage, thinly sliced on a diagonal

2 ounces (1 to 2 links) Chinese cured duck liver sausage, thinly sliced on a diagonal

3 ounces Chinese cured pork belly, thinly sliced

FOR THE SAUCE

2 teaspoons sugar

4 teaspoons water

2 teaspoons light soy sauce

1 teaspoon dark soy sauce

¼ teaspoon toasted sesame oil

⅛ teaspoon white pepper powder

PREPARE THE RICE: Place the rice in a medium bowl, cover with 2 inches of water, and soak for 1 hour. Drain the rice, then transfer to a 10-inch cast-iron or nonstick skillet. Stir in the 1⅔ cups water, 3 teaspoons of the neutral oil, and the salt. Gently shake the pan to even out the rice. Scatter the sliced sausages and pork belly on top.

Bring the rice and water to a simmer over medium-high heat. When the mixture begins to slowly bubble, cover with a tight-fitting lid, reduce the heat to medium-low, and cook for 15 to 17 minutes, until the rice is tender.

Remove the lid from the skillet and increase the heat to medium. Drizzle the remaining 2 teaspoons neutral oil around the perimeter of the pan. You should hear the rice sizzling and crackling; if not, increase the heat to medium-high. Cook, uncovered, for an additional 7 to 10 minutes to crisp the bottom of the rice. Use a thin spatula to check the bottom periodically, and rotate the pan a few times to ensure the rice is cooking evenly.

MAKE THE SAUCE AND SERVE: In a small saucepan, combine the sugar, water, light soy sauce, dark soy sauce, sesame oil, and white pepper. Bring to a simmer over medium heat and stir to dissolve the sugar. When the sugar is dissolved, turn off the heat.

When the bottom of the rice is golden brown, drizzle half the sauce over the dish. Serve with the remaining sauce on the side.

How to Make
Perfect Rice

White Rice

Here's how to make perfectly tender rice every time, whether it's with a rice cooker or on the stovetop. We cook long grain jasmine rice most often, but we also have instructions for brown rice and sticky rice, both of which require soaking before cooking (at least 2 hours for brown rice and 6 hours for sticky rice).

RICE COOKER METHOD: This is easy! Use the cup that came with your rice cooker (most are generally equivalent to a US ¾ cup measure) to add however many cups you need to the rice cooker pot. The ratio of uncooked rice to cooked rice is 1:3, so keep your rice cooker's capacity in mind.*

Cover the rice in the rice cooker pot with cold water and rinse, agitating the grains with your hands. Carefully pour off the starchy water. Then add water up to the fill line that corresponds with the number of cups you used. Place the pot in the cooker, close the lid, and turn it on.**

STOVETOP METHOD: To a deep pot, add 1 cup rice (or whatever number of cups you want). Cover the rice with 2 inches of cold water, and soak for 20 minutes. After soaking, carefully pour off the water. Measure 1 cup of fresh water (or the same volume of water as rice) and add it to the pot. Bring to a boil (uncovered) over medium-high heat. Reduce the heat to low, cover, and cook until the water is absorbed, 12 to 15 minutes for white rice.

Bonus Method: How to Cook Rice in a Steamer

Brown Rice

For brown rice, soak it at least 2 hours (or up to 12 hours) before carefully pouring off the water and following the rice cooker or stovetop methods. Note that brown rice takes longer to cook (20 to 25 minutes on the stove).

Sticky Rice

Add 2 cups glutinous rice (sometimes labeled "sweet rice") to a large bowl. Cover with 2 inches of water and soak for 6 to 24 hours. Drain the rice and arrange it in an even layer in a shallow heatproof bowl. If you want your sticky rice *extra* sticky (ideal for desserts like Eight Treasures Sticky Rice, page 297), add 1 cup of water to the rice. Place the dish on a metal steaming rack in a wok with simmering water. Cover and steam for 40 minutes. Turn off the heat and keep the rice covered (to prevent it from drying out) until ready to use.

*Note that elsewhere in this book, when we use cup measures for rice, we mean a standard US cup.

**Whatever you do, don't forget to press the On button! Forgetting to press the button has derailed many a meal.

福建萝卜饭 fújiàn luóbo fàn

Fujian-Style **Daikon Rice**

This dish represents a taste of home for many people from the coastal cities of southeast China. Dried shrimp, shiitake mushrooms, pork belly, Chinese cured sausage, and both preserved and fresh daikon all meld seamlessly, with rice as the shared vehicle. Our favorite way to prepare it is in a rice cooker, but we also include stovetop instructions if you don't have one. You may also see this dish made with kohlrabi instead of daikon.

Serves 4

FOR THE PORK BELLY

4 ounces boneless pork belly, cut into ½-inch pieces

1 teaspoon Shaoxing wine

1 teaspoon light soy sauce

½ teaspoon minced fresh ginger

½ teaspoon dark soy sauce

⅛ teaspoon five-spice powder

⅛ teaspoon white pepper powder

FOR THE DRIED MUSHROOMS AND SHRIMP

5 medium dried shiitake mushrooms

1½ cups hot water

3 tablespoons dried shrimp

½ cup water

TO COMPLETE THE DISH

1½ tablespoons neutral oil

1 star anise

1½ teaspoons minced fresh ginger

1 tablespoon minced garlic (from about 3 cloves)

2 ounces (1 to 2 links) Chinese cured pork sausage, thinly sliced

¼ cup finely diced Chinese preserved radish

12 ounces fresh daikon radish, peeled and cut into ½-inch cubes

2 scallions, white and green parts separated and finely chopped

2 teaspoons Shaoxing wine

2 teaspoons oyster sauce

¼ teaspoon white pepper powder

1 cup uncooked long-grain white rice (preferably jasmine)

Fine sea salt

MARINATE THE PORK BELLY: Combine the pork belly with the Shaoxing wine, light soy sauce, ginger, dark soy sauce, five-spice powder, and white pepper. Marinate for at least 30 minutes, or up to 2 hours.

PREPARE THE MUSHROOMS AND SHRIMP: Soak the dried shiitake mushrooms in the 1½ cups hot water for 2 hours, until rehydrated. Squeeze any excess water from the mushrooms, trim off any tough stems, and finely dice the mushrooms. Reserve the soaking liquid.

Rinse the dried shrimp and soak them in the ½ cup room-temperature water for 1 hour. Finely chop the shrimp. Add the shrimp soaking liquid to the reserved mushroom soaking liquid.

ASSEMBLE THE DISH: Heat a wok over medium heat until it begins to smoke lightly. Swirl the oil around the perimeter of the wok, then add the star anise, ginger, and marinated pork belly. Stir-fry for 1 to 2 minutes, or until the pork turns opaque.

Add the prepared mushrooms and rehydrated shrimp to the wok, along with the garlic, Chinese sausage, preserved radish, fresh daikon cubes, and the white parts of the scallions. Stir-fry for 5 minutes over medium heat. Add the Shaoxing wine and continue cooking for another 5 minutes, until the radish cubes turn translucent. There should be no standing liquid at this point. Stir in the oyster sauce and white pepper. Turn off the heat. Remove the star anise and discard.

IF USING A RICE COOKER: Rinse the rice in your rice cooker pot, carefully draining off the starchy water. Add 1¼ cups of the soaking liquid from the mushrooms and shrimp, avoiding any sediment. Spoon the stir-fry mixture on top of the rice, close the lid, and turn on the rice cooker.

IF USING A POT: Put the rice in a deep medium pot and cover with 2 inches of water. Soak for 20 minutes to 1 hour. Thoroughly drain off all the water, then add 1 cup of the soaking liquid from the mushrooms and shrimp. Place the pot over medium heat and bring to a boil. Immediately turn down the heat to low, spoon the stir-fry mixture on top of the rice, cover tightly, and cook over low heat for 15 to 20 minutes, until the rice is cooked through.

When the rice is done, let it sit in the rice cooker or covered pot for another 5 minutes to allow the other ingredients to continue steaming (10 minutes if your rice cooker cooks in 15 minutes or less). Open the lid and stir in the green parts of the scallions, add salt to taste, and serve.

特色黄金炒饭 tèsè huángjīn chǎofàn

Special Golden Fried Rice

This is one of our favorite fried rice dishes. The name Golden Fried Rice references the process of coating the rice in egg yolks prior to cooking. Another reason it's called golden rice is the addition of "rich" ingredients like Chinese cured ham and dried scallops (also known as conpoy). If you can't find Chinese cured ham, you can substitute dry-cured American country ham or even Serrano ham. As for the scallops, larger dried scallops will have a more burnt golden color and deeper flavor, but the small dried bay scallops are fine to use and more affordable. The final touch? An occasional hint of sweetness from golden raisins—a trick we learned from New York City's Wu's Wonton King. This fried rice is golden in every sense of the word.

Serves 4

⅓ **cup dried scallops** (1¼ ounces)

1 cup hot water

6 large egg yolks

1 tablespoon Shaoxing wine

½ **teaspoon fine sea salt**

¼ **teaspoon white pepper powder**

5 cups cooked and cooled long-grain white rice (preferably jasmine; see page 123)

¼ **cup neutral oil**

⅓ **cup very finely diced Chinese cured ham** or other dry-cured ham (1¾ ounces)

1 tablespoon finely minced fresh ginger

1 teaspoon minced garlic

⅓ **cup golden raisins**

3 scallions, thinly sliced

Place the dried scallops in a small bowl, cover with the hot water, and soak for 1 hour, until rehydrated (see Tip). Shred the scallops into smaller pieces with your fingers, then drain and set aside.

In a small bowl, lightly beat 3 of the egg yolks. In a large bowl, lightly beat the remaining 3 egg yolks, along with the Shaoxing wine, salt, and white pepper. Add the cooked rice to the egg mixture and mix thoroughly.

Preheat a wok over medium-high heat until it starts to smoke lightly. Add the oil. When little bubbles form around the tip of a bamboo or wooden chopstick dipped into the oil, add the beaten egg yolks (not the rice coated in egg yolk) and rapidly stir them in wide circles, breaking them up into tendrils with your wok spatula. Turn off the heat and remove the egg using a fine-mesh strainer, letting any excess oil drip back into the wok.

With the wok over medium heat, add the scallops and fry for 8 to 10 minutes, until crisp, golden brown, and fragrant. Add the ham and fry for 1 to 2 minutes, until crisp around the edges. Add the ginger and garlic and cook for another minute. Increase the heat to high and add the egg yolk–coated rice. Stir-fry continuously for 2 minutes, until the rice is heated through. Add the fried egg yolks, the raisins, and scallions. Stir-fry for 1 minute. Serve.

TIP! For a more tender texture, you can steam the scallops after soaking them and do the same with the Chinese cured ham for similar effect. Steam them both in a heatproof dish over medium-high heat for 15 minutes, either on a metal steaming rack or in a bamboo steamer with enough water in the wok to come ½ inch up the bottom rim of the steamer (you may need to add boiling water during steaming to keep the water at this level). Then incorporate the scallops and ham as instructed in the recipe.

卤肉饭 lǔ ròu fàn

Braised Pork Rice

While we were living in China, we found this beloved home-cooked dish just about everywhere, particularly in places where "home" might feel very far away, like fast-food chains, airport and train-station restaurants, and even in ready-to-eat packages. Bits of pork belly and mushrooms are braised with Shaoxing wine, soy sauce, and aromatic spices, with hard-boiled eggs added in the last 30 minutes of cooking. The result is like a gravy that gets ladled over rice. Try to find skin-on pork belly, as it makes the sauce particularly sticky and delicious. You'll also need cheesecloth (or two coffee filters) and kitchen string to make the spice sachet!

Serves 4

8 fresh or dried shiitake mushrooms

2½ cups hot water if using dried mushrooms

1 pound boneless pork belly (ideally skin-on), cut into ½-inch pieces

6 whole cloves

3 dried bay leaves

3 star anise

2 (⅛-inch-thick) slices fresh ginger

2 strips dried mandarin orange peel

1 Chinese cassia cinnamon stick, about 2 inches long

2 teaspoons whole Sichuan peppercorns

2 teaspoons neutral oil

1½ tablespoons sugar or 20g rock sugar

1 cup diced white or yellow onion (from 1 medium)

¼ cup Shaoxing wine

3 tablespoons light soy sauce

2 tablespoons dark soy sauce

4 large eggs

6 cups cooked long-grain white rice (preferably jasmine; see page 123), for serving

If using fresh shiitakes, trim off any woody stems, dice, and set aside. If using dried shiitakes, soak them in the hot water for 2 hours, until rehydrated. Trim off any tough stems and dice into ½-inch pieces. Reserve the water they soaked in.

To a medium pot, add the pork belly with enough water to cover it. Bring to a boil, then drain through a colander and rinse the pieces of any foam or impurities.

Make a spice sachet by combining the cloves, bay leaves, star anise, ginger, orange peel, cinnamon stick, and Sichuan peppercorns in a piece of cheesecloth and tie closed with kitchen string. (Alternatively, place the spices in a coffee filter and fold to close. Place into another coffee filter and tie with kitchen string.)

Heat the oil in a wok over low heat and add the sugar. Cook until the sugar melts, then increase the heat to medium-high and add the onion. Stir-fry until the onion begins to brown at the edges, about 1 minute. Add the shiitakes and stir-fry for 2 minutes, until fragrant. Add the pork, the Shaoxing wine, light soy sauce, dark soy sauce, and 2 cups of the mushroom-soaking water (leaving behind any sediment at the bottom of the bowl). If you didn't use dried mushrooms, add 2 cups fresh water. Stir and bring to a boil, then add the spice sachet. Cover, reduce the heat to medium-low, and simmer for 1 hour, stirring occasionally.

Meanwhile, make the hard-boiled eggs. Bring a large pot of water to a rapid boil. Use a spoon to carefully lower in the eggs and boil for 1 minute. Cover, reduce the heat to low and simmer for 9 minutes. Transfer the eggs to an ice bath to cool.

When the pork has simmered for 1 hour, peel the eggs and submerge them in the pork mixture. Remove the sachet. Cover and simmer over low heat for another 30 minutes.

Uncover and increase the heat to medium-high. Continue cooking for 5 minutes, stirring occasionally, until the sauce is thick enough to coat a spoon. Serve over steamed rice.

Lessons *in* Grocery Shopping

SARAH / **WHILE MY MOM'S** first experience with an American grocery store may have made her feel like a fish out of water (see page 246), as her daughter I only ever saw a calm, cool, collected couponing machine. After fifteen years in America, she was no longer that wide-eyed girl fresh off the plane from Shanghai. She was an absolute master of the supermarket circular.

As a child of the '90s—perhaps the golden age of junk food—walking through the grocery store with my mom was an exercise in persuasion and not-so-subtle manipulation. Nine-year-old me wasn't thinking about preserving family recipes or the importance of fresh ingredients. I was obsessed with the Backstreet Boys *Millennium* album, and my pastimes included watching Nickelodeon shows and attempting to learn the choreography to "Baby One More Time." My TV-addled brain only had eyes for Fruit Roll-Ups and Dunkaroos, Marie Callender's frozen chicken Alfredo, and those rectangular crackers with the fake cheese that you would spread on with a tiny red plastic stick. If it was highly processed and could be dipped, dunked, microwaved, or otherwise assembled, I wanted it.

I would snatch a box of Bagel Bites out of the freezer case and hold it aloft like it was Simba and I was wise, old Rafiki, explaining to my mother that when pizza's on a *bagel*, we could eat it *anytime*. I seized any opening I saw, making a habit of helping her clip coupons from the Sunday newspaper inserts . . . my mildly obsessive-compulsive brain relishing the task of placing each strip of glossy barcoded paper into the correct slot of her coupon organizer. I knew that it was harder for her to resist a good deal, so during these seemingly innocuous Sunday afternoons I would tuck a few items for my sister and me into the organizer. When we went shopping the next week, I could casually "discover" a coupon for Hot Pockets and say, "Hey, these are on sale! And look! You get fifty cents off if you buy two!"

I didn't realize it at the time, but my mom had her own agenda on those weekly grocery shopping trips: to make her daughters understand the value of money. One of

Above: A rare night of hot dogs for dinner during a camping trip—notice how happy I am! Right: My mother, who can't believe she ended up with kids who sometimes wanted Kraft mac and cheese instead of chive dumplings.

us would put a jar of something in the cart, and she would immediately snatch it up and put it back on the shelf. "Not today. Next week is double coupon."

She would send me to grab something in the produce section, and if I came back with an orange that wasn't heavy enough with juice, a barely bruised apple, or a potato that looked a little soft or wrinkly, I would be sent back. Whenever I did successfully return to our cart with something she'd asked for, I'd be quizzed on the price. If I couldn't give her the right number, she'd make me go back to the aisle in question to look (bonus points if I could name the unit price).

Having grown up with scarcity, my mom would buy things in bulk whenever they were on sale, filling the pantry to the brim (and, in preparation for Y2K, the basement, where we had a truly impressive stockpile of rice, ramen noodles, water, and pet food).

In my elementary school years, we rarely went out to eat. While I longed for fast food and restaurants, it was home-cooked meals every night. (Quelle nightmare!) At the time, I couldn't stand the idea of waiting a whole week to stock up on canned goods. I didn't understand why my mother scoffed every time I asked for Lunchables pizza kits, or why ordering takeout was such a hard sell.

But eventually, I realized that although I didn't grow up under the same circumstances as she did, she was teaching me many of the same lessons she'd learned as a child in Hubei and Shanghai—not just how to stretch a dollar, but also how to value food. As I explored food outside our home, I began to appreciate my mom's (and dad's, for that matter) plates of fresh vegetables, lovingly braised dishes, and expedient, tasty stir-fries. In high school, I went to a friend's house for dinner, and our meal was a slice of cheese pizza, a glass of whole milk, and a Centrum vitamin. No offense to the vitamins (or the friend's family), but suddenly my mom's way of preparing meals looked a lot better than food that came out of a box.

I've realized that her frugality in those years taught me how important and precious food is—how to cook according to what the best-looking produce might be and how to repurpose leftover ingredients to make something entirely new and tasty. These days, I get a deep sense of satisfaction from creating a "fridge clean-out meal," something both my parents had always done to salvage the last of the refrigerator's contents at the end of the week. I can also play an impromptu game of *The Price Is Right* and tell you how much a bag of flour is and what the price might be when it goes on sale.

So basically, I've turned into my mother. But that's not such a bad thing.

阿姨的炒年糕 āyí de chǎo niángāo
Ayi's Rice Cake Stir-Fry

SARAH Our parents both worked when we were young, and for some time in elementary school, we had a Chinese nanny (or ayi, "auntie" in Chinese) to help care for us. Every day after school, she'd fix us something delicious to eat, and this tasty rice cake stir-fry became my favorite "snack." Sometimes she added napa cabbage or bok choy, but this version with lots of sweet scallions was what we liked best. Rice cakes, or niángāo, have the texture of a chewy noodle. Made by steaming and pounding cooked rice into a sticky paste, or by using rice flour and water, their shapes can vary. Look for the oval discs in the refrigerated or frozen section of your local Asian grocery store; if frozen, there is no need to thaw before using. You may also find dried rice cakes, which need to be soaked overnight before use; after reconstituting, they can be refrigerated in a bowl of water for up to 1 week.

Serves 4

FOR THE PORK

6 ounces boneless pork shoulder, butt, or loin, thinly sliced

1 tablespoon water

1 teaspoon cornstarch

2 teaspoons Shaoxing wine

1 teaspoon neutral oil

1 teaspoon oyster sauce

FOR THE SAUCE

½ cup water

1 tablespoon oyster sauce

1 teaspoon light soy sauce

1 teaspoon dark soy sauce

¼ teaspoon sugar

⅛ teaspoon white pepper powder

FOR THE REST OF THE DISH

2 tablespoons neutral oil

2 (⅛-inch-thick) slices fresh ginger

8 scallions, white and green parts separated and cut on a diagonal into 2-inch pieces

1 tablespoon Shaoxing wine

1 pound Chinese rice cakes (preferably oval)

MARINATE THE PORK: In a medium bowl, combine the pork with the water, cornstarch, Shaoxing wine, oil, and oyster sauce. Let marinate for 20 minutes.

PREPARE THE SAUCE: In a small bowl, combine the water, oyster sauce, light soy sauce, dark soy sauce, sugar, and white pepper.

ASSEMBLE THE DISH: Heat a wok over high heat until it starts to lightly smoke, then add 1 tablespoon of the oil. Spread it around the wok and add the pork. Stir-fry just until the pork turns opaque, about 1 minute. Remove the pork from the wok and set on a plate.

Reduce the heat to medium and add the remaining tablespoon oil. Add the ginger slices and the white parts of the scallions. Cook for 30 seconds, until the ginger begins to crisp at the edges and the scallions begin to turn golden brown.

Increase the heat to high and add the Shaoxing wine. It will hiss and bubble vigorously! Stir for 15 seconds. Then add the rice cakes, the prepared sauce, and the pork. Stir-fry for 30 seconds, using your wok spatula to scoop the rice cakes and sauce up from the bottom of the wok so nothing sticks and everything is thoroughly combined. Cover and reduce the heat to medium-low to cook the rice cakes through.

Uncover the wok after 2 minutes. The rice cakes should be cooked but still al dente, and there will be standing sauce pooling at the bottom of the wok. Increase the heat to high, add the green parts of the scallions, and stir-fry until there is very little standing sauce, about 1 minute. Serve.

快手滑鸡粥 kuàishǒu huá jī zhōu

Quick Chicken Congee

Congee is the common English term for a Chinese rice porridge, but most families know it as jook (Cantonese) or zhōu (Mandarin). While it normally takes hours for the rice to break down and create that familiarly smooth texture, we have a secret to making flavorful congee in a fraction of the time: rinsing and freezing the rice before cooking. The moisture in the frozen rice expands and fractures the grains, so your congee needs to simmer only for 25 minutes. Keep a large batch of frozen rice in your freezer, and you can make a batch of congee in under an hour whenever the mood strikes. We like to use long-grain white rice (like jasmine), but if you want yours to be extra creamy, use medium or short-grain white rice.

Serves 4 to 6

1 cup uncooked long-grain white rice (preferably jasmine)

6 ounces boneless, skinless chicken breast, partially frozen

2 tablespoons plus 2 cups water

1 teaspoon cornstarch

1 teaspoon neutral oil

1½ teaspoons oyster sauce

½ teaspoon toasted sesame oil

¼ teaspoon fine sea salt, plus more for serving

¼ teaspoon white pepper powder, plus more for serving

5 cups low-sodium chicken stock or Chicken & Pork Stock (page 268)

3 (⅛-inch-thick) slices fresh ginger, julienned, plus more for serving

1 scallion, white and green parts finely chopped

3 tablespoons finely chopped fresh cilantro

Rinse the rice, drain, and repeat twice more. Transfer the rice to a freezer-safe container, cover, and freeze overnight, or at least 8 hours.

Slice the chicken into ¼-inch-thick strips (this is much easier when the chicken is partially frozen). In a medium bowl, combine the chicken with 2 tablespoons of the water, the cornstarch, neutral oil, oyster sauce, sesame oil, ¼ teaspoon salt, and ¼ teaspoon white pepper. Marinate for 15 to 20 minutes.

In a deep medium pot, add the remaining 2 cups water, the chicken stock, and the frozen rice. Bring to a boil, cover, and reduce the heat to medium-low. Keep it at a slow simmer until thickened, 20 to 25 minutes. Do not stir, as doing so will release starch and cause the rice to stick to the pot.

Uncover the pot, increase the heat to medium-high, and bring the congee to a slow boil (small bubbles). Now, stir continuously for 5 minutes to release the starch and thicken the congee. (If you like your congee even thicker, stir for an additional 5 minutes.) If at any point you find it is too thick, add water or stock to achieve your preferred consistency.

Stir in the ginger and the chicken. Increase the heat to high; the congee should be bubbling. Boil for 2 minutes to cook the chicken through, stirring often to prevent sticking. Stir in more salt and white pepper to taste. Serve piping hot, garnished with more fresh ginger and the scallion and cilantro.

广式五花肉炒饭 guǎng shì wǔhuāròu chǎofàn

Cantonese
Pork Belly Fried Rice

KAITLIN　For me, a plate of Cantonese roast pork belly, or siu yuk, will forever be a sign of the weekend. After Sarah and I finished Chinese school on Saturday mornings (the star pupil of our class was a 4-year-old who could run circles around us), our mom would take us to the hot bar of our local Chinese market for lunch. My order of choice was glorious piles of crispy roast pork and garlicky cabbage. No longer occupied with pencils and workbooks, my mind could go gloriously blank, wiped clean by the aroma of pork fat. This fried rice dish captures all those flavors in less time. Unctuous pork belly is seasoned with five-spice powder, while cabbage, ginger, and scallions—stand-ins for the requisite sides of cabbage and a ginger-scallion oil (page 278)—are stir-fried right into the rice. For the traditional version of siu yuk, see Sarah's recipe on page 180.

Serves 4

10 ounces boneless pork belly, cut into ½-inch pieces

4 teaspoons Shaoxing wine

1 teaspoon fine sea salt

1 teaspoon rice vinegar

½ teaspoon five-spice powder

¼ teaspoon sugar

⅛ teaspoon white pepper powder

2 tablespoons neutral oil

1 tablespoon minced fresh ginger

5 cups cooked and cooled long-grain white rice (preferably jasmine; see page 123)

2 teaspoons dark soy sauce

2 cups shredded napa cabbage

2 scallions, white and green parts finely chopped

In a medium bowl, marinate the pork belly with 1 teaspoon of the Shaoxing wine, ½ teaspoon of the salt, the rice vinegar, five-spice powder, sugar, and white pepper for 30 minutes.

Heat a dry wok over high heat until it's just beginning to smoke. Add the oil, quickly followed by the pork belly. Fry until golden and crispy at the edges, about 8 minutes. (Reduce the heat to medium-high, if needed, to avoid burning.) Turn off the heat and remove the pork belly, leaving any excess oil in the wok. (Scoop the pork up along the side of the wok and hold it in place for a few seconds with your spatula to allow the oil to drain.)

Reset the heat to medium-high, add the ginger, and cook until slightly crisped, about 30 seconds. Increase the heat to high and add the rice. Stir-fry to coat it in the oil and ginger. Spread the rice evenly across the bottom of the wok and allow it to fry for 30 seconds. Stir and repeat three more times, for a total of about 2 minutes.

Stir in the dark soy sauce. Add the remaining 3 teaspoons Shaoxing wine around the hot exposed perimeter of the wok. Add the cabbage and stir-fry until it's just wilted, about 2 minutes.

Finally, add the scallions, pork belly, and remaining ½ teaspoon salt. Stir-fry until thoroughly combined. Taste for seasoning and adjust with additional salt before serving, if desired.

Poultry & Eggs

In China, poultry is usually cooked on the bone (skin on, of course) to preserve moisture and flavor, and every part of the bird gets used. As a little girl, I remember how happy we were when my father once caught a wild chicken and brought it home for dinner. We certainly weren't going to waste any of it! In this chapter, we show you how to cook a whole bird the Chinese way, like Bill's classic Cantonese Roast Duck (page 153). If you're not yet ready to confront a whole bird or learn the way of the cleaver, we've got you covered with easy stir-fries you can make on any weeknight, as well as a few classic and beloved egg dishes that will stretch your ingredients—and your dollar.
JUDY

三杯鸡 sān bēi jī

Three-Cup Chicken

JUDY

Three-cup chicken gets its name from its three main ingredients: one cup each of soy sauce, Shaoxing wine, and sesame oil. I've since adjusted the 1:1:1 ratio; while poetic and easy to remember, that amount of sesame oil would overwhelm the dish! I first learned how to make three-cup chicken from my friend Karen. We met at work, both in our first jobs and with little ones at home (back when "mom jeans" were just jeans and headbands had their first heyday). When I saw how easy it was to make—and tasted it—it quickly became a go-to at home. The girls remember me slapping a bowl of this chicken down in front of them often. (They weren't complaining!)

Serves 4 to 6

2 pounds bone-in, skin-on chicken thighs, boned with skin left on

1 tablespoon neutral oil

6 (⅛-inch-thick) slices fresh ginger

5 medium garlic cloves, smashed

2 scallions, white and green parts separated and cut into 2-inch pieces

1 dried red chili, cut in half lengthwise

1 tablespoon toasted sesame oil

¼ cup Shaoxing wine

¼ cup water

1½ tablespoons light soy sauce

2 teaspoons sugar

2 teaspoons dark soy sauce

1 cup fresh Thai basil leaves

Use a sharp knife to carefully cut the chicken thighs into large 2-inch chunks, keeping the skin on the meat.

Place a wok over high heat until it begins to smoke lightly. Add the neutral oil and swirl to coat the wok evenly. Add the chicken pieces in one layer and sear for 1 minute without stirring. When seared enough to release from the hot wok, stir the chicken, then add the ginger, garlic, white parts of the scallions, chili, and sesame oil. Stir for another 30 seconds.

Add the Shaoxing wine, water, light soy sauce, sugar, and dark soy sauce. Stir and cover the wok. Turn the heat down to medium and simmer for 10 minutes, stirring occasionally.

Remove the cover and increase the heat to medium-high. Rapidly reduce the sauce, stirring often to prevent burning, for 4 to 8 minutes, until the sauce clings to the chicken and gives it a rich, dark color.

Add the Thai basil and the green parts of the scallions and stir for another 30 seconds. Serve.

How to Debone Chicken Thighs

蒜香鸡翅 suàn xiāng jīchì

Garlic Fried Chicken Wings

BILL At Sun Hing restaurant, you could always tell what was really good on the menu by looking at what we—the employees—ate after a long and grueling dinner shift. For us, fried chicken wings were often the highlight of our staff meals. This is a new take on the classic version from our blog, with garlic added to the crispy coating. Note that these *must* be fried twice to be extra crispy; after the initial fry, we let them rest for 10 minutes and then fry them a second time right before serving. Another trick is to use potato starch for extra crispness, though cornstarch will do if you can't find it.

Serves 4 to 6

12 whole large chicken wings (about 3 pounds)

1 large egg, lightly beaten

3 tablespoons finely chopped garlic (from 9 to 10 cloves)

1 tablespoon Shaoxing wine

2 teaspoons fine sea salt

1 teaspoon sugar

1 teaspoon garlic powder

2 teaspoons light soy sauce

1 teaspoon toasted sesame oil

½ teaspoon onion powder

½ teaspoon white pepper powder

2 tablespoons all-purpose flour

2 tablespoons cornstarch

1 tablespoon potato starch (or more cornstarch)

Peanut oil (or other neutral oil), for frying

Pat the chicken wings dry with paper towels. In a large bowl, combine the wings, beaten egg, garlic, Shaoxing wine, salt, sugar, garlic powder, light soy sauce, sesame oil, onion powder, and white pepper. Mix everything with a rubber spatula until the wings are evenly coated. Add the flour, cornstarch, and potato starch, and mix again to coat. Marinate the wings in the refrigerator overnight for best results or for at least 2 hours at room temperature. (If you refrigerate your wings overnight, let them come back up to room temperature, about 1 to 2 hours, before frying.)

Fill a medium pot about two-thirds of the way with peanut oil (enough to fully submerge the wings) and heat the oil until it reaches 325°F on an instant-read thermometer. Line a sheet pan with paper towels and place a wire rack on top, if you have one.

Mix the wings thoroughly again to ensure they're evenly covered with a thin, batter-like coating and the garlic bits are evenly distributed. Drop the wings into the hot oil and fry in small batches for 5 minutes per batch, or until light golden brown. Be sure to flip them once halfway through, or as needed for even color. (When adding the wings to the oil, the temperature will drop immediately. Increase the heat to bring the temperature back up and keep it at 325°F using an instant-read thermometer.) Remove the fried wings to the prepared sheet pan to drain. After this first frying, rest each batch of wings for 10 minutes before the second fry.

With the oil again at 325°F, fry the wings in batches a second time for 3 minutes, or until crispy. Drain on paper towels and serve.

白切鸡 bái qiē jī

Poached "White Cut" Chicken

BILL

My mom was a generous woman, known for giving out $20 red envelopes on Chinese New Year (this was the 1970s, when you could buy a loaf of bread for 25 cents!). So when she hosted her friends for mahjong on weekends, true to form, she went all out, cooking a dinner as extravagant as a Chinese New Year meal. There would always be a baak chit gai (Cantonese for "white cut chicken"), a dish that amplifies chicken to its purest form. A poached chicken may not sound like much, but it's Cantonese home cooking at its best, featuring silky meat (described as waat, meaning "slippery" in Cantonese) that gets dipped into a ginger-scallion oil. The quality of the chicken matters here, so buy the best you can find. We buy fresh Buddhist-style chickens at our local Chinese market, which still have the head and feet on. A whole chicken symbolizes family unity and prosperity, and because none of the skin has been torn or removed, the meat is protected from drying out during cooking.

Serves 4 to 6

1 (4-pound) whole chicken (optionally, head and feet still on)

2 scallions, trimmed

5 (⅛-inch-thick) slices fresh ginger

Raw Ginger-Scallion Oil (page 277), for serving

Remove any giblets from the chicken and rinse the cavity to thoroughly clean it out (depending on how your chicken was processed, it may still contain some organ tissue in the cavity). Set the chicken on a large plate and leave out at room temperature for 1 hour. Be sure to disinfect your sink and work surface after handling the raw chicken.

Carefully place the chicken in a tall, narrow stockpot (tall and narrow is ideal, as less water is then required, which yields a more concentrated stock, though any deep stockpot will work). Be careful not to rip any of the chicken skin—you don't want the meat exposed to the boiling water as it cooks. Fill the pot with just enough water to submerge the chicken completely. Remove the chicken from the pot and set back on the plate.

To the water, add the whole scallions and ginger, and bring to a boil over high heat. Slowly lower the chicken into the pot, legs down. (It's okay if the breast is peeking out of the water a bit.) The water will cool down and stop boiling when you add the chicken, so bring it up to a boil once again. Don't step away from the stove.

As soon as the water comes back to a boil, immediately lift the chicken out of the water. You can do this by carefully sliding two wooden spoons under the wings or using a roasting fork stuck in the underside of the wing joint. Allow any water inside the cavity to pour back into the pot, then lower the chicken back into the boiling water. This step is key, as it ensures there are no cold spots that could result in uneven cooking.

Bring the water to a boil once again, keeping a close eye on the pot. Once boiling, immediately reduce the heat to the lowest setting, keeping the water at barely a simmer (there should be barely any movement in the

(RECIPE CONTINUES)

water). Cover the pot and cook the chicken for 40 to 45 minutes (10 to 11 minutes per pound).

When the chicken is almost done, prepare a large bowl of ice water. To check for doneness, poke a chopstick or skewer into the thickest part of the thigh. If the juices run clear, it's done.

Carefully lift the chicken out of the pot (using the same method as before), and transfer the chicken to the ice bath, carefully flipping it a few times to ensure the whole chicken gets cooled and the texture of the skin becomes snappy. (Save the stock in the pot and refrigerate or freeze for other uses.)

When the chicken has cooled, remove it from the ice bath. (For extra wow factor, brush the chicken lightly with neutral oil or some of the chicken grease floating at the top of the poaching liquid for an extra enticing, shiny look.)

Using a sharp cleaver or chef's knife, cut the chicken in half lengthwise, from the top of the breast down through to one side of the backbone. Next, take the half of the chicken with the backbone still attached, and make a lengthwise cut along the other side of the backbone to remove it. You can cut it into bite-size pieces to serve, or use it for chicken stock. Cut off the leg quarters and wings, chop the wings in half at the joint, chop each drumstick into two pieces, and chop each thigh into three pieces. Then chop the chicken breasts into bite-size pieces, using your cleaver to drive through the soft bones. Serve with the ginger-scallion oil.

DOCTORING THE DIPPING SAUCE
When it comes to dipping sauces for this chicken, Raw Ginger-Scallion Oil (page 277) is traditional. My dad, ever the good Cantonese son, prefers it as is, while my mom, ever the Shanghai gal, loves to add light soy sauce (just add 1 tablespoon of light soy sauce to 1 tablespoon of the ginger-scallion oil—she sometimes adds a few drops of sesame oil too). Sarah and I are somewhere in the middle. Splitting the oil into two small bowls to get the best of both worlds is the perfect compromise.
—KAITLIN

香酥鴨 xiāng sū yā

Chinese Crispy Salted Duck

JUDY In the 1990s, my mother worked at a company in Manhattan that beaded evening gowns. Many of her colleagues were Chinese, and someone brought in this crispy duck for lunch one day, singing its praises. Like any smart home cook, she immediately asked for the recipe. Involving just a handful of ingredients, it wasn't hard to memorize, and the recipe spread like wildfire. There was a moment in the '90s when it felt like everyone in our circle was making it! Toasted Sichuan peppercorns don't have a numbing effect in this recipe, but they add great flavor. The salt level here is similar to that of cured ham, making a helping of steamed rice the perfect companion.

Serves 4

1 tablespoon fine sea salt	**1 teaspoon water**
1 tablespoon whole Sichuan peppercorns	**⅛ teaspoon dark soy sauce**
4 meaty duck legs (about 2½ pounds)	

MARINATE: In a wok or small pan, toast the salt and Sichuan peppercorns over low to medium-low heat for about 5 minutes, until the salt turns a pale yellow and the Sichuan peppercorns are fragrant. Transfer to a small bowl and let cool completely.

Pat the duck legs dry with a paper towel and place them in a medium bowl or baking dish. (Do not trim away any skin or fat.) Rub the salt and Sichuan peppercorns evenly over the duck legs. Cover and marinate in the refrigerator for at least 24 hours or up to 48 hours.

STEAM: Brush any Sichuan peppercorns off the duck legs and discard. Place the legs in a rimmed heatproof dish (a 9-inch pie plate works well), as there will be juices and fat rendered out during steaming. Place a 2-inch-tall metal steaming rack in the bottom of your wok (or any pot with a lid that will accommodate the steaming dish) and fill with enough water to come up to about 1 inch below the rack. Bring the water in the wok to a simmer over medium-high heat. Place the dish of duck onto the rack, cover, and steam over medium-high heat for 30 minutes.

PAN-FRY: Remove the duck legs from the steaming dish and lay them skin side up on a separate plate. In a small bowl, combine the water and dark soy sauce, then brush the sauce onto the skin of each duck leg, avoiding the meat.

Pour the juices from the steaming dish into a fat separator and separate the juices from the fat. Heat a large cast-iron skillet or Dutch oven over medium heat, and add some of the rendered duck fat so there is a ⅛-inch layer in the pan. (Save the remaining fat and juices for use in other cooking.)

Add the duck legs skin side down and cook over medium heat for 15 minutes without disturbing them (or the skin may break), until the skin is crispy and a deep golden brown. (If the legs are darkening too quickly, reduce the heat to medium-low.) Flip the legs and fry for another 10 to 15 minutes on the other side, until they are deeply golden brown all over. During the frying, carefully spoon the hot fat over any pale patches of skin to even out the color. Serve.

DON'T WASTE THAT FAT!
Save it for roasting potatoes or using in place of cooking oil for extra flavor (note that duck fat has a smoke point of about 375°F). It will keep in the refrigerator for up to 6 months.

宫保鸡丁 gōng bǎo jī dīng

Kung Pao Chicken

Is it just us, or are people "kung pao-ing" the heck out of everything these days? While kung pao chicken traditionally includes peanuts (they do make the dish great), you can't just go throwing peanuts into any wok full of meat and sauce and call it kung pao! The interplay of flavors and textures in this dish is key. The chicken, peanuts (which are wok-roasted), and scallions are all kept at about the same size, creating a unique mix of textures in every bite. The flavors should be balanced across spicy heat, sweetness, and tanginess, with no standing sauce. A small sprinkling of ground Sichuan peppercorns at the end balances the heat from the chilies and marks it as a Sichuan classic. It's time to set things straight—to use peanuts responsibly—and return to this classic recipe.

Serves 4

FOR THE CHICKEN

12 ounces boneless, skinless chicken breasts, cut into ½-inch cubes

1 tablespoon water

1 teaspoon cornstarch

1 teaspoon neutral oil

1 teaspoon Shaoxing wine

⅛ teaspoon fine sea salt

⅛ teaspoon white pepper powder

FOR ROASTING THE PEANUTS

1 teaspoon neutral oil

1 cup raw shelled peanuts

FOR THE SAUCE

1 tablespoon rice vinegar

1 tablespoon light soy sauce

1 teaspoon cornstarch

1 teaspoon sugar

½ teaspoon dark soy sauce

FOR THE REST OF THE DISH

3 tablespoons neutral oil

3 medium garlic cloves, smashed and sliced

2 to 4 dried red chilies, seeded and sliced into small pieces

½ cup diced scallions, white parts only (from 6 to 7 scallions)

2 teaspoons minced fresh ginger

½ teaspoon ground Sichuan peppercorns

MARINATE THE CHICKEN: In a medium bowl, combine the chicken, water, cornstarch, oil, Shaoxing wine, salt, and white pepper. Marinate for 20 minutes.

ROAST THE PEANUTS: Heat the oil in a wok over medium heat, then add the peanuts. Stirring constantly to prevent burning, roast the peanuts for 3 minutes. Turn off the heat and roast for another minute using the residual heat of the wok. Let cool.

PREPARE THE SAUCE: In a small bowl, combine the rice vinegar, light soy sauce, cornstarch, sugar, and dark soy sauce.

ASSEMBLE THE DISH: Heat your wok over high heat until lightly smoking. Add 2 tablespoons of oil to coat the surface of the wok. Add the chicken in one layer and sear it undisturbed for 30 seconds. Stir-fry for 1 minute, until the chicken turns opaque. Remove the chicken from the wok.

Reduce the heat to low and add the remaining tablespoon oil. Add the garlic, chilies, scallions, ginger, and ground Sichuan peppercorns. Stir-fry for 1 to 2 minutes, until the aromatics are fragrant and the scallions are lightly browned around the edges.

Add the chicken back to the wok and increase the heat to high. Stir-fry for 1 minute. Re-stir the sauce so the cornstarch is incorporated, then add the sauce to the wok and stir-fry for 1 minute, until the sauce has thickened and clings to the chicken. Stir in the peanuts and serve.

广东烧鸭 guǎngdōng shāo yā

Cantonese Roast Duck

BILL

Turn the corner into a Chinatown in any city, and you'll be greeted with the sight of gleaming roast ducks hanging in restaurant windows. A Cantonese duck is all about the spices, and while the skin isn't crispy like a Peking duck's, the flavor is out of this world. Becoming a master at roasting a whole duck will require patience—and an air pump. The former because the process takes two days and has lots of steps (all worth it, I promise), and the latter because forcing air under the skin lifts it off the meat, creating even browning and allowing excess fat to render out (pale spots on your duck are a telltale sign that the skin didn't properly separate). For best results, use an electric air pump for a steadier, stronger flow of air, and get a fresh duck with the head and neck still attached to ensure a tight seal. If you can only get a duck without the head, don't worry. We include instructions for both scenarios. I think this recipe goes toe-to-toe with some of the best restaurants out there. It may not be easy, but the greater the challenge, the greater the reward!

Serve 4 to 6

1 (5- to 6-pound) Long Island (Pekin) duckling

½ cup hot water, for the roasting pan

FOR SEASONING THE DUCK CAVITY

1½ tablespoons fine sea salt

2½ teaspoons five-spice powder

2 teaspoons sugar

1 teaspoon sand ginger powder or galangal powder

2 tablespoons Shaoxing wine

FOR THE COOKED MARINADE

2 tablespoons chee hou sauce

2 tablespoons warm water

1 tablespoon ground bean sauce

1 tablespoon hoisin sauce

1 tablespoon oyster sauce

1 tablespoon red fermented bean curd (a mix of solids and liquid)

2 teaspoons neutral oil

2 (⅛-inch-thick) slices fresh ginger

2 medium garlic cloves, sliced

1 scallion, white and green parts cut into 2-inch pieces and smashed

2 dried bay leaves

2 star anise, segments broken apart

1 Chinese cassia cinnamon stick, about 3 inches long, broken into small pieces

1 (2-inch) piece dried mandarin orange peel, broken into a few small pieces

FOR THE WATER AND VINEGAR BATHS

6 cups water

3 tablespoons Chinese red vinegar (Koon Chun brand)

2 tablespoons (40g) maltose or corn syrup

1½ teaspoons fine sea salt

TRIM AND CLEAN THE DUCK: Trim any excess fat from the cavity of the duck, leaving the skin intact. Remove the wing tips using a sharp cleaver or kitchen shears. If you have a whole duck, remove the feet at the joints between the feet and legs. Traditionally, Chinese roast ducks come with the head on, but you can remove the head if you prefer. Leave the entire neck—it's good for roasting and leaving it on makes the inflation process easier in later steps. Use tweezers to remove any pinfeathers and remove any of the remaining internal organs (there may still be parts of the lung in the upper cavity or the kidneys next to the cavity opening). Then rinse the outside and cavity of the duck, and pat both the outside and cavity dry with a paper towel. (Disinfect your sink and work surfaces after this process.)

SEASON THE DUCK CAVITY: Combine the salt, five-spice powder, sugar, and sand ginger powder. Rub the cavity of the duck with the Shaoxing wine, followed by the dry spice mixture, until thoroughly coated. Refrigerate for 1 hour, uncovered.

(RECIPE CONTINUES)

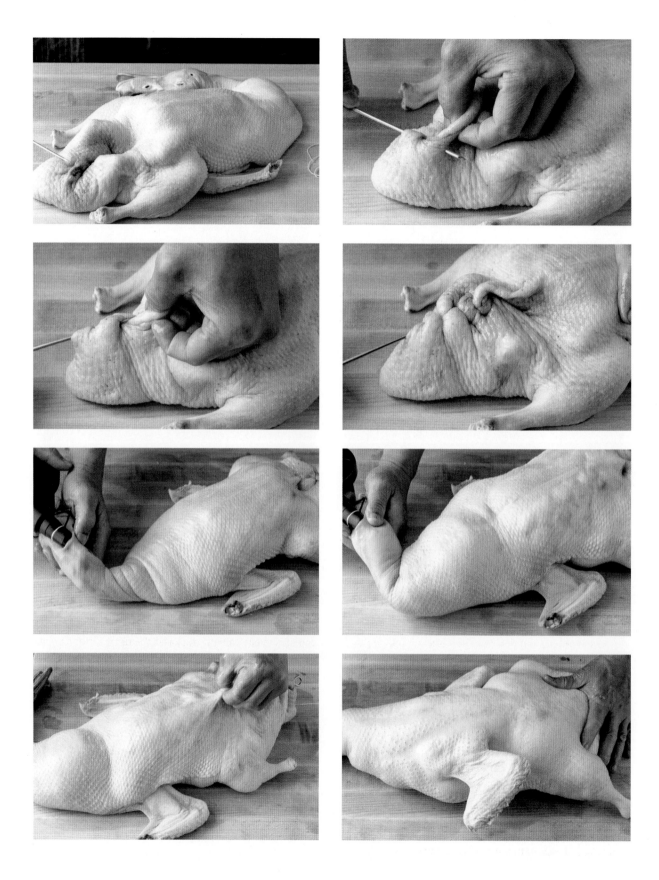

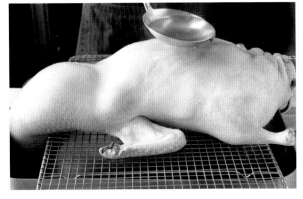

MAKE THE COOKED MARINADE: In a medium bowl, combine the chee hou sauce, warm water, ground bean sauce, hoisin sauce, oyster sauce, and red fermented bean curd. Heat the oil in a saucepan over medium-low heat. Add the ginger and cook for 20 to 30 seconds, until fragrant. Stir in the garlic, scallion (both white and green parts), bay leaves, star anise, cinnamon stick, and orange peel. Cook for another 20 to 30 seconds. Add the sauce mixture you made earlier, and bring to a simmer over medium heat, stirring often. Once simmering, remove from the heat and let cool completely.

MARINATE AND SEAL THE CAVITY: After the duck has sat in the fridge for 1 hour, pour the cooled marinade into the cavity. Use your hands to coat the entire cavity with the marinade, taking care to keep the outside of the duck clean.

Use a metal skewer to carefully seal the cavity and make it completely airtight. At the base of the tail, insert the skewer crosswise through the flaps of skin on either side of the cavity, poking the skewer through so that only about 1 inch of the sharp end is sticking out the other side. Turn the skewer over the skin back the way it came from, and insert the skewer again, just above where you initially inserted it. Repeat, weaving the skewer across the skin around the cavity until you've sealed it completely. Push any remaining length of the skewer into the cavity. (You can also perform these steps with butcher's twine and a trussing needle; just make sure you get a tight seal.)

INFLATE THE DUCK: Now for the part that makes this a distinctively Chinese duck recipe! Insert a clean plastic tube attached to a small electric air pump between the folds of skin on the neck and close your hand around the tube and neck to create a seal. There should be a cut on the neck where the duck was slaughtered, where you can insert the tube. If your duck does not have the neck still attached, and the opening at the neck is very large, seal a portion of the opening using skewers or butcher's twine before inserting the tube.

(RECIPE CONTINUES)

SWEET SOY DIPPING SAUCE
In addition to the duck juices, you can serve this duck with a sweet soy sauce on the side: Heat 2 teaspoons dark soy sauce, 2 teaspoons light soy sauce, 2 teaspoons sugar, and 2 tablespoons water in a small saucepan, stirring until the sugar dissolves and the mixture comes to a simmer.

Pump air in until you see the skin separating from the meat, all the way down to the drumsticks. As the air is pumped under the skin, it will look like an inflated balloon (albeit a lumpy one). Maintain a tight seal; it will deflate if the air is released.

If the seal over the cavity (where you used the metal skewer earlier) opens, use your other hand (or ask someone to help!) to hold it closed so that the duck inflates. In stubborn areas where the skin is still sticking to the meat, use your fingers to pull the skin up off the meat (especially around the breast), and then reinflate. *Thorough separation of the skin from the meat is key to even roasting.* Flip the duck over and repeat this process.

When the duck has been completely inflated on both sides, it's time to tie it off. Grab someone to help you with this step to make it easier! With the pump still running, take a 6- to 8-inch length of kitchen string and tie a knot around the neck of the duck. Do your best to seal in as much air as possible.

APPLY THE WATER AND VINEGAR BATHS: Bring 4 cups of the water to a boil. Turn off the heat. Place a rack crosswise over the top of a deep roasting pan or wok and place the duck on top of the rack. One ladle at a time, pour half the boiled water evenly over the duck. You'll see the skin immediately shrink and tighten up as the hot water is applied. Carefully flip the duck over and repeat with the remaining boiling water. Set the duck aside on a sheet pan and discard the water.

Next, make the vinegar bath, which will give the duck that signature dark color after roasting. In a medium saucepan over medium-high heat, heat the remaining 2 cups water, along with the red vinegar, maltose, and salt. Bring to a simmer, stirring to dissolve the salt, and remove from the heat.

Place the duck back on the rack (over the roasting pan or wok) breast side down, and carefully ladle all the hot vinegar solution over the duck to coat it completely, just as you did with the boiling water. Make sure to cover all the exposed skin.

Set the duck on the sheet pan once again and pour the used vinegar solution into a bowl. Then repeat this procedure with the duck back on the rack breast side up, pouring the reused hot vinegar liquid over this side of the duck. Any missed areas won't have that signature Chinese roast duck color, so thoroughness is important!

AIR-DRY AND MARINATE OVERNIGHT: Leave the duck to air-dry for 30 minutes. Then place the duck breast side down on a clean, dry sheet pan or roasting pan, and refrigerate overnight, uncovered.

ROAST THE DUCK AND SERVE: 4 hours before serving, take the duck out of the fridge, flip it breast side up, and let it sit for 2 hours at room temperature. (A cold duck won't roast evenly.)

Position a rack in the center of the oven, then preheat the oven to 350°F. Line a large roasting pan with heavy-duty foil, with a roasting rack on top (a V-shaped rack is ideal). Place the duck on the rack breast side down and use a paper towel to wipe away any marinade that may have leaked onto the skin (it will burn in the oven or result in uneven coloring). Add the ½ cup hot water to the bottom of the pan to prevent any drippings from smoking as the duck roasts.

Roast breast side down for 25 minutes. Rotate the pan 180 degrees and continue to roast for another 25 minutes. At this point, the skin should be a uniform reddish, dark brown. Remove the duck from the oven and use clean kitchen towels or heat resistant cooking gloves to flip the duck over so it is breast side up.

Roast for 20 minutes, then rotate the pan 180 degrees and roast for another 20 minutes, or until the duck is a uniform dark brown color. Remove the duck from the oven, tent it with a piece of aluminum foil, and let it rest for 20 minutes.

When ready to serve, remove the skewer sealing the cavity and carefully pour all the fat and juices into a fat separator. Then pour the juices through a fine-mesh strainer into a bowl to serve with the duck. (Reserve the rendered duck fat for other uses.)

Using a sharp cleaver, cut the duck in half lengthwise from the top of the breast down through to one side of the backbone. Remove any aromatics in the cavity and discard. Next, take the half of the duck with the backbone still attached and make a lengthwise cut along the other side of the backbone to remove it. Cut off the wings and leg quarters. Chop the wings in half at the joint, chop each drumstick into two pieces, and chop the thighs crosswise into three pieces. Then, chop the remaining duck into bite-size pieces, using your cleaver to drive through the soft bones. Serve with the reserved sauce on the side.

手撕鸡 *shǒu sī jī*

Hand-Shredded Chicken

This simple hand-shredded chicken, or shǒu sī jī, is a light but satisfying meal. While many recipes call for steaming the chicken, we poach it instead, leaving it in a pot of hot water with the heat off to finish cooking. This not only prevents overcooking, it also gives the chicken a silky texture. We also like the addition of raw red onion at the end, which contributes freshness and bite. And because we know the spice fiends will be asking—yes, you can use a couple Thai chilies in the sauce if you prefer more heat. For those prone to profuse chili sweats, omit them to keep it mild.

Serves 4

FOR THE CHICKEN

1 pound chicken drumsticks or boneless, skinless chicken breasts

6 cups water

3 (⅛-inch-thick) slices fresh ginger

1 scallion, cut in half crosswise

FOR THE SAUCE

2 tablespoons finely chopped scallions, white parts only (from 1 to 2 scallions)

1 heaping tablespoon minced garlic (from 3 to 4 cloves)

1 tablespoon minced fresh ginger

1 or 2 fresh Thai bird's-eye chilies, finely chopped (optional)

3 tablespoons neutral oil

2 tablespoons light soy sauce

2 teaspoons Chinese black vinegar

1½ teaspoons oyster sauce

1 teaspoon toasted sesame oil

½ teaspoon ground Sichuan peppercorns

½ teaspoon sugar

FOR SERVING

½ small red onion, thinly sliced

¼ cup chopped fresh cilantro

2 teaspoons toasted sesame seeds

Fine sea salt

PREPARE THE CHICKEN: Let the chicken sit at room temperature for 1 to 2 hours so it isn't cold when you begin the cooking process. In a medium pot, bring the water to a boil along with the ginger slices and scallion. Lower the chicken into the pot (it should be completely submerged) and bring to a boil again. Don't step away from the stove. Once boiling, immediately reduce the heat to the lowest setting, cover, and simmer the chicken: 9 to 11 minutes for drumsticks or 3 to 5 minutes for breasts, depending on the size and thickness of your chicken pieces. Turn off the heat and keep the pot untouched on the stove for 10 to 15 minutes so the chicken can continue to cook without risk of drying out.

To check the chicken for doneness, pierce the thickest part of the meat with a sharp skewer. If the juices run clear, it's done. (If not, cover and leave in the hot water for a bit longer.) Transfer the chicken to a bowl of ice water for 5 minutes. Remove from the ice bath, shred the meat, and transfer to a serving plate.

MAKE THE SAUCE: In a medium heatproof bowl, add the scallions, garlic, ginger, and chilies (if using). Heat the neutral oil in a wok or small saucepan until shimmering, and carefully pour it over the aromatics in the bowl. The oil will sizzle and immediately smell fragrant. Mix in the light soy sauce, black vinegar, oyster sauce, sesame oil, ground Sichuan peppercorns, and sugar.

ASSEMBLE THE DISH: Toss the chicken in the sauce, along with the onion, cilantro, and sesame seeds. Add salt to taste. Serve cold or at room temperature.

BONUS BROTH
After you've poached the chicken, you'll be left with a light broth. Use it instead of water to make a more flavorful batch of jasmine rice (see page 123) or add it to other recipes that call for chicken broth or water.

盐焗鸡, 简易版 *yán jú jī, jiǎnyì bǎn*

Easy Salt-Baked Chicken

To make salt-baked chicken, or yim guk gai in Cantonese, a whole chicken is marinated, wrapped in a parcel, placed in a wok or ceramic pot that is then filled with heated salt, and roasted. The purpose of the salt is not to flavor the chicken, but rather to transfer the heat evenly to the chicken, cooking it gently and resulting in silky, juicy meat. While the traditional method is great (you can find it on the blog), we also like adapting old-school recipes so they are easier to make—in this case, replicating the flavor of a traditional salt-baked chicken without having to deal with a few pounds of sea salt. This easy version is well seasoned with the requisite sand ginger, Shaoxing wine, and just a few teaspoons of salt before it's baked to juicy perfection.

Serves 4 to 6

- **1 (4- to 5-pound) whole chicken,** giblets and neck removed
- **1 tablespoon Shaoxing wine**
- **1 tablespoon neutral oil**
- **3 to 3½ teaspoons fine sea salt**
- **2 teaspoons sand ginger powder** or galangal powder
- **1 teaspoon sugar**
- **½ teaspoon ground Sichuan peppercorns**
- **½ teaspoon white pepper powder**
- **¼ teaspoon five-spice powder**
- **1 teaspoon mushroom powder** or chicken powder (optional)
- **3 medium garlic cloves,** smashed
- **2 (⅛-inch-thick) slices fresh ginger,** smashed
- **1 scallion,** white part only, cut into 2-inch pieces and smashed
- **1 dried bay leaf**
- **1 small or ½ medium yellow onion,** thinly sliced

Remove any giblets from the chicken and rinse the cavity to thoroughly clean it out (depending on how your chicken was processed, it may still contain some organ tissue in the cavity). Pat the chicken and the cavity dry with a paper towel. Be sure to disinfect your sink and work surface after handling the raw chicken.

Place the chicken in a baking dish (or any vessel you can marinate it in). Rub the entire chicken with the Shaoxing wine, inside and out. In a small bowl, combine the oil, salt, sand ginger powder, sugar, ground Sichuan peppercorns, white pepper, five-spice powder, and mushroom or chicken powder (if using). Thoroughly rub the chicken inside and out with the spice mixture. Place the garlic, ginger, scallion, and bay leaf in the cavity. Tie the legs together with kitchen string and tuck the wing tips under the back. Cover and marinate the chicken overnight in the refrigerator.

3½ to 4 hours before serving, take the chicken out of the fridge and let sit at room temperature for 2 hours. (Cooking a chicken straight out of the refrigerator will result in undercooking or uneven cooking.)

Set a rack in the middle of the oven, and preheat the oven to 375°F. Line a large cast-iron pan (it will help the chicken roast quickly and evenly) with the onion slices to protect the skin on the bottom of the chicken. Place the chicken in the pan breast side up.

Roast the chicken for 75 to 85 minutes, rotating the pan halfway through. When a meat thermometer in the thickest part of the thigh reads 165°F, remove the chicken from the oven and tent it lightly with aluminum foil. Let it rest for 15 minutes before carving. The drippings are delicious—a bit salty, but perfect to dip the chicken pieces in. (And the bones and carcass make a tasty stock.)

芝麻鸡 zhīma jī
Classic Sesame Chicken

KAITLIN When we decide to order Chinese takeout (yes, sometimes we don't feel like cooking, and we're just as nostalgic about Chinese takeout as any other American family!), I'm usually the one to pipe up with the question, "Should we get the sesame chicken?!," along with a few eyebrow-wiggling glances around the table to get everyone on board. When our order arrives and we crack open that container of orange jewels sprinkled with sesame seeds, no one has any regrets. If you're wondering why you'd ever want to make sesame chicken yourself, consider this: Yes, many Chinese takeout joints make great sesame chicken, and you should absolutely order it from your favorite spots. But those willing to spend a little time in the kitchen will be able to control the sweetness level and go heavier on the chicken and lighter on the batter, resulting in the juiciest sesame chicken you've ever had.

Serves 4

FOR THE MARINADE

1 pound boneless, skinless chicken thighs or breast, cut into 1-inch pieces

1 teaspoon Shaoxing wine

½ teaspoon fine sea salt

½ teaspoon toasted sesame oil

¼ teaspoon white pepper powder

¼ teaspoon MSG (optional)

⅛ teaspoon garlic powder

⅛ teaspoon onion powder

FOR THE BATTER

6 tablespoons cornstarch

3 tablespoons all-purpose flour

6 tablespoons water

1 tablespoon neutral oil

½ teaspoon baking soda

FOR THE SAUCE AND CORNSTARCH SLURRY

¾ cup low-sodium chicken stock or water, heated

3 tablespoons sugar

1½ tablespoons oyster sauce

1 tablespoon honey

1 tablespoon clear rice wine or Shaoxing wine

1 tablespoon light soy sauce

1½ teaspoons rice vinegar

1½ teaspoons toasted sesame oil

⅛ teaspoon white pepper powder

2 teaspoons cornstarch

1 tablespoon water

FOR FRYING AND SERVING

Neutral oil, for frying

1 garlic clove, minced

1 teaspoon toasted sesame seeds

MARINATE THE CHICKEN: In a medium bowl, combine the chicken pieces with the Shaoxing wine, salt, sesame oil, white pepper, MSG (if using), garlic powder, and onion powder. Marinate for 30 minutes.

MAKE THE BATTER: In a large bowl, whisk together the cornstarch, flour, water, neutral oil, and baking soda. Add the marinated chicken and mix thoroughly to coat.

MAKE THE SAUCE AND SLURRY: In a medium bowl, combine the hot chicken stock, sugar, oyster sauce, honey, rice wine, light soy sauce, rice vinegar, sesame oil, and white pepper. In a small bowl, mix the cornstarch with the water to make a slurry.

DOUBLE-FRY THE CHICKEN: Fill a small, deep pot until one-half to two-thirds full with neutral oil, and heat over medium-high heat until it reaches 335°F on an instant-read thermometer. Set a wire cooling rack on a sheet pan or line a plate with paper towels.

Carefully drop the chicken pieces into the oil in three batches. The oil temperature will drop after the chicken is added, so use your thermometer and adjust the heat as needed to keep the oil at 335°F. Fry for 5 to 6 minutes per batch, stirring and flipping the chicken in the oil for even coloring, until the chicken is light golden

brown. Transfer to the rack or plate to drain. Let the chicken pieces cool for 10 minutes before moving on to the second fry.

After the chicken has cooled for 10 minutes, heat the oil to 335°F and fry the chicken in batches a second time, for 3 to 4 minutes or until crispy. Drain the chicken well on your wire rack or plate.

SAUCE THE CHICKEN AND SERVE: Heat a wok over medium heat, then add 2 teaspoons of the oil you fried the chicken in, along with the garlic. After 5 to 10

seconds, add the sauce mixture and bring to a simmer. Re-stir the cornstarch slurry, then, while stirring constantly, gradually add it to the sauce. Simmer for 10 to 20 seconds, until the sauce is just thick enough to coat a spoon. (If the sauce is too thick, add a splash of water.)

Turn off the heat and toss in the fried chicken, stirring until it's evenly coated. There should be little to no standing sauce. Sprinkle the chicken with toasted sesame seeds and serve.

鸡肉菌菇蒸蛋 *jīròu jūn gū zhēng dàn*

Steamed Eggs
with Chicken & Oyster Mushrooms

Steamed eggs are comforting and easy on the stomach (and teeth, for our elderly family members!). If we don't have quite enough dishes planned for dinner, we'll whip up this recipe to make sure everyone at the table walks away satisfied. This recipe is also a great way to stretch a few eggs. Equal parts water and stock are added to create a smooth, pudding-like texture, made even better by a savory topping of chicken and oyster mushrooms. To scale up the recipe, increase the steaming time by 1 minute per added egg.

Serves 2

FOR THE CHICKEN

4 ounces ground chicken

1 tablespoon minced fresh ginger

1 tablespoon water

1 teaspoon Shaoxing wine

1 teaspoon light soy sauce

½ teaspoon cornstarch

¼ teaspoon sugar

FOR THE REST OF THE DISH

3 large eggs

1 teaspoon toasted sesame oil

¼ teaspoon fine sea salt

About ⅔ cup water (same volume as eggs)

About ⅔ cup low-sodium chicken stock or vegetable stock (see page 269; same volume as eggs)

1 tablespoon neutral oil

1 cup finely chopped oyster mushrooms (about 3 ounces)

½ teaspoon dark soy sauce

2 tablespoons finely chopped scallions, green and white parts

SEASON THE CHICKEN: In a medium bowl, combine the ground chicken, ginger, water, Shaoxing wine, light soy sauce, cornstarch, and sugar.

STEAM THE EGGS: Crack the eggs into a liquid measuring cup and note the volume (it should be around ⅔ cup). Pour the eggs into a large bowl, add the sesame oil and salt, and beat for 30 seconds.

Measure out the same volume of water as the eggs and do the same with the stock (so you have one part eggs, one part water, and one part stock). Whisk the water and stock into the eggs for 30 seconds, until well combined.

Pour the egg mixture through a fine-mesh strainer into a shallow heatproof bowl (like a 9-inch glass pie plate) to remove air bubbles.

Place a 2-inch-tall metal steaming rack in the bottom of your wok (or any pot with a lid that will accommodate the dish of eggs) and fill with enough water to come up to about 1 inch below the rack. Bring to a simmer over medium-high heat.

Place the dish of eggs on the steamer rack and cover. Reduce the heat to medium and steam for 3 minutes. Then turn off the heat, keeping the eggs tightly covered. Let stand for 14 minutes (exactly!). The eggs are done when they wobble like Jell-O when you shake the bowl. Remove from the wok, and cover to keep warm.

COOK THE CHICKEN AND SERVE: Dry your wok and place it over medium-high heat. When the wok is smoking lightly, add the neutral oil and the chicken. Stir-fry for 2 to 3 minutes, breaking the chicken into small crumbles, until it is cooked through and begins to crisp. Add the oyster mushrooms and cook for another 3 minutes, until the mushrooms are lightly caramelized.

Add the dark soy sauce and scallions to the wok. Cook for 30 seconds to 1 minute more, until the scallions are wilted. Top the steamed eggs with the chicken and mushroom mixture and serve.

芙蓉蛋 *fúróng dàn*

Hong Kong "Furong" Omelet

SARAH This recipe for fúróng dàn is the grand-daddy of Chinese takeout egg foo young, those deep-fried egg patties smothered in brown gravy. Egg foo young has gone a bit out of style, but we're hoping we can give this original Hong Kong version the comeback it deserves. A "true" Hong Kong–style omelet is more like a frittata than a deep-fried patty and is usually served on its own without the gravy. As the resident gravy-obsessed cook of the family, though, I couldn't forgo the gravy entirely. But instead of the old-school thick brown version, I've made a light sauce to drizzle over the omelet, which is packed with juicy shrimp, char siu, and crunchy vegetables.

Serves 4

FOR THE SHRIMP

4 ounces peeled and deveined jumbo or extra-jumbo shrimp

¼ teaspoon cornstarch

⅛ teaspoon fine sea salt

⅛ teaspoon sugar

⅛ teaspoon white pepper powder

FOR THE EGGS

4 large eggs

½ teaspoon fine sea salt

½ teaspoon sugar

½ teaspoon toasted sesame oil

¼ teaspoon white pepper powder

2½ teaspoons cornstarch

1 tablespoon water

FOR THE SAUCE (OPTIONAL)

¼ cup water

2 teaspoons sugar

2 teaspoons oyster sauce

1 teaspoon light soy sauce

FOR THE REST OF THE DISH

5 tablespoons neutral oil

⅔ cup julienned Char Siu Roast Pork (page 173) or ham (about 3 ounces)

½ cup Chinese yellow chives, cut into 2-inch pieces (or 2 scallions, cut into 2-inch pieces, then white parts halved lengthwise)

1 cup mung bean sprouts

PREPARE THE SHRIMP: Pat the shrimp dry, then combine with the cornstarch, salt, sugar, and white pepper.

PREPARE THE EGGS: In a large bowl, beat the eggs with the salt, sugar, sesame oil, and white pepper. In a small bowl, mix the cornstarch with the water until combined, and then add it to the egg mixture and beat for 30 seconds.

MAKE THE SAUCE: If serving your omelet with the sauce, add the water, sugar, oyster sauce, and light soy sauce to a small saucepan over medium-low heat. Bring to a simmer, and simmer for 2 minutes, until reduced by half. Turn off the heat and set aside.

PRECOOK THE SHRIMP AND PORK: Heat a wok until it's just starting to smoke. Add 1 tablespoon of the neutral oil and swirl it around the perimeter of the wok. Add the shrimp and stir-fry for 45 seconds, until the shrimp just turn color and are around 75 percent cooked. Transfer the shrimp to a plate. Add the pork to the wok and stir-fry for 30 seconds, just to warm it through. Remove from the wok and transfer to the plate with the shrimp.

ASSEMBLE THE DISH: Stir the pork and the shrimp into the egg mixture in the bowl, along with the yellow chives and bean sprouts. Heat the wok again over high heat until it starts to smoke. Add the remaining

4 tablespoons neutral oil, and again swirl it around the sides of the wok to coat.

Toss the egg mixture again in the bowl to redistribute the ingredients, then pour the mixture into the wok. Immediately reduce the heat to medium-low. Spread the egg mixture evenly over the surface of the wok so you have a circle 8 to 9 inches in diameter. When the bottom of the egg is cooked enough to release easily from the

wok, rotate the omelet so it cooks evenly. When the egg looks almost set, it's time to flip it over.

Either use two spatulas to flip the omelet in one big piece or break up the omelet into 4 sections and flip each piece individually. Cook 1 to 2 minutes more, until the egg is cooked through. Remove from the wok, drizzle with the sauce, if desired, and serve.

番茄炒鸡蛋 fānqié chǎo jīdàn

Tomato Egg Stir-Fry

JUDY This dish probably holds the record for most appearances on Chinese family dinner tables around the world. It's made with everyday ingredients—eggs, tomatoes, scallions—and is easy to execute. The combination of eggs with tart tomatoes (tempered with a little sugar) tastes like home to me. (I guess there's something to Kaitlin's childhood habit of eating scrambled eggs with ketchup.) When Sarah studied abroad in China, this was the dish that all the international students wanted to order at humble restaurants churning out simple home-cooked meals, and we know why. It's comfort food, whether you grew up with it or not. My go-to weekday lunch is a noodle soup version of this dish, which you can find on the blog. You might prefer it sweeter or saltier, so feel free to make it your own!

Serves 2

4 large eggs

1 teaspoon Shaoxing wine

¾ teaspoon fine sea salt, or to taste

½ teaspoon toasted sesame oil

¼ teaspoon white pepper powder

3 tablespoons neutral oil

3 ripe medium tomatoes (about 1 pound), each cut into 6 to 8 wedges

¼ cup water, or as needed

2 teaspoons sugar or to taste (see Tip)

1 scallion, white and green parts finely chopped

Crack the eggs into a medium bowl and add the Shaoxing wine, ¼ teaspoon of the salt, the sesame oil, and white pepper. Beat for 1 minute.

Preheat a wok over medium heat until it just starts to smoke. Add 2 tablespoons of the neutral oil and immediately add the eggs. Lightly scramble the eggs, then remove from the wok immediately while the eggs are still tender and slightly runny.

Add the remaining tablespoon oil to the wok, increase the heat to high, and add the tomatoes. Stir-fry for 1 minute, then add the ¼ cup water, the sugar, and the remaining ½ teaspoon salt. If your stove gets very hot and liquid tends to cook off very quickly in your wok, add more water, up to ½ cup total. Bring to a simmer and cook for 1 minute, until the tomatoes begin to wilt.

Add the scrambled eggs. Mix everything together, reduce the heat to medium-low, cover the wok, and cook for 1 minute, until the tomatoes are completely softened. Uncover, add the scallions, and continue to stir over high heat until the sauce thickens to your liking. Serve.

TIP! While sugar is a key ingredient in this dish, the amount you need hinges on your tomatoes. Tomatoes vary in acidity and sweetness, depending on the variety and growing season. Taste your tomatoes as they cook, and adjust the amount of sugar accordingly. If you're using ripe summer tomatoes, you may need less sugar!

Pork, Beef & Lamb

Growing up in upstate New York, meat and potatoes were a way of life (or in our case, meat and rice). My stepfather was a master at preparing meats to perfection. As a roast cook at Grossinger's Catskill Resort Hotel, he prepped rows of prime rib for 1,000 guests on a holiday weekend. (Some of the tastiest bites I've ever eaten were the unwanted end cuts he'd bring home in a gallon-size industrial tomato can.) When I was old enough to land a job in his kitchen we cooked countless pieces of glistening red Char Siu Roast Pork (page 173) together at the Holiday Inn. The recipes in this chapter encompass a medley of pork, beef, and lamb dishes from our family archives. Yes, there are roast meats, but there are also braises, stir-fries, and meats simmered in broth, grilled, and even steamed. BILL

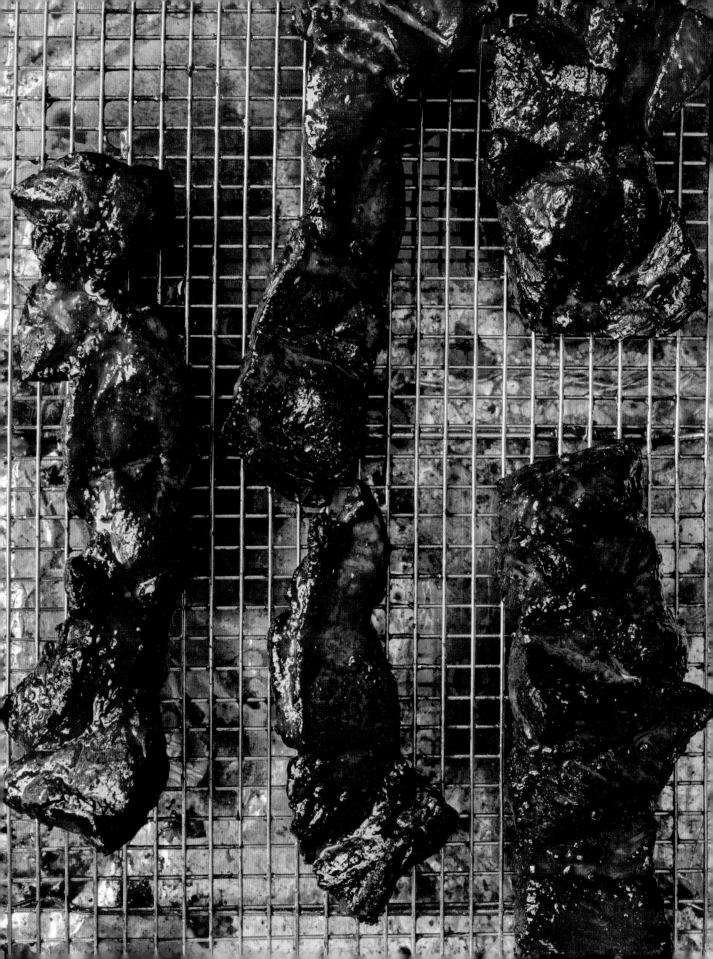

叉烧 chāshāo

Char Siu Roast Pork

BILL

I first learned how to make char siu (叉烧) from my stepfather at the Holiday Inn where he worked as head chef. The hotel restaurant featured both Chinese and American menus, and my father's char siu BBQ pork was legendary. I don't think guests knew they were getting a taste of southern China in that hotel dining room, but he knew how to replicate the flavor of Hong Kong's and Shenzhen's best roasted-meat restaurants. It's much easier than you might think—just a simple overnight marinade and less than an hour in the oven. For best results, it's worth searching a local Chinese market or online vendor for maltose, a sticky, viscous syrup produced from fermented grains—a couple spoonfuls give char siu its signature shiny glaze.

Serves 6

3 medium garlic cloves, finely minced

¼ cup sugar

1 tablespoon hoisin sauce

1 tablespoon Shaoxing wine

1 tablespoon light soy sauce

2 teaspoons fine sea salt

2 teaspoons molasses

½ teaspoon five-spice powder

½ teaspoon toasted sesame oil

¼ teaspoon white pepper powder

⅛ teaspoon red food coloring (optional)

3 pounds boneless pork shoulder or butt (large pieces with plentiful fat)

1½ cups plus 1 tablespoon hot water, plus more as needed

2 tablespoons (40g) maltose or barley malt syrup, corn syrup, or honey

In a medium bowl, combine the garlic, sugar, hoisin sauce, Shaoxing wine, light soy sauce, salt, molasses, five-spice powder, sesame oil, white pepper, and food coloring (if using) to make the marinade. Set 2 tablespoons aside in a small covered container and refrigerate.

Cut the pork into long strips or chunks 2 to 3 inches thick and ¾ to 1 pound each (pieces any smaller will cook too quickly and dry out). Do not trim off any excess fat—it adds flavor as it renders during roasting. Add the pork to the marinade and thoroughly coat all the pieces. Cover the pork and refrigerate for at least 8 hours or preferably overnight (or up to 48 hours).

Position an oven rack in the upper third of the oven, then preheat the oven to 475°F. Line a sheet pan with aluminum foil and place a metal rack on top (the rack helps the pork roast more evenly). Place the pork pieces on the rack, leaving as much space as possible between them. Pour 1½ cups of the hot water into the pan below the rack to prevent any drippings from burning or smoking. (Never let the roasting pan dry out.)

Transfer the pork to the oven and roast for 10 minutes. Reduce the oven temperature to 375°F and roast for an additional 15 minutes. Flip the pork; if the pan is dry, add another cup of water. Rotate the pan 180 degrees and roast the pork for another 15 minutes. During this time, check the char siu every 5 minutes or so. If it begins to scorch around the edges, tent it lightly with aluminum foil to prevent burning.

Meanwhile, combine the reserved marinade, the maltose (maltose is extremely sticky and viscous—you can heat it in the microwave to make it more pliable), and the remaining tablespoon of hot water. This will be the sauce you'll use to baste the pork.

(RECIPE CONTINUES)

MAKE AHEAD
You can stash cooked char siu pork in the freezer for up to 3 months to make recipes like Mini Char Siu Bao (page 29) or a tasty Hong Kong "Furong" Omelet (page 166) whenever the mood strikes. Freeze your char siu in large pieces so it doesn't dry out, and thaw completely before slicing.

GET TO KNOW YOUR OVEN
It's amazing how much oven temperatures can vary by model, or even in different spots in the oven. Temperatures can sometimes be up to 50°F off the mark! There are also variations in how ovens preheat and then maintain their heat. We recommend using an oven thermometer to check the accuracy of your oven temperatures—if the oven runs hot or cold, account for it by adjusting the setting as needed or recalibrate it. Keep an eye on your char siu as it roasts. If you have a convection oven and like to use that method, keep in mind that the char siu will roast and caramelize faster, so watch it closely, tent it with aluminum foil earlier if necessary, and reduce the oven temperature if it's browning too quickly.

After 40 minutes of total roasting time, remove the pan from the oven. Baste the pork with the maltose mixture, then flip and baste the other side. You should still have some basting sauce remaining. Return the pork to the oven and roast for another 10 minutes.

By now, the pork should be caramelized on top. An instant-read thermometer should register an internal temperature of 145°F (take the temperature at one of the thickest pieces and remember that the pork will continue to cook as it rests, ultimately reaching an internal temperature of 150° to 155°F). If it's not caramelized to your liking, put it under the broiler for 1 to 2 minutes, until the edges of the pork are caramelized. (Don't walk away from the oven. The sweet char siu sauce can burn quickly.)

Remove the pan from the oven and baste the pork with any remaining maltose sauce. Tent with aluminum foil and let the meat rest for 10 minutes before slicing and serving.

Hong Kong Beef Brisket
in Clear Broth

BILL This recipe is based on one of the best meals I ever had in Hong Kong: tender beef in a rich, clear broth, usually served with rice or wide rice noodles. Some believe the dish originated at Sister Wah's, a restaurant tucked away in the Tin Hau metro station. While the dish is usually translated as "beef brisket in clear broth," it's often made with several cuts: a full brisket (both the lean flat and the fatty "point"), as well as tripe, tendon, and rough flank (牛腩, niúnǎn in Mandarin; ngau lam in Cantonese), a cut of meat with tough connective tissue that's prized for stews. Because it's difficult to find the fatty brisket point, I recommend using rough flank or brisket, along with bone-in short ribs, which provide plenty of marbled, lean, and flavorful connective tissue (the hallmark of a great Cantonese beef braise). This dish does take some time to make, but you'll find that it's well worth it.

Serves 8

FOR THE SPICE SACHET

4 white cardamom pods

3 dried bay leaves

3 whole cloves

2 star anise

2 small pieces dried sand ginger

2 small slices dried Chinese licorice root

1 black cardamom pod

1 Chinese cassia cinnamon stick, about 2 inches long

½ teaspoon coriander seeds

½ teaspoon whole Sichuan peppercorns

¼ teaspoon whole white peppercorns

FOR THE BEEF

3 pounds boneless beef rough flank or brisket

2 pounds bone-in beef short ribs

13 cups water, plus more for preparing the beef

3 large garlic cloves, smashed

3 (⅛-inch-thick) slices fresh ginger, smashed

1 medium shallot, quartered and smashed

3 tablespoons clear rice wine

1 tablespoon sugar

1½ tablespoons fine sea salt, plus more as needed

1 medium daikon radish (about 1¼ pounds)

⅓ cup chopped fresh cilantro

2 scallions, white and green parts finely chopped

Ultimate Chili Oil (page 275), for serving (optional)

PREPARE THE SPICE SACHET: On a square of cheesecloth, combine the white cardamom pods, bay leaves, cloves, star anise, sand ginger, licorice root, black cardamom pod, cinnamon stick, coriander seeds, Sichuan peppercorns, and white peppercorns. Bring the cheesecloth up into a bundle and tie with kitchen string. (Alternatively, place the spices in a coffee filter and fold to close. Place that packet into another coffee filter and tie with kitchen string.)

SOAK AND PRECOOK THE BEEF: In a large bowl, cover the beef with lukewarm water. Soak and agitate for 1 minute, then drain off the water. Repeat twice more, until the impurities are washed off and the water is somewhat clear.

Add the beef to a stockpot or Dutch oven and cover with water. Bring to a boil over medium heat, then turn off the heat and let sit for 2 minutes. Transfer the beef to a large bowl, and rinse thoroughly with warm water to wash off any foam or other impurities.

(RECIPE CONTINUES)

COOK THE BEEF: Wash out the stockpot, then place the beef back in it, along with the 13 cups of water, the garlic, ginger, shallot, rice wine, sugar, and salt. Add the spice sachet.

Spread the beef out in an even layer so everything is covered with the liquid. Bring to a boil over medium-high heat, then reduce the heat to low (it should be at a slow simmer). Skim off any foam that rises to the surface, cover tightly, and simmer for 1 hour.

Gently stir the beef and flip the pieces over for even cooking. Continue to simmer for 2 hours if using the mix of rough flank and short ribs, or for 1 hour if using brisket and short ribs. When the beef is fork-tender, it's ready. Transfer the beef to a large bowl and cover with an overturned plate to keep the meat warm.

OPTIONAL STEP FOR A CLEAR BROTH: You may need to take an extra step to ensure a super-clear broth. If you see tiny particles floating on the soup or sediment in the bottom after you have removed the beef, take the pot off the heat and let the liquid "rest" for 20 to 30 minutes, covered, until the particles settle to the bottom of the pot. Carefully ladle out the clear soup into another pot, leaving the sediment behind. Qing tang (清汤) means "clear broth," but if you are not finicky about it, you can skip this step.

COOK THE DAIKON RADISH: Peel the daikon radish and cut into 1½-inch chunks. Add the radish to the pot of clarified stock, along with the beef. Bring to a boil and immediately reduce the heat to low. Simmer for 20 minutes, until the daikon is tender.

SERVE: Skim off any grease floating on top of the broth. Salt the broth to taste (keeping in mind that you can always add salt at the table, but you cannot remove it once it's added).

Slice the beef into ¾- to 1-inch-thick slices and discard any bones from the short ribs. Ladle the broth, beef, and daikon radish into bowls, and finish with a sprinkle of the chopped cilantro and scallions. Serve with chili oil for dipping if desired.

羊肉串 yángròu chuàn

Grilled Lamb Skewers

KAITLIN These crispy Xinjiang-style lamb kebabs (yángròu chuàn, or "chuan'r" if you say it with a heavy Beijing accent) are a wildly popular street food in northern China. They are cooked on narrow charcoal grills, where vendors sprinkle the kebabs enthusiastically with giant shakers of chili flakes, cumin, fennel, and salt, flipping them over by the fistful. The lamb fat mingles with the spices as they toast right on the grill. In college, I'd often visit my grandparents in Flushing, Queens, where there is a vibrant and renowned China-town. They would wave me down at the Flushing Main Street stop of the #7 subway train and immediately thrust three lamb skewers into my hands from the street vendor on the corner of Main Street and 41st Avenue—which I would then happily eat on the walk back to their apartment. The key to great results here is to use well-marbled lamb. Lean cuts won't lead you to the true chuan'r experience.

Makes about 12 skewers

2 pounds well-marbled boneless lamb shoulder

2 teaspoons untoasted sesame seeds

1½ tablespoons cumin seeds

1 tablespoon fennel seeds

1½ tablespoons Sichuan chili flakes

1½ teaspoons fine sea salt

2 tablespoons neutral oil

Metal skewers or bamboo skewers soaked overnight or for at least 1 hour

Cut the lamb into ¾-inch pieces. Do not trim any of the fat, which will baste the lamb as it cooks and ensure the kebabs get crispy on the grill without drying out. Transfer the lamb to a medium bowl.

Toast the sesame seeds in a small dry pan over medium heat for 2 to 3 minutes, until lightly golden. Transfer to a small bowl.

Toast the cumin and fennel seeds in the same pan over medium-low heat until fragrant, 2 to 3 minutes. Grind the toasted cumin and fennel seeds into a coarse powder using a mortar and pestle or a spice grinder. Add the ground cumin and fennel to the sesame seeds, then mix in the chili flakes and salt.

Preheat a grill. If using a gas grill, crank up the heat to the highest setting. If using a charcoal grill, let the coals preheat until you see white ash on the coals. For best results, use a charcoal grill with natural hardwood lump charcoal (rather than briquettes).

Add the oil to the lamb in the bowl and toss to coat. Thread the lamb onto the skewers so the pieces are just touching each other. Sprinkle the skewers evenly with about half the spice mixture.

Put the skewers on the grill (no need to oil the grates as long as your lamb is nice and fatty). Grill for 4 to 6 minutes, turning every minute or so and sprinkling the skewers with the remaining spice mixture with every turn, until the skewers are lightly charred on all sides and the fat is crispy. Remove from the grill and serve immediately.

广式烧肉 guǎng shì shāo ròu

Cantonese Roast Pork Belly *(Siu Yuk)*

SARAH

Growing up, weekends were for grocery shopping at the Chinese market. Like Kaitlin (see page 137), I remember it as a much-anticipated family activity, because it meant we were having lunch at the market's hot bar before starting the shopping. While they had a wide assortment of vegetable, meat, and seafood dishes, steamed buns, and even Vietnamese noodle soups to enjoy in the utilitarian seating area with a view of the parking lot, it was this crispy skinned roast pork that I looked forward to most.

To me, the best part was always the crackly, bubbly skin, which is achieved by poking the skin with holes deep enough to just reach the layer of fat below and then letting the pork air-dry in the fridge overnight. Poking holes through the leathery raw pork skin can be difficult, even with special tools. We've solved the problem by blanching just the skin side of the belly in a very shallow pan of water, making it easier to pierce through.

Serves 8

1 (3-pound) slab boneless, center-cut, skin-on pork belly (as lean as possible, ideally with an even thickness of about 2 inches)

1 tablespoon Shaoxing wine

2 teaspoons fine sea salt

1 teaspoon sugar

½ teaspoon five-spice powder

¼ teaspoon white pepper powder

¼ cup coarse salt

Cooked Ginger-Scallion Oil (page 278), Chinese hot mustard, and/or sugar, for serving

BLANCH THE PORK SKIN: Rinse the pork belly and place it skin side down in a wide, shallow pan that will accommodate it lying flat. Fill the pan with just enough water so that only the skin portion of the belly is submerged. Ensure that the water level is even all around the pork belly.

Place the pan over medium heat and bring the water to a simmer. Cook for 3 minutes, using a spatula to press the pork down, if needed, to ensure the skin remains submerged. Carefully remove the pork belly from the pan and thoroughly dry it with paper towels.

MARINATE THE PORK: Place the belly skin side down on a plate or tray that will fit in your refrigerator. Mix the Shaoxing wine, salt, sugar, five-spice powder, and white pepper. Thoroughly rub this spice mixture into the meat only (not on the skin).

Flip the pork belly skin side up and dry the skin off once again. Use a sharp dinner fork or metal skewer to poke small holes all over the skin (this will help it puff and crisp rather than stay smooth and leathery). Take your time and make sure you cover the entire surface of the pork belly skin with small holes, all the way to the edges.

Pat the skin dry with a paper towel once again, then place the pork belly skin side up in the refrigerator, uncovered, for 12 to 24 hours.

PREPARE THE PORK FOR ROASTING: 2 hours before you plan to roast the pork belly, remove it from the refrigerator to allow it to come to room temperature. Position a rack in the center of the oven, then preheat the oven to 375°F.

(RECIPE CONTINUES)

Place a large piece of heavy-duty aluminum foil on a baking sheet, and lay the pork skin side up in the center of the foil. Fold up the foil around the sides of the pork snugly, so that you've created a box all around it, with a 1-inch-high border on all sides.

Ideally, your pork belly will be an even thickness from end to end, but if one side is thicker than the other, use a piece of balled-up aluminum foil to prop up the thinner side so the top is level (you want the skin across the pork belly to be the same distance from the heat for even roasting).

Carefully spread the coarse salt over the top of the pork belly, so it's sitting on top of the skin, ensuring the salt doesn't get between the meat and the foil.

ROAST THE PORK AND CRISP THE SKIN: Roast the pork belly for 90 minutes. Take the pork out of the oven and increase the temperature to 475°F. Carefully unfold and flatten the foil around the pork belly. Scrape off the salt layer (discard it or save it to add a porky flavor to other dishes). Use a pair of tongs to lift up the pork belly, and quickly place a wire rack on the sheet pan (you can either place it on top of the foil you just unfolded or discard the foil beforehand). Place the pork belly skin side up in the center of the rack.

When the oven temperature reaches 475°F, put the pork belly back in the oven and continue to roast for 10 to 15 minutes, until the skin has puffed up with bubbles. (If your skin isn't puffing up, the meat may not be close enough to the heat source. You can move the oven rack higher or turn on the broiler, but watch it carefully to avoid burning!) If certain areas are blistering and browning faster than others, tent the blistered or brown areas lightly with foil.

When the skin has puffed up and gotten crispy, remove from the oven. Let the pork belly rest for 15 minutes before slicing into 1-inch pieces. (To cut through the crispy pork skin more easily, turn the pork belly on its side or skin-side down before slicing.) Serve with the ginger-scallion oil, mustard, and/or sugar.

黑椒士的球 hēi jiāo shì dì qiú

Black Pepper Beef
(Steak Kow)

The word kow in Cantonese means "ball" (qiú, in Mandarin). You'll find this word in the name of Cantonese dishes where proteins—often extravagant ones like scallops, fresh fish fillets, or in this case, tender filet mignon—are cut into large chunks and stir-fried with vegetables. The ingredients are bound together with a light sauce and, in this case, a healthy dose of black pepper. While black pepper is a constant companion for salt in many American kitchens, you don't see it very often in Chinese cooking (it's almost always white pepper). However, Chinese cooks do like to pair black pepper with beef. They are indeed a great combination in this special banquet-style dish.

Serves 4

FOR VELVETING THE STEAK

1 pound beef filet mignon, cut into 1¼-inch cubes

2 tablespoons water

1 tablespoon neutral oil

1 teaspoon cornstarch

¼ teaspoon fine sea salt

FOR THE PEPPER SEASONING

1½ to 2 tablespoons coarsely ground black pepper

½ teaspoon coarsely ground white pepper

½ teaspoon ground Sichuan peppercorns

¼ teaspoon fine sea salt

FOR THE SAUCE

½ cup low-sodium beef stock or water, heated

1 tablespoon oyster sauce

1 tablespoon light soy sauce

1 teaspoon tomato ketchup

½ teaspoon sugar

¼ teaspoon toasted sesame oil

FOR THE REST OF THE DISH

2 tablespoons neutral oil

½ teaspoon minced fresh ginger

2 medium garlic cloves, finely chopped

1 small green bell pepper, cut into 1-inch pieces (about 1¼ cups)

1 small red bell pepper, cut into 1-inch pieces (about 1¼ cups)

½ medium red onion, cut into 1-inch pieces (about 1¼ cups)

1¼ cups quartered fresh cremini or button mushrooms (about 4 ounces)

2 tablespoons Shaoxing wine

2 teaspoons cornstarch

1 tablespoon water

VELVET THE BEEF: Add the beef to a medium bowl, along with the water, neutral oil, cornstarch, and salt. Toss to coat.

MAKE THE PEPPER SEASONING: In a small bowl, combine the black pepper, white pepper, ground Sichuan peppercorns, and salt.

SEASON THE BEEF: Sprinkle two-thirds of the pepper seasoning over the beef (reserve the rest for later), pressing the spices into the meat.

MAKE THE SAUCE: In a small bowl, combine the hot beef stock, oyster sauce, light soy sauce, ketchup, sugar, and sesame oil. Stir until the sugar dissolves.

SEAR THE BEEF: Heat your wok over high heat until smoking. Add 1 tablespoon of the neutral oil around the perimeter to coat the wok. Add the beef chunks in a single layer (fat side down for any pieces with visible fat). Do not disturb the beef cubes for 20 to 30 seconds, until browned on one side.

(RECIPE CONTINUES)

Flip the beef chunks over and sear on the other side for another 20 seconds. Then stir-fry continuously for 30 to 60 seconds to brown all sides of the meat. The beef should be just under your desired doneness, as it will cook again in the wok. Transfer the beef to a plate.

ASSEMBLE THE DISH: Add the remaining tablespoon neutral oil to the wok over medium-high heat. Add the ginger and cook for 5 to 10 seconds. Then add the garlic and bell peppers. Stir-fry for 1 minute, until the peppers are browned at the edges and slightly tender.

Add the red onion, mushrooms, and remaining pepper seasoning. Pour the Shaoxing wine around the perimeter of the wok, then stir-fry for 1 minute. Add the sauce mixture, and stir it around to deglaze, loosening any browned bits in the wok. Bring the sauce to a simmer. Combine the cornstarch and water in a small bowl to make a slurry. Drizzle half the slurry into the sauce, stirring constantly until it is thick enough to coat a spoon. Add the beef to the wok, along with any juices. Gently toss with the sauce and vegetables until evenly coated. At this point, if the sauce is not thick enough, add the remaining cornstarch slurry and stir-fry for another 10 to 15 seconds to thicken. Serve.

椒盐排骨 *jiāoyán páigǔ*

Salt & Pepper Pork Chops

"Salt and pepper pork chops" is the first thing we rattle off whenever we order food at a Cantonese restaurant. By now, we've eaten this dish in so many different places that we know at first bite whether or not it's up to scratch. For us, the best versions are always light and crispy (and stay that way), have the perfect balance of salt and white pepper, and are finished off with a "relish" of thinly sliced green peppers, shallots, and fried garlic. Of course, the type of chop matters too; shoulder blade chops work best, as they have a good amount of fat and more flavor than lean center cut chops. They are also cut just ⅜ to ½ inch thick (into 4- to 5-inch pieces so they're easy to pick up with chopsticks), giving you plenty of crispy surface area with every bite. You can either cut around the bones or use a heavy-duty cleaver to cut through them so each piece has a bit of bone to keep it moist. We also double-fry the chops to ensure they're extra crisp. If you can't find shoulder blade chops, you can substitute boneless pork shoulder.

Serves 4

FOR THE PORK AND MARINADE

1¼ pounds thin pork shoulder blade chops or boneless pork shoulder, cut ½ inch thick into 4- to 5-inch pieces

3 tablespoons water

1½ tablespoons Shaoxing wine

½ teaspoon fine sea salt

½ teaspoon sugar

½ teaspoon toasted sesame oil

¼ teaspoon baking soda

¼ teaspoon MSG (optional)

¼ teaspoon white pepper powder

⅛ teaspoon five-spice powder

FOR THE SEASONED SALT

1 teaspoon fine sea salt

¾ teaspoon white pepper powder

⅛ teaspoon sugar

FOR THE COATING

⅓ cup cornstarch

⅓ cup water

1 tablespoon all-purpose flour

1½ tablespoons neutral oil

½ teaspoon baking soda

FOR THE REST OF THE DISH

Peanut oil or other neutral oil, for frying

2 tablespoons chopped garlic (from 5 to 6 cloves)

1 long hot green pepper or Anaheim pepper, seeded and sliced crosswise into thin rounds

1 small shallot, thinly sliced

MARINATE THE PORK CHOPS: In a large bowl, combine the pork chops, water, Shaoxing wine, salt, sugar, sesame oil, baking soda, MSG (if using), white pepper, and five-spice powder. Use your hands to mix everything until the pork is evenly coated. Marinate for 1 to 2 hours at room temperature.

MAKE THE SEASONED SALT: In a small bowl, combine the salt, white pepper, and sugar.

MAKE THE COATING: In a medium bowl, combine the cornstarch, water, flour, neutral oil, baking soda, and 1¼ teaspoons of the seasoned salt. Mix until you have a loose batter. Add the batter to the marinated pork and mix until the pork is well coated.

(RECIPE CONTINUES)

PREPARE TO FRY: Fill a small, deep pot until one half to two thirds full with peanut oil, and place over medium heat until it reaches 250°F, or until a piece of garlic added to the oil bubbles gently.

CRISP THE GARLIC: Line a plate with paper towels. Add the garlic to the pot and cook, turning occasionally with a fine-mesh strainer, until it just begins to turn a very light golden color, 2 to 4 minutes (no longer or it may become bitter). Use the strainer to transfer the garlic to the plate. (As you prepare the rest of the dish, the moisture in the garlic will evaporate and the garlic will become crisp.)

DO THE FIRST FRY: Place a wire cooling rack on a sheet pan or line a large plate with paper towels. Increase the heat under the pot to medium-high to bring the oil temperature to 325°F.

Swish a piece of pork around in any of the loose batter that's pooled at the bottom of the bowl and carefully place the pork in the hot oil. Do the same with 1 to 2 more pork pieces and fry until light golden brown—flipping as needed for even coloring—for 3 to 4 minutes, depending on the size and thickness of the pieces. Transfer to the wire rack or plate to drain. Continue frying the pork pieces, 2 to 3 at a time, maintaining the oil temperature at 325°F (the temperature will drop every time you add new pieces, so increase the heat as needed) and turning the pork to fry evenly.

Let the pork rest and drain for at least 5 minutes before moving on to the second fry. This lets the juices settle and distribute through the meat, resulting in an extra crispy exterior after the second fry.

DO THE SECOND FRY: Check the oil temperature to be sure it is at 325°F, then add the once-fried pork chops to the oil in two or three batches, frying each batch for 2 minutes, until the pork chops are very crispy.

ASSEMBLE THE DISH: Transfer the pork to a large serving plate. Sprinkle evenly with ¼ teaspoon of the remaining seasoned salt.

Heat a clean, dry wok over high heat until it just begins to smoke. Reduce the heat to medium-low and add the hot pepper. Toss for 20 seconds or so to lightly sear, until it is fragrant. Turn off the heat and add the shallot, then the fried garlic and the remaining seasoned salt. Gently toss everything to mix. Scoop up the seasoned aromatics and sprinkle them evenly on top of the pork chops. Serve immediately.

红烧肉卤蛋 hóngshāo ròu lǔ dàn
Red Braised Pork Belly
with Eggs

JUDY Red braised pork belly is one of China's most popular dishes. "Red braising," or "red cooking," refers to stewing in a mixture of light soy sauce, dark soy sauce, rock sugar, and Shaoxing wine to create a rich reddish-brown sauce. While you can "red cook" fish, beef, or even vegetables, pork belly is by far the favorite medium for this technique. My mother makes this hearty homestyle variation with hard-boiled eggs for family gatherings, without fail. When we visit her apartment in Queens, we arrive to the sight of platters on the small table just beyond the foyer, all covered with overturned plates. When we uncover the largest plate, we always find shining chunks of pork belly with amber-colored eggs underneath.

Serves 4 to 6

1½ pounds lean boneless pork belly (ideally skin-on), cut into 1-inch-thick pieces

2 tablespoons neutral oil

25g rock sugar or 2 tablespoons granulated sugar

3 (⅛-inch-thick) slices fresh ginger

⅓ cup Shaoxing wine

2 tablespoons light soy sauce

1 tablespoon dark soy sauce

3 cups water (see Tip), plus more for preparing the pork and eggs

6 large eggs

Put the pork belly in a medium pot and cover with water. Bring to a boil and boil for 1 minute. Remove from the heat, drain the pork in a colander, and rinse thoroughly to wash off any foam or other impurities.

In a wok over medium-low heat, add the oil and rock sugar. Cook until the sugar melts into the oil. It will look syrupy and amber in color. Take care not to burn it; if it starts to burn, immediately remove the wok from the heat or start over with a clean wok if it is beyond saving. Add the pork pieces and the ginger, and increase the heat to medium. Cook, stirring occasionally, until the pork pieces are lightly browned around the edges, about 3 to 5 minutes.

Add the Shaoxing wine, light soy sauce, dark soy sauce, and the 3 cups of water. Stir with a spatula; you will likely have residual sugar on your spatula, so leave it in the liquid to dissolve, then bring the liquid to a simmer. Remove the spatula, cover the wok, and simmer the pork over medium heat for 30 minutes, stirring every 10 minutes.

Meanwhile, cook the eggs. Bring a large pot of water to a rapid boil, then carefully lower in the eggs. Allow the eggs to boil vigorously for 1 minute, and then cover the pot and reduce the heat to low. Simmer for 9 minutes. Prepare a large bowl of ice water. Lift the eggs out of the pot using a slotted spoon and transfer them to the ice water to cool. Once cooled, peel the eggs.

After the pork has cooked for 30 minutes, submerge the eggs in the sauce and continue cooking, covered, for another 15 to 30 minutes, until the pork is fork-tender.

At this point, there will still be some liquid in the wok. Turn up the heat to medium-high to reduce the sauce, stirring continuously, until it coats the pork belly and eggs. (Be gentle with the eggs and patient as the sauce reduces.) When the sauce has thickened to a glistening coating, it's ready to serve.

TIP! FOR EXTRA-TENDER PORK BELLY!
Add 4 cups of water instead of 3 and braise the pork longer, until it is as tender as you like.

From top, left to right: A celebratory Chinese New Year meal at the restaurant after the dinner shift; Judy, my oldest sister, and my parents spending a weekend at the restaurant; celebrating a birthday at Sun Hing—this was probably in between chores, as you can tell by the stains on my shirt; with my mother, finally sitting down after a long shift—we're eating lobster, because my parents always tried to prepare something special when I would return on the weekends from college or work; my parents with Sarah; my parents, retired from their restaurant days, enjoying time with all of their grandkids.

The Friday Night Rush *at* Sun Hing

BILL

SUN WAS MY uncle's first name and Hing was my stepfather's middle name. Together, Sun Hing means "new prosperity." And so the family restaurant was born.

When I was twenty-three years old, I was working as a software engineer in Binghamton, New York. On Friday evenings when my regular work week wrapped up, I'd switch gears and rush back to New Jersey—a three-hour drive—to arrive at Sun Hing around 7:30 p.m., the restaurant's busiest time. Here's how it would go.

"Hi, Mom!"

I run past the counter where she's taking an order from a customer, and as I push open the double doors to the kitchen, the temperature spikes a few degrees from the combined heat of the deep-fryer, broiler, and blue flames blasting from beneath the line of woks. I greet my father's back ("Hi, Daddy!"), as he tends to all four stations. Though he had a thin build with lean, wiry arms, he could nonetheless deftly maneuver heavy woks full of food.

I check the tickets and see what's cooking—or more important, what isn't yet cooking—and head straight to manning the third wok station, pausing here and there to work the deep-fryer for the steady stream of egg rolls for the dining room and for stuffing into wax paper bags for takeout.

Just as I start to feel like things are under control, a new order comes in: beef lo mein, five chicken wings, three egg rolls. I drop the wings and egg rolls into the deep-fryer, but not before wrapping the single egg roll sitting in the basket, a spare from the last batch.

新 興 樓
Sun Hing Chinese Restaurant
ORDERS TO TAKE OUT OR EAT IN

Specializing in Chinese Cuisine

**10 SOUTH ESSEX AVENUE
ORANGE, NEW JERSEY 07050**

TEL.:(201) 674-4544

Monday through Thursday:
11:00 a.m.–10:30 p.m.
Friday and Saturday:
11:00 a.m.–11:30 p.m.
Sunday: Closed

SOUPS
1. Wonton Soup	1.20	2.10
2. Chicken Egg Drop Soup	1.00	1.80
3. Chicken Consumme Soup	1.10	2.00
4. *Hot and Sour Soup	1.45	2.55
5. Chicken Yat Gaw Mein		2.50
6. Pork Yat Gaw Mein		2.50

APPETIZERS
7. Fried Crab Stick	.65
8. Gried Filet of Sole (w. tartar sauce)	2.35
9. Fantail Shrimp	.80
10. Egg Roll	.80
11. Barbecued Spare Ribs	7.50
	4.25
12. Shrimp Toast (4 pcs.)	3.25
13. Fried Steamed Dumplings (8 pcs.)	3.25
14. Fried Chicken Wings (5 pcs.)	2.25
15. Assorted Fried Chicken (5 pcs.)	3.25
16. Shrimp Roll	.85

CHOW MEIN
(with Crispy Noodles & White Rice)
	Sm.	Lg.
17. Chicken Chow Mein	2.20	3.95
18. Pork Chow Mein	2.20	3.95
19. Beef Chow Mein	2.55	4.65
20. Shrimp Chow Mein	2.95	5.45
21. Vegetable Chow Mein	2.40	4.15
22. Lobster Chow Mein	3.65	6.75

CHOP SUEY
(with White Rice)
	Sm.	Lg.
23. Roast Pork Chop Suey	2.75	5.25
24. Chicken Chop Suey	2.75	5.15
25. Beef Chop Suey	2.85	5.35
26. Shrimp Chop Suey	3.45	5.95
27. Vegetable Chop Suey	2.65	4.95

EGG FOO YOUNG
(with White Rice)
28. Pork Egg Foo Young	3.85
29. Chicken Egg Foo Young	3.85
30. Shrimp Egg Foo Young	4.65
31. Lobster Egg Foo Young	6.95
32. Beef Egg Foo Young	4.55
33. Ham Egg Foo Young	4.25
34. Vegetable Egg Foo Young	3.75

LO MEIN
	Sm.	Lg.
35. Chicken Lo Mein	2.75	4.75
36. Roast Pork Lo Mein	2.75	4.75
37. Beef Lo Mein	2.95	4.95
38. Shrimp Lo Mein	2.95	5.25
39. Lobster Lo Mein	3.95	6.95
40. Vegetable Lo Mein	2.65	4.50

COMBINATION DINERS
(Served w. Roast Pork Fried Rice & Egg Roll)
1. Chicken Chow Mein	4.05
2. Roast Pork Chow Mein	4.05
3. Beef Chow Mein	4.25
4. Roast Pork with Chinese Vegetable	4.95
5. Spare Ribs (4 pcs.)	5.45
6. Pepper Steak	4.95
7. Shrimp with Lobster Sauce	5.95
8. Shrimp Chow Mein	4.75
9. Egg Foo Young (beef, chicken or shrimp)	4.95
10. Beef with Broccoli	5.25

FRIED RICE
	Sm.	Lg.
41. Roast Pork Fried Rice	2.35	4.15
42. Chicken Fried Rice	2.35	4.15
43. Beef Fried Rice	2.55	4.75
44. Ham Fried Rice	2.55	4.75
45. Shrimp Fried Rice	2.85	5.15
46. Lobster Fried Rice	3.95	6.95
47. Subgum Fried Rice	2.95	5.75
48. Young Chow Fried Rice	3.35	6.45
49. Vegetable Fried Rice	2.35	4.15
50. Plain Fried Rice	1.75	3.25

SHRIMP
(with White Rice)
	Sm.	Lg.
51. Shrimp with Bean Sprouts	2.85	5.45
52. Shrimp with Lobster Sauce	3.85	7.25
53. Shrimp w. Black Bean Sauce	3.85	7.25
54. Shrimp with Chinese Vegetable	3.75	7.25
55. Shrimp with Snow Peas	3.80	7.45
56. Shrimp with Almond Ding	3.15	5.95
57. Shrimp with Tomatoes and Pepper	3.80	7.25
58. Shrimp with Curry Sauce	3.25	6.35

CHICKEN
(with White Rice)
	Sm.	Lg.
59. Chicken with Snow Peas	3.40	6.50
60. Chicken with Bean Sprouts	2.55	4.75
61. Moo Goo Gai Pan	2.95	5.65
62. Chicken with Almond Ding	3.15	5.95
63. Chicken with Curry Sauce	2.95	5.75

PORK
(with White Rice)
	Sm.	Lg.
64. Roast Pork with Mushroom	3.65	6.25
65. Roast Pork with Chinese Vegetable	2.95	5.65
66. Roast Pork with Snow Pea Pods	3.40	6.50
67. Roast Pork with Bean Sprouts	2.55	4.75
68. Roast Pork with Tomatoes and Peppers	3.15	5.95
69. Roast Pork with Almond Ding	3.15	5.95

BEEF
(with White Rice)
	Sm.	Lg.
70. Beef with Chinese Vegetable	2.95	5.65
71. Beef with Onion	2.95	5.45
72. Pepper Steak	2.95	5.65
73. Beef with Snow Peas	3.60	6.75
74. Beef with Mushrooms	2.95	6.75
75. Beef with Bean Sprouts	2.55	4.75
76. Beef with Curry Sauce	2.95	5.65
77. Beef with Tomatoes and Pepper	3.40	6.50
78. Beef with Oyster Sauce	3.45	5.95

SWEET AND SOUR
(with White Rice)
79. Sweet and Pungent Shrimp	7.25
80. Sweet and Pungent Pork	5.45
81. Sweet and Pungent Chicken	5.45

* HOT & SPICY

SPECIAL HOUSE DISHES
(with White Rice)
	Order
82. Lobster with Shrimp	7.95
83. Butterfly Shrimp (with Bacon)	7.75
84. Lobster Cantonese (Whole)	Seasonal
85. Chow Har Kew (Jumbo Shrimp)	7.25
86. Roast Pork with Broccoli	3.25 5.75
87. Shrimp with Broccoli	3.80 7.25
88. Beef with Broccoli	3.55 6.25
89. Chicken with Broccoli	3.25 6.25
90. Boneless Chicken Cantonese	6.25
91. Lobster with Chicken	7.55
92. Baby Shrimp with Green Peas	6.25
93. Wor Su Duck	6.75
94. Pineapple Duck	6.75
95. Subgum Pan Fried Noodle (no rice)	6.75
96. Beef with Scallion	7.25
97. Beef with Fresh Scallops	7.95
98. Chicken with Cashew Nuts	6.25
99. Shrimp with Cashew Nuts	6.75
100. Chinese Vegetable Delight	4.50

HUNAN AND SZECHUAN
(with White Rice)
	Order
101. Moo Shu Shrimp	6.25
102. Moo Shu Beef	5.75
103. Moo Shu Pork	5.65
104. Moo Shu Vegetable	5.65
105. *Kung Po Beef	5.95
106. *Kung Po Chicken	5.75
107. *Kung Po Shrimp	6.25
108. *Chicken with Hoisin Sauce	5.95
109. *Shrimp with Garlic Sauce	6.75
110. *Beef with Garlic Sauce	5.75
111. *Chicken with Garlic Sauce	5.95
112. *Chicken with Garlic Sauce	5.95
113. *Shrimp with Spicy Sauce Szechuan Style	6.95
114. *General Tso's Chicken	6.95
115. *Double Sauteed Sliced Pork	5.75
116. *Hunan Beef	6.75
117. *Shredded Beef with Spicy Sauce Szechuan Style	6.25
118. *Szechuan Style Lobster	Seasonal
119. *Lobster with Garlic Sauce	Seasonal
120. *Double Delight	7.45
121. *Bean Curd in Hot Sauce	4.75
122. *Broccoli with Garlic Sauce	4.75

EXTRA ITEMS
White Rice (Small)	.50
(Large)	1.00
French Fries	1.00
Soda	.60
Fried Noodles (Small)	.25
(Large)	.50
Fortune Cookies (6)	.30
Almond Cookies (2)	.55

NAME

AMOUNT $

TAX $

TOTAL $

05602

05602

The original menu from the family restaurant in Orange, NJ.

The Top 5 Most Popular Orders at Sun Hing:
1. Beef with Broccoli
2. Chicken Wings with Fried Rice
3. Barbecued Spare Ribs
4. Shrimp Fried Rice
5. Chicken Egg Foo Young (extra gravy!)

Then I see, in my mom's scribble, a small order of ribs. I cut six off the full rack, already roasted, but cold. I leave the extra end piece as a bonus for the customer and slide the ribs under the broiler to reheat.

Back to that last item—beef lo mein, large. I assemble the ingredients in the takeout container first, cherry-picking the noodles, cabbage, and onions from the countertop food-prep refrigerator where everything is laid out and ready. Before I can make it back to the station, my father calls out that he needs a shrimp with lobster sauce. I briefly pause to prep it for him, snatching up a handful of shrimp, peas, ground pork, chopped scallions, and an egg, so it's on deck for him to run through the wok.

Back to the lo mein. I crank up the fire. I've been sweating since I stepped into the kitchen, but good wok hei is key to great lo mein. Just then, my father finishes one dish and pounces on the broiler to flip my spareribs just before they get scorched. I'd been the one to put them in, but had forgotten about them! Nothing went unnoticed in his kitchen.

With his chef's instinct and flawless efficiency, he turns to the fryer to give my chicken wings and egg rolls a quick shake, lifting them up to drain before returning to his wok station to finish and plate that shrimp with lobster sauce. When the lo mein is done, I grab a takeout carton and load it with noodles, taking care not to get stray sauce on the outside of the carton. I put it under the heat lamps, wash my wok, and rush over to cut and bag the ribs—just in time.

Next, I bag the egg rolls and chicken wings, which have drained and are perfectly crispy. I haven't eaten anything yet, and the egg rolls smell mighty fine, but I can't think about that right now. I head back to the waiter's station on the other side of the double doors to help my mom, who rushes to the counter and cash register while I pack my orders: the small order of ribs—check. Beef lo mein—check. Chicken wings and the egg rolls on top—check, check. Sauce packets. Utensils. Fortune cookies. Staple everything shut. My brain is on autopilot.

I run the orders out to the counter and grab the receipt my mom just took from the last customer, along with some dirty dishes. At the bussing cart, I realize a couple who was just seated needs tea and a bowl of fried noodles. They ask for sodas, so I reach into the fluorescent glow of the Coke fridge, and the cold air is heaven after the inferno of the kitchen.

We continue like this for four hours through dinner service, moving in and out of the kitchen, losing track of how many platters of beef and broccoli get shuttled out to the tables or shoved into brown paper bags. By the time the dinner rush ends, we're all dead tired. There's $1,500 in the register—a very good day. My parents can rest easier knowing they made a decent profit. After emptying the register, my mom holds up the cash and says, "Here's our blood and sweat money." My father throws together the last order of beef lo mein and chicken wings of the night (our favorites), and some Chinese leafy greens he had stashed away. We pack a quart of rice to go and enjoy our dinner at home while watching late-night TV.

While my parents had pride in being able to say they ran their own restaurant, make no mistake: It was grueling work. After my Friday-night shift, I'd pick up Judy (just my girlfriend at the time), and she would join in to work a full Saturday. We were back in the restaurant by 8:00 a.m. to replenish what we'd sold out of the night before, to wrap egg rolls, and to make dumplings and moo shu pancakes for the week ahead. On top of that was the inescapable daily chore of peeling shrimp and slicing meat and vegetables.

We were always short-handed. Everyone did whatever was needed: waiting tables, answering the phone, working the wok or the deep-fryer, or washing dishes and mopping the floor at the end of the night. On more than one occasion, we arrived in the morning to broken glass. We'd tape up the door with cardboard, then figure out what had been stolen. Other times, the water heater would break or the kitchen drain would clog, and I would have to make a run to the hardware store and crawl into grimy corners of the kitchen to make the fix. If it wasn't something like that, the roasting oven was busted, and I would call the Chinatown restaurant suppliers on Manhattan's Lower East Side to figure out who could come out and fix it. Some nights, a few folks who had indulged in too much drink would come in for a meal, rowdy and dangerous, and we'd have to call the police to help escort them out of the restaurant. Other times, people just were out of it. But they never failed to ask for extra gravy on their egg foo young.

When Judy and I got married, we both still helped out at the restaurant. When Sarah and Kaitlin came along, we were busier than ever. I was working full time and putting in weekends at the restaurant, while Judy stayed home to take care of the girls. The truth is, I always felt guilty that I couldn't help my parents *more*. They were getting on in years and had only two part-time employees other than us.

After about ten years running it, my parents sold the restaurant. Judy still can't help but smile when she thinks back on my father's fried chicken wings. We sold dozens of orders each day, but even after a tiring shift with grease staining our aprons, those wings were still one of the best things we'd ever tasted.

西兰花炒牛肉 xī lánhuā chǎo niúròu

Beef and Broccoli

BILL In my parents' restaurant, this was one of the most-ordered items on the menu. It also happens to be one of our family's favorite takeout dishes. There are countless recipes for it—made on sheet pans, in slow cookers, and in pressure cookers. If you've ever wondered why the beef and broccoli recipe you've tried doesn't taste like what you get when you order out, we're here to show you how to get restaurant-quality results. I cranked out many orders in my day, so I've had plenty of practice!

Serves 4

FOR THE BEEF

1 pound beef flank steak, sliced against the grain into ⅛- to ¼-inch-thick pieces

3 tablespoons water

¼ teaspoon baking soda (optional tenderizer)

1½ teaspoons cornstarch

2 teaspoons neutral oil

1 teaspoon oyster sauce

FOR THE SAUCE

⅔ cup low-sodium chicken stock, heated

1½ tablespoons light soy sauce

1 tablespoon oyster sauce

1½ teaspoons granulated sugar or brown sugar

1 teaspoon dark soy sauce

½ teaspoon toasted sesame oil

⅛ teaspoon white pepper powder

FOR THE REST OF THE DISH

4 cups broccoli florets (about 10 ounces)

3 tablespoons neutral oil

2 teaspoons minced garlic (about 2 cloves)

¼ teaspoon minced fresh ginger (optional)

1 tablespoon Shaoxing wine

2½ tablespoons cornstarch

3 tablespoons water

MARINATE THE BEEF: In a medium bowl, combine the beef, water, baking soda (if using), cornstarch, neutral oil, and oyster sauce. Mix until the beef has absorbed all the liquid and let marinate for 30 minutes.

MAKE THE SAUCE: In a medium bowl, combine the chicken stock, light soy sauce, oyster sauce, sugar, dark soy sauce, sesame oil, and white pepper.

BLANCH THE BROCCOLI: Fill a wok halfway with water, bring to a boil, then cook the broccoli for 30 to 60 seconds, depending on whether you like your broccoli crisp or more tender. Drain in a colander.

SEAR THE BEEF: Clean the wok and wipe it dry. Place it over high heat until smoking. Add 2 tablespoons of the neutral oil, then add the beef in a single layer. Sear for 1 minute, then flip and sear for 1 minute on the other side. Turn off the heat, then remove the beef from the wok and into a bowl.

ASSEMBLE THE DISH: Over medium heat, add the remaining tablespoon neutral oil, then the garlic and ginger (if using). Stir for 10 seconds, then pour the Shaoxing wine around the perimeter of the wok. Add the sauce and stir it around the sides of the wok to deglaze, loosening up any browned bits, and bring the sauce to a simmer. Combine the cornstarch with the water in a small bowl to make a slurry, then drizzle three-quarters of the slurry into the sauce while stirring constantly. Simmer for 20 seconds, until thickened enough to coat a spoon.

Toss in the blanched broccoli and seared beef (along with any juices). Mix everything over medium heat until the sauce coats the beef and broccoli. If the sauce seems thin, turn up the heat and reduce it further, or add the remaining slurry. If the sauce is too thick, add a splash of stock or water. When the sauce has thickened to your liking, remove from the wok and serve.

咖喱炒牛肉 gālí chǎo niúròu

Quick Curry Beef

SARAH

Anytime our family ventured into Manhattan's Chinatown, we'd grab takeout from a Cantonese restaurant before heading back to New Jersey via the Holland Tunnel. As we drove home, I couldn't stop myself from digging through the red plastic bag of takeout containers in search of my usual order of beef curry over rice. As I dug in, I would balance the steaming-hot foam container on my lap, trying not to drip sauce onto the cloth car seats. Rather than the version I've posted on the blog, which is a long-braised stew, this recipe is more expedient: stir-fried slices of tender flank steak in a flavorful curry sauce that comes together in minutes rather than hours.

Serves 4

FOR THE BEEF

1 pound beef flank steak, thinly sliced against the grain

3 tablespoons water

1 teaspoon cornstarch

2 teaspoons neutral oil

2 teaspoons oyster sauce

1 teaspoon light soy sauce

½ teaspoon baking soda

FOR THE REST OF THE DISH

3 tablespoons neutral oil

1 medium onion, halved and then sliced into small wedges

½ green bell pepper, seeded and cut into 1-inch pieces

½ red bell pepper, seeded and cut into 1-inch pieces

1½ cups low-sodium chicken stock, plus more as needed

5 teaspoons curry powder (preferably Madras)

1 teaspoon turmeric powder

½ teaspoon fine sea salt, or to taste

½ teaspoon sugar

2 teaspoons cornstarch

1 tablespoon water

MARINATE THE BEEF: In a medium bowl, combine the flank steak with the water, cornstarch, oil, oyster sauce, light soy sauce, and baking soda. Marinate for 20 minutes.

SEAR THE BEEF: Heat a wok over high heat until smoking. Add 2 tablespoons of the oil, then add the flank steak in one layer. Sear the flank steak undisturbed for 30 seconds, then stir-fry just until it turns opaque (it's okay if it's still slightly rare; it will be cooked again). Turn off the heat and transfer the beef to a plate, leaving behind any residual fat.

ASSEMBLE THE DISH: Reduce the heat to medium and add the remaining tablespoon oil, along with the onion and bell peppers. Stir-fry for 1 minute. Stir in the chicken stock, curry powder, turmeric, salt, and sugar. Bring to a simmer.

Combine the cornstarch and water in a small bowl to make a slurry. Add about three-fourths of the slurry to the wok and simmer for 1 minute, until the sauce has thickened enough to coat a spoon. If the sauce isn't thick enough, add more slurry. If it's too thick, add more chicken stock. Check the seasoning and add salt if needed. Stir in the cooked beef and cook for another 30 seconds. Serve.

农家小炒肉 nóngjiā xiǎochǎo ròu

Farmhouse Pork Stir-Fry

Chinese city-dwellers searching for a glimpse back to simpler times have sparked a renaissance in rural tourism across China. When we lived in Beijing, we went on several of these trips. The cramped bus ride was never much of a picnic, but what more than made up for it was that in every village, we were greeted by mom-and-pop restaurants specializing in simple family-style cooking. Nóngjiā cài (农家菜), or farmhouse cuisine, is the Chinese answer to farm-to-table cooking in the West. This stir-fry is the epitome of that style of cooking, in which vegetables are the emphasis and meat is used judiciously. If spice is not your thing, try substituting milder cubanelle peppers for the long hots.

Serves 2 to 4

- **8 ounces boneless pork belly,** partially frozen
- **1 teaspoon cornstarch**
- **1 teaspoon light soy sauce**
- **2 tablespoons neutral oil**
- **8 long hot green peppers** or Anaheim peppers (about 6 ounces), seeded and thinly sliced on the diagonal
- **4 medium garlic cloves,** thinly sliced
- **3 (⅛-inch-thick) slices fresh ginger**
- **1 tablespoon Shaoxing wine**
- **1 teaspoon spicy bean sauce**
- **½ teaspoon dark soy sauce**
- **½ teaspoon sugar**

Cut the pork belly into thin slices (this is much easier when the meat is partially frozen), then put it in a medium bowl. Add the cornstarch and light soy sauce. Mix well.

Heat a wok over high heat until smoking. Add 1 tablespoon of the oil, and then add the pork belly. Stir-fry for 2 to 3 minutes, until the pork belly is lightly browned around the edges. Remove the pork from the wok and set on a plate.

Over medium-high heat, add the remaining tablespoon oil, along with the peppers, garlic, and ginger, and fry for 30 seconds to 1 minute. The peppers should be beginning to blister from the heat, but adjust the heat if necessary to avoid burning the garlic! Add the Shaoxing wine to deglaze the wok, stirring to loosen any browned bits on the bottom, and then add the spicy bean sauce. Stir for another 10 seconds.

Return the pork belly to the wok, along with the dark soy sauce and sugar. Stir-fry for another few seconds over high heat, then serve.

香煎羊排 xiāngjiān yáng pái

Restaurant-Style Pan-Fried Lamb Chops

When we go to a Cantonese restaurant, no one looks at the menu, because we already know what we want. Every once in a while, though, branching out can pay off big time. One evening, we glimpsed a plate of lamb chops at a neighboring table and decided to take a chance. Since then, this dish has been added to the regular rotation. (It isn't over-ordering if you eat all the leftovers the next day, right?) The spice rub and quick cornstarch dredge give these chops a flavorful crisp exterior, while the dry-fried peppers, garlic, shallots, and celery offer a fresh contrast to the rich meat. After pan-frying, they're blushing pink inside—not rare—which allows you to really taste the meat and spices. While you can buy individual rib chops, it's a better value to buy a whole rack of lamb and divide the chops yourself.

Serves 4

1 (2-pound) rack of lamb or 2 pounds lamb rib chops

1½ teaspoons fine sea salt

1 teaspoon garlic powder

¾ teaspoon five-spice powder

½ teaspoon sugar

¼ teaspoon white pepper powder

4 to 5 tablespoons cornstarch

Neutral oil, for frying

5 medium garlic cloves, thinly sliced

½ green bell pepper, seeded and very thinly sliced

½ red bell pepper, seeded and very thinly sliced

½ cup thinly sliced Chinese celery or regular celery (cut on an angle)

½ cup thinly sliced shallots (from 2 to 3 medium)

If using a rack of lamb, trim away all but a ⅛-inch layer of fat from the cap. Stand the rack up so the ribs are pointing upward. Slice between the rib bones, following the curvature of the ribs, to cut chops of even thickness.

Pat the chops dry with a paper towel and place on a large plate. In a small bowl, combine the salt, garlic powder, five-spice powder, sugar, and white pepper. Set aside 1 teaspoon of this mixture for later, and then use the remainder to evenly sprinkle over both sides and the outer edges of the chops. Marinate the chops at room temperature for 45 minutes. (You don't want to fry cold lamb chops right out of the refrigerator.)

Add the cornstarch to a shallow bowl. Dredge the lamb chops in the cornstarch, coating both sides, then thoroughly shake off any excess to achieve a thin layer.

Heat ¼ to ½ inch of oil in a large cast-iron skillet or Dutch oven over medium-high heat. The oil is ready when bubbles immediately form around a bamboo chopstick dipped into the oil.

Add half the lamb chops to the skillet and cook for 3 to 4 minutes per side, until golden brown. (Watch them closely, and peek underneath to check the progress and color.) When the first batch is done, transfer the chops to a plate and cook the second batch.

Place a clean dry wok over medium-low heat and add the reserved 1 teaspoon spice mix. Toast the spices for 10 to 20 seconds (make sure the wok isn't too hot, or they will burn), and add the garlic, bell peppers, and celery. Increase the heat to medium-high, and dry-fry the vegetables for 30 seconds. Add the shallots and the lamb chops to the wok. Toss for another 30 seconds over medium-high heat, until the shallots begin to wilt. Serve.

梅干菜蒸肉饼 méigān cài zhēng ròu bǐng

Steamed Pork Patty
with Preserved Mustard Greens

BILL
A steamed patty of seasoned ground pork is total Cantonese comfort food. Every time I eat one, breaking off pieces to spoon over rice with some of the sauce pooling on the bottom of the dish, I am transported back in time to my childhood on Chestnut Street in Liberty and the weeknight dinners my mom would make. This version uses store-bought dried preserved mustard greens (méigān cài, in Mandarin, or moy choy, in Cantonese), which have a unique, salty flavor. Note that the pork needs to marinate for at least 30 minutes—or better yet, overnight—before steaming.

Serves 4

10 ounces ground pork (70% to 80% lean)

¼ cup water, plus more for soaking the preserved greens

1 tablespoon oyster sauce

2 teaspoons Shaoxing wine

¾ teaspoon fine sea salt

¾ teaspoon sugar

½ teaspoon cornstarch

½ teaspoon grated fresh ginger

¼ teaspoon toasted sesame oil

Pinch of baking soda

½ cup (30g) dried preserved mustard greens (méigān cài, 梅干菜)

1 tablespoon neutral oil

¼ teaspoon white pepper powder

Pinch of five-spice powder

Chopped scallion or fresh cilantro, for garnish

SEASON THE PORK: In a medium bowl, combine the ground pork, ¼ cup water, the oyster sauce, Shaoxing wine, salt, sugar, cornstarch, ginger, sesame oil, and baking soda. Mix with a fork or chopsticks until all the ingredients are blended. Continue mixing vigorously in one circular direction, until the meat takes on a sticky, paste-like texture, 2 to 3 minutes. Let marinate for at least 30 minutes at room temperature (or overnight in the refrigerator, covered).

PREPARE THE MUSTARD GREENS: Pour the preserved mustard greens into a large bowl and cover with water. Use your hands to agitate the mustard greens, then soak for 30 minutes, until rehydrated.

Scoop the mustard greens into a fine-mesh colander to drain. Pour off the water, and if there is sand at the bottom of the bowl, then repeat the rinsing process until there is no more sand present. Drain the preserved mustard greens thoroughly in the colander.

Roughly chop the mustard greens, transfer them to a medium bowl, and add the neutral oil, white pepper, and five-spice powder. Toss until well combined.

STEAM THE PORK AND MUSTARD GREENS: Add the pork to the mustard greens and mix until uniformly combined. Transfer the mixture to a shallow rimmed heatproof dish about 8 inches in diameter. Spread the meat in an even layer, to form a meat patty about 1 inch thick.

Place a 2-inch-tall metal steaming rack in a wok (or any pot with a lid that will accommodate the rack with the dish on top of it) and fill the wok with enough water to come up to about 1 inch below the rack. (You can also use a bamboo steamer if your dish fits in it with enough clearance for the steam to rise around the dish; fill the wok with enough water to come ½ inch up the sides of the steamer. You may need to add more boiling water during steaming to keep the bottom rim of the steamer submerged.) Bring the water to a simmer over medium-high heat and place the dish into your steaming set-up. Cover and steam for 20 minutes. Garnish with the scallion and serve.

蒙古牛肉 ménggǔ niúròu

"Mongolian" Beef

BILL Our blog readers have been known to obsess over this recipe. My armchair theory about the dish's wayward origins is that someone in an American Chinese restaurant forgot to put the orange in a batch of orange beef. Another theory is that it evolved from the Taiwanese invention of "Mongolian BBQ" in the mid-twentieth century—a style of cooking on a large flat griddle similar to Japanese teppanyaki. However it happened, somewhere in the messy history of fusing cuisines, Mongolian beef came to be. It's not Mongolian, but it's a beloved mainstay of American Chinese food.

Serves 4

FOR MARINATING THE BEEF

1 pound beef flank steak, sliced against the grain into ¼-inch-thick slices

2 teaspoons neutral oil

2 teaspoons Shaoxing wine

1 teaspoon light soy sauce

1 tablespoon cornstarch

1 tablespoon water

¼ teaspoon baking soda

FOR THE SAUCE

¼ cup light brown sugar

¾ cup hot water

¼ cup light soy sauce

1 teaspoon dark soy sauce

FOR COATING AND SEARING THE BEEF

½ cup cornstarch

⅔ cup neutral oil

FOR THE REST OF THE DISH

1 teaspoon minced fresh ginger

8 dried red chilies (optional)

3 medium garlic cloves, finely chopped

4 scallions, white and green parts separated and cut on an angle into 2-inch pieces

1½ tablespoons cornstarch

2 tablespoons water

MARINATE THE BEEF: Combine the beef with the neutral oil, Shaoxing wine, light soy sauce, cornstarch, water, and baking soda. Marinate for 1 hour.

MAKE THE SAUCE: In a small bowl, dissolve the brown sugar in the hot water. Mix in the light soy sauce and dark soy sauce.

COAT AND SEAR THE BEEF: Dredge the marinated beef slices in the ½ cup cornstarch until thoroughly coated.

Heat the neutral oil in a wok over high heat. Just before the oil starts to smoke, spread the flank steak pieces evenly in the wok and shallow-fry them undisturbed for 1 minute on each side to achieve a crusty coating. Turn off the heat and transfer the beef to a plate.

ASSEMBLE THE DISH: Drain most of the oil from the wok, reserving 1 tablespoon (the rest can be strained and used for other cooking). Wipe the wok clean with a paper towel, then add the reserved tablespoon of oil. Over medium-high heat, add the ginger and whole dried chilies (if using—if you'd like the dish spicier, break 1 or 2 chilies in half). After 15 seconds, add the garlic and the scallion whites. Stir-fry for another 15 seconds. Add the sauce and simmer for 2 minutes.

Combine the cornstarch with the water to make a slurry, then slowly stir it into the wok.

Add the beef and the green parts of the scallions. Toss everything together for 30 seconds, until the scallions are wilted and there is almost no standing sauce. Serve.

Fish & Shellfish

When I was a kid, I was in awe of my dad's easygoing mastery when he showed me how to prepare a whole fish or a banquet-style shellfish dish. Our lessons continued at the table. If we had Cantonese steamed fish for dinner, Sarah and I would eagerly spoon the oily seasoned soy sauce over our rice while my dad showed us how to pick out choice pieces free of bones. My mom warned us of little superstitions: Flipping the whole fish was a no-no, as it meant sailors at sea might suffer choppy waters or capsizing! My maternal grandma never failed to claim the fish head, with the eyeballs and tender cheeks. There are recipes in this chapter suitable for any level of expertise, from beginning seafood cooks to experienced ones, so you too can prepare fish and other seafood dishes like a master. **KAITLIN**

Ginger Scallion Lobster

姜葱炒龙虾 jiāng cōng chǎo lóngxiā

This ginger scallion lobster is usually served as twin lobsters on a plate, as a symbol of abundance and good luck (lobsters are the "dragons" of the sea after all!). The lobsters are divided into easy-to-grab pieces so everyone can nab their favorite, be it the tender claw or the meaty tail. After flash-frying the lobster to seal in the juices, it's "baked" in a covered hot wok with Shaoxing wine, ginger, and scallion. That's why this dish sometimes goes by the name of "ginger scallion baked lobster," or jiāng cōng jú lóngxiā (姜葱焗龙虾) in Chinese. The end result is a glossy, saucy coating on every piece. Don't be turned off if you have an urge to lick the lobster shells clean. We'd be offended if you didn't.

Serves 4

2 (1¼- to 1½-pound) live lobsters	¼ teaspoon sugar
3 tablespoons cornstarch	¼ teaspoon toasted sesame oil
1 tablespoon all-purpose flour	⅛ teaspoon white pepper powder
3 cups peanut oil (or other neutral oil, for frying	6 (⅛-inch-thick) slices fresh ginger
2½ tablespoons hot water, plus more as needed	3 scallions, white and green parts cut into 2-inch pieces
2 teaspoons oyster sauce	2 tablespoons Shaoxing wine
1½ teaspoons light soy sauce	

PREPARE THE LOBSTERS: Put the lobsters in the freezer for 10 minutes. This will sedate them and make preparation easier. Work with one lobster at a time, and move quickly and confidently through these next steps for the sake of a humane dispatch. In one firm motion, remove the head shell. (You can later discard it or trim it so it sits upright on the plate—a classic restaurant-style lobster presentation.) Position your cleaver or chef's knife crosswise just behind the mouth portion of the lobster head, and drive the knife down in one firm motion to cut off the mouthparts and claws at the same time. Then cut off the smaller legs, and set those aside. *(If you're worried you won't be able to move quickly enough through these steps, point the tip of the knife in the center of the lobster head just behind the eyes and plunge the knife down vertically all the way through to dispatch the lobster immediately.)*

Remove and discard the lobster gills, which are inedible. Remove the green tomalley and any innards. You can discard the tomalley, use it in another dish, or include it in this dish; we leave it out, since some people don't like the strong flavor. If you find any lobster roe, also known as the "coral," remove it. (Use it in another recipe, if you like!)

Rinse the remaining lobster pieces under a thin stream of cold running water. Split the lobster lengthwise from the head portion to the end of the tail so you have two halves. With your hands, remove the dark vein running down the center of the tail. Cut each half into 4 pieces crosswise. (The tail portion should be in 3 pieces, leaving the remaining upper section as the fourth piece.)

Separate the elbow joint from the claws and split each claw and elbow piece in half with a heavy cleaver. Gently rinse all the lobster pieces, drain in a colander, and pat dry with a paper towel. Repeat with the second lobster.

DREDGE AND FLASH-FRY THE LOBSTERS: Mix the cornstarch and flour in a large shallow dish. Add the lobster pieces a few at a time and lightly dredge them, making sure to coat any exposed lobster meat. Shake off any excess coating.

Heat the peanut oil in a wok to 350°F. Drop the lobster into the wok a few pieces at a time, cooking for 15 to 20 seconds per batch. The shells should turn bright red almost instantly. Use a slotted spoon or a frying spider to

(RECIPE CONTINUES)

transfer the pieces to a sheet pan to drain (no need for a wire rack). Remove the oil from the wok, but reserve 2 tablespoons to finish the dish.

ASSEMBLE THE DISH: Prepare the seasoning by combining the hot water, oyster sauce, light soy sauce, sugar, sesame oil, and white pepper in a small bowl. Mix to dissolve the sugar.

Place a clean wok over high heat. When it's just beginning to smoke, add the reserved oil, along with the ginger. Fry for 15 to 20 seconds, until the ginger is fragrant and golden brown at the edges. Add the white portions of the scallions and all the lobster. Stir-fry for 20 seconds, keeping the heat cranked up as high as it'll go.

Pour the Shaoxing wine around the perimeter of the wok and immediately cover the wok. Cook for about 2 minutes, until any remaining dark spots on the lobster have turned bright red. This step infuses, or "bakes," the lobster with the ginger and scallion flavor.

Uncover the wok and add the prepared seasoning mixture along with the green parts of the scallions. Stir-fry for 1 minute. If the wok is dry, add a couple tablespoons of water, but the lobster should be glossy, with little to no standing sauce. Serve immediately.

清蒸鱼 qīngzhēng yú

Cantonese Steamed Fish

BILL No fish preparation has played a bigger role on our dinner table than Cantonese steamed fish. After fishing trips out of Montauk, Long Island, with my cousins, at least one fish from the day's catch is immediately prepared with this familiar mixture of soy sauce, ginger, scallions, and cilantro. We even once steamed some largemouth bass on a camping trip, huddled over a campfire next to our tents. (Have soy sauce, will travel!) You can steam virtually any whole delicate white fish of good eating size (1 to 1½ pounds), such as striped bass or branzino. Flat fish like flounder or grey sole are also great for steaming. I always say the best way to eat fish is to choose what's in season (and sustainable)— and the best way to do that is to just ask your fishmonger. If you can't get a whole fresh fish, use fillets!

Serves 4

1 (1- to 1½-pound) whole striped bass or other delicate white fish, scaled and cleaned

5 tablespoons neutral oil

3 tablespoons finely julienned fresh ginger

4 scallions, white and green parts separated and finely julienned

¼ cup light soy sauce

¼ cup water

¾ teaspoon sugar

¼ teaspoon fine sea salt

Pinch of white pepper powder

8 sprigs fresh cilantro, torn into smaller pieces (about ⅔ cup)

Give the fish a quick once-over to make sure it's thoroughly cleaned (see page 213). Rinse it and shake off any excess water (no need to pat it dry). Transfer the fish to an oval heatproof plate. Note: No salt, seasoning, or wine should be used on the fish before steaming.

Place a 2-inch-tall metal steaming rack in a wok (or any pot with a lid that will accommodate the fish) and fill the wok with enough water to come up to about 1 inch below the rack. Turn on the heat to high and bring the water to a simmer. Place the plate of fish on the rack, cover the wok, and steam for 9 minutes. After 9 minutes, test the fish for doneness using a butter knife. If the knife slides into the center of the fish without resistance, it's done. You know the fish is cooked perfectly when the flesh is opaque down to the bone, but the bone is slightly translucent. (Remember, you will not be eating the bone, and the fish will continue to cook as it rests— while you're preparing the sauce. Trust us on this one!)

Carefully pour off any liquid that has accumulated on the plate during steaming and discard. (Don't skip this step. The steaming liquid has a strong fishy taste.)

In a small saucepan, heat 2 tablespoons of the oil and 1½ tablespoons of the ginger over medium heat, until the ginger begins to sizzle. Next, add the white parts of the scallions, the soy sauce, water, sugar, salt, and white pepper. Bring the mixture to a simmer and spoon the mixture evenly over the fish. Then spread the green portions of the scallions, the remaining 1½ tablespoons of the ginger, and all the cilantro on top of the fish.

Heat the remaining 3 tablespoons oil in the saucepan until shimmering. Pour the hot oil over the raw ginger and herbs—they will sizzle on contact. Serve immediately.

> **TIP!** If using fillets, adjust the cooking time accordingly—as little as 3 to 4 minutes for very thin sole or flounder fillets to 7 minutes for fillets of medium thickness, or up to the full cooking time of 9 minutes for thicker fillets. Use the butter knife test to check for doneness, as described in the recipe!

MAKE SURE YOUR FISH IS CLEAN!

While the fish you buy from your fishmonger is likely already cleaned and scaled, it's always a good idea to run through these steps after you bring your fish home:

○ Use a fish scaler or serrated steak knife to pass over the sides of the fish for any stray scales. Pay special attention to the belly and edges, including near the dorsal fins and the head.

○ Use a pair of kitchen shears to remove any fins. They can be pretty tough or even sharp, so be careful. Leave the tail and head intact for presentation.

○ Look into the cavity. Since the fish has been gutted, you should see the backbone. You may also see a white membrane along the backbone—if you do, pierce and cut it to reveal a blood line near the bone. Run your finger or a spoon across it and rinse to clean it thoroughly.

○ Check the head and gills. You should not see any gills left. If there are any, remove them with kitchen shears and rinse clean. Folks who like dining on the fish head will appreciate this step.

核桃虾 hétáo xiā
Walnut Shrimp

This is everyone's favorite Cantonese-style banquet dish. Large shrimp are dredged in cornstarch, fried, and tossed in a luxurious savory-sweet mayonnaise-based sauce with candied walnuts and crunchy broccoli. Sometimes, banquet waiters have to dish out the excess of the less popular dishes so they can serve the next round of items. No such problems with this shrimp—it always disappears quickly! Serve this at your next party, and your friends will be talking about it for days. Oh, and if you want to minimize chopstick battles at the table, don't skimp on the walnuts—which are, incidentally, great in salads or as a snack, so consider making a double batch! The walnuts and shrimp are fried in the same small pot of oil to minimize oil usage.

Serves 4

FOR THE CANDIED WALNUTS

Neutral oil, for frying

2½ tablespoons sugar

2½ tablespoons water

⅛ teaspoon fine sea salt

⅔ cup large walnut halves (about 20)

FOR THE SHRIMP

1 pound peeled and deveined jumbo shrimp

2 teaspoons Shaoxing wine

½ teaspoon toasted sesame oil

⅛ teaspoon fine sea salt

⅛ teaspoon white pepper powder

⅓ cup cornstarch

FOR THE MAYONNAISE SAUCE

2 tablespoons sweetened condensed milk

1 teaspoon honey

1 teaspoon rice vinegar

Pinch of fine sea salt

¼ cup mayonnaise, at room temperature

FOR THE BROCCOLI

1 teaspoon fine sea salt

1 teaspoon neutral oil

8 ounces broccoli crowns, cut into 2-inch florets

CANDY THE WALNUTS: Line a sheet pan with parchment paper. Add 3 to 4 inches of the neutral oil to a small saucepan and heat to 325°F. In another small saucepan, heat the sugar, water, and salt over medium-low heat, stirring until the sugar is dissolved. Then cook for 5 minutes, stirring often with a rubber spatula, until the mixture reduces to a thin syrup.

Meanwhile, when the oil has reached 325°F, add the walnuts and fry for 3 to 4 minutes, until they turn golden brown. Immediately scoop the nuts out with a slotted spoon, and transfer them to the saucepan with the syrup. Still over medium-low heat, stir until most of the syrup has coated the nuts in a thin, translucent layer. Spread the walnuts on the lined sheet pan so they are not touching. Let cool completely.

PREPARE THE SHRIMP: Make the existing cuts on the back of the shrimp deeper without cutting all the way through. This gives the shrimp a plump shape and more surface area for the cornstarch coating. If the shrimp still have the tails on, you can remove them or keep them on, per your preferences.

Toss the shrimp in a medium bowl with the Shaoxing wine, sesame oil, salt, and white pepper. Put the cornstarch in another medium bowl, then dredge the shrimp in the cornstarch a few at a time, until they are covered with a light layer. Reserve the remaining cornstarch.

PREPARE THE SAUCE: In a medium microwaveable bowl, combine the condensed milk, honey, rice vinegar, and salt. Microwave for 15 seconds to make it easier to stir. Stir in the mayonnaise until smooth (the sauce should be slightly warm or at room temperature).

COOK THE BROCCOLI: Have a large bowl of cold water nearby. Fill your wok (or a medium pot) halfway with water and bring to a boil, then add the salt and neutral oil. Add the broccoli florets and blanch for 30 seconds, then immediately scoop them out. Transfer

the broccoli to the bowl of cold water to stop the cooking process for 10 seconds, then drain thoroughly in a colander. The broccoli should still be quite warm, but the shock of the cold water will keep them green.

FRY THE SHRIMP: Heat the pot of oil you used for the walnuts to 325°F.

Dredge the shrimp for a second time in the remaining cornstarch. Moving quickly, drop the shrimp one at a time into the hot oil, adding just enough to fry without touching. Fry the shrimp until golden brown, 2 to 3 minutes, using a slotted spoon to move them around gently so they fry evenly. Use the slotted spoon to transfer the fried shrimp to a large stainless-steel mixing bowl and repeat with the remaining shrimp.

ASSEMBLE THE DISH: When all the shrimp have been fried, pour the creamy sauce over them and gently toss until evenly coated. Arrange the broccoli florets around the perimeter of a large serving platter, then transfer the shrimp to the center of platter. Top with the candied walnuts and serve immediately!

油爆虾 *yóu bào xiā*

Oil-Crackling Shrimp

Wok-fried in a generous amount of hot, ginger-infused oil, these shrimp (usually whole, head and shell on) crackle and "explode" in the wok. While we've shared the traditional version on the blog, this recipe is even easier, as we use peeled shrimp (no need to trim the legs or devein them yourself). In both recipes, the signature step is wok-frying the shrimp in oil at a high temperature to form a delicious crispy crust that the savory, slightly tangy sauce can cling to.

Serves 4

FOR DREDGING THE SHRIMP

1 pound peeled and deveined jumbo shrimp, with the tails intact

1½ tablespoons cornstarch

FOR THE SAUCE

1 medium garlic clove, minced

⅓ cup hot water

1 tablespoon Shaoxing wine

1 teaspoon sugar

2 teaspoons light soy sauce

1 teaspoon ketchup

1 teaspoon oyster sauce

½ teaspoon toasted sesame oil

½ teaspoon Worcestershire sauce

¼ teaspoon dark soy sauce

⅛ teaspoon white pepper powder

FOR THE REST OF THE DISH

1 cup neutral oil for frying

3 (⅛-inch-thick) slices fresh ginger

2 scallions, white parts cut into 2-inch pieces and halved lengthwise, and green parts chopped

1 tablespoon roughly chopped fresh cilantro

PREPARE THE SHRIMP: Pat the shrimp dry with a paper towel. In a large bowl, toss the shrimp with the cornstarch until evenly coated.

PREPARE THE SAUCE: In a medium bowl, combine the garlic, hot water, Shaoxing wine, sugar, light soy sauce, ketchup, oyster sauce, sesame oil, Worcestershire sauce, dark soy sauce, and white pepper.

ASSEMBLE THE DISH: Add the neutral oil to a wok over high heat and stir until the oil begins to smoke lightly.

You will need to fry the shrimp in two batches. Carefully lower half the shrimp into the hot oil all at once, shallow-frying them for about 5 seconds. Flip them and cook for another 5 seconds. Scoop them up with a spider or metal strainer and let the excess oil drain back into the wok. Set the shrimp on a plate and let the oil heat back up until it's just beginning to smoke once again. Repeat with the second batch of shrimp.

Repeat this flash-frying two more times to give the shrimp a crispy coating.

Turn off the heat and scoop the oil into a medium heatproof bowl, leaving about 1 tablespoon in the wok.

With the wok over medium heat, add the ginger and white parts of the scallions. Cook for 30 seconds, until fragrant and caramelized. Add the sauce mixture and turn up the heat, bringing the sauce to a simmer. Stir for 30 seconds to sear the sauce against the hot wok, creating wok hei and reducing the liquid slightly.

Add the shrimp, scallion greens, and cilantro to the wok and stir-fry for 15 to 20 seconds, until there is little to no standing sauce. Serve.

虾龙糊 xiā lóng hú

Shrimp with Lobster Sauce

Shrimp with lobster sauce is one of those dishes that took a meandering route through Chinese American restaurant kitchens to become what we know it as today. The light, translucent sauce was inspired by the flavors of Cantonese-style lobster, but shrimp was a more cost-effective and widely available option. If you really want this dish to shine (and get that old-school American takeout taste), serve it with some pork fried rice made with our char siu (see page 173).

Serves 2

4 ounces ground pork

2 tablespoons neutral oil

1 large garlic clove, minced

12 ounces peeled and deveined jumbo or extra-jumbo shrimp

1 tablespoon Shaoxing wine

1½ cups low-sodium chicken stock

½ teaspoon fine sea salt

½ teaspoon toasted sesame oil

¼ teaspoon sugar

¼ teaspoon MSG (optional)

⅛ teaspoon white pepper powder

½ cup frozen peas

2½ tablespoons cornstarch

2 tablespoons water, plus more for boiling the pork

1 large egg, lightly beaten

1 scallion, white and green parts chopped

Add water to your wok until it's about one-third full, and bring to a boil over high heat. Stir in the pork and break up any clumps. Cook for about 1 minute, until the pork is no longer pink. Use a fine-mesh strainer to remove the pork and give it a quick rinse. (This step will give you a cleaner sauce.)

Clean the wok, then heat over medium-high heat until the wok is completely dry and just begins to smoke. Add the neutral oil, garlic, shrimp, and the ground pork. Stir-fry for 10 to 20 seconds. Add the Shaoxing wine and stir-fry for another 10 seconds. Add the chicken stock, salt, sesame oil, sugar, MSG (if using), and white pepper. Stir in the peas and bring to a simmer.

Combine the cornstarch and the 2 tablespoons of water to make a slurry, then add it to the wok a little bit at a time, stirring constantly. Let the mixture bubble and thicken to a gravy-like consistency. If it's too thick for your liking, add a little more chicken stock. If it's too thin, add more slurry.

Without stirring, pour the lightly beaten egg evenly over the sauce and sprinkle on the scallion. Don't stir yet; just simmer for 5 seconds. Then use your spatula to fold the egg into the sauce with a few strokes. Serve.

THE KEY TO PERFECT LOBSTER SAUCE
Adding the egg to the sauce at the end seems simple, but it's an art that takes practice! The egg is lightly beaten so you get streaks of both egg white and yellow yolk. Allowing the egg to simmer briefly before stirring ensures that the egg doesn't disappear into the sauce or make it cloudy, but you don't want to end up with large chunks of cooked egg either. Eggs that resemble ribbons in the sauce mark success!

糯米蒸膏蟹 nuòmǐ zhēng gāo xiè

Steamed Crab with Sticky Rice

Although you can use any crab for this dish, Dungeness crab—with its large chunks of firm, sweet meat—is ideal. Abundant in the Pacific Northwest, Dungeness crab is generally most affordable in the winter months when the crabs tend to be more abundant, though prices can fluctuate widely based on supply and demand. It's not uncommon to pay a per-pound price for the live crabs you see in the tanks at Chinese seafood restaurants. Here, fresh Dungeness crab is placed on top of sticky rice—studded with Chinese ham, dried scallops, and shallot—and steamed to perfection in a lotus leaf (or bamboo/reed leaves). The crab flavor seeps into the rice and the lotus leaf adds a subtle aroma. Note that you need to soak the lotus leaf, as well as the glutinous rice and dried scallops overnight before steaming.

Serves 2 to 4

FOR THE RICE

1 large dried lotus leaf or 6 dried bamboo or reed leaves

2 cups uncooked short-grain glutinous rice (also called sweet rice or sticky rice)

2 tablespoons (15g) dried scallops

¼ cup water, plus more for soaking and steaming

1 tablespoon oyster sauce

¼ teaspoon toasted sesame oil

¼ teaspoon dark soy sauce

⅛ teaspoon white pepper powder

1 tablespoon neutral oil

¼ cup finely diced Chinese cured ham or other dry-cured ham (about 1¼ ounces)

2 tablespoons minced shallot

1 (2- to 2½-pound) live Dungeness crab, refrigerated for at least 1 hour

FOR THE SAUCE

2 tablespoons neutral oil

1½ teaspoons minced shallot

½ teaspoon finely minced garlic

6 tablespoons hot water

4 teaspoons light soy sauce

2 teaspoons oyster sauce

¾ teaspoon sugar

1 tablespoon finely chopped scallion, green part only

SOAK THE LOTUS LEAF, RICE, AND DRIED SCALLOPS: Place the lotus leaf in a large bowl, cover with water, and weight it down with something heavy. (Do the same if using dried bamboo or reed leaves.) In another large bowl, cover the glutinous rice with 2 inches of water. In a small bowl, add the dried scallops and enough water to submerge them. Soak the lotus leaf, rice, and dried scallops overnight.

PREPARE THE RICE: Rinse the lotus leaf and use it to line the bottom of a 10-inch bamboo steamer (or a heatproof dish in a similar size and shape). If the leaf is very large, trim away any excess around the edges of the steamer. If using bamboo or reed leaves, trim 1 inch of tough stem off the bottom of each leaf, then line them across the steamer so they're overlapping.

Strain the glutinous rice and place it in a shallow heatproof bowl, evening it out so it's in a flat layer. Strain the soaked scallops, reserving ¼ cup of the soaking liquid. Distribute the scallops over the rice in the bowl, and drizzle the scallop-soaking water evenly over the rice.

(RECIPE CONTINUES)

Place a 2-inch-tall metal steaming rack in a wok (or any pot with a lid that will accommodate the bowl of rice and scallops) and fill with enough water to come up to about 1 inch below the rack. Bring to a simmer over medium-high heat, then place the bowl of rice and scallops onto the rack, cover, and steam for 30 minutes.

Transfer the scallops to a plate, lifting them off the rice, and set the bowl of rice aside. When cool enough to touch, use your hands to shred the scallops.

In a small bowl, make the rice seasoning mixture by combining the ¼ cup water, oyster sauce, sesame oil, dark soy sauce, and white pepper.

Heat a wok over medium heat and add the neutral oil, ham, shallot, and shredded scallops. Stir-fry for 1 to 2 minutes, or until the shallots are translucent. Increase the heat to high and stir in the sticky rice. Mix until everything is well combined, then pour in the rice seasoning mixture. Continue stir-frying the rice, breaking up any clumps, until the seasoning is uniformly mixed in. Transfer the rice mixture to the lined bamboo steamer (or heatproof dish, if that's what you used).

PREPARE THE CRAB: Having the crab cold will make it less active and easier to handle. You can wear protective gloves to shield your hands from the sharp parts of the shell. Place the crab on a large cutting board or in your sink. The crab is desensitized at this point, but for the sake of a humane dispatch, move quickly and confidently through these next steps.

Hold the crab's legs on one side and use your other hand to grab the shell on the same side. Use steady force to pull the top shell off the body.

Flip the rest of the crab body over. Remove the narrow flap, or apron, on the underside by peeling it back and pulling it off. Use a cleaver or chef's knife to cut the crab in half down the middle so you have two pieces with the legs attached to each side.

Flip the crab shell so the inside is facing up, and use your thumb to press down on the mouthparts on the shell to crack and remove them. Then carefully remove

the stomach sac inside the shell. Clean and rinse out the inside of the crab shell, leaving most of the membrane since it will add flavor to the rice. Use your knife to scrape any hairs from the underside of the shell to create a smooth, clean surface.

Take each half of the crab body, and remove the remaining mouthparts and the inedible gills and organs by pulling them off. You can use running water to rinse away the green tomalley (also called mustard). We recommend discarding the tomalley for Dungeness crab, since it has a very strong flavor, but this is a personal preference. All commercially sold Dungeness crabs are male, so don't worry about discarding any roe!

Take the two crab halves and use a cleaver to cut each half into 4 pieces: one with the claw only, one with 2 legs, and two other pieces each with 1 leg attached.

ASSEMBLE AND STEAM: Place the crab pieces on top of the prepared sticky rice with the legs and claws facing out in the original shape of the crab and the shell on top.

Add enough water to the wok so that it submerges the bottom of the bamboo steamer by ½ an inch. (You may need to add more boiling water during steaming to maintain this water level.) If using a heatproof dish instead, set a steaming rack in the wok as you did before to steam the rice and scallops. Bring the water to a slow boil, then place the bamboo steamer (or heatproof dish) into the wok, cover, and steam for 13 to 16 minutes. (For larger crabs, cook for the longer end of the time range, and vice versa for a smaller crab.)

MAKE THE SAUCE AND SERVE: In a small saucepan over low heat, add the oil, shallot, and garlic. Cook for 30 seconds, until fragrant. Add the hot water, light soy sauce, oyster sauce, and sugar. Bring to a simmer and turn off the heat. Stir in the scallion.

Remove the large crab shell and spoon the sauce over the crab and rice below. Replace the shell for presentation and serve.

干煎鱼 gān jiān yú

Crispy Pan-Fried Fish Fillets

KAITLIN

Coming from a line of restaurant chefs and masterful home cooks, I sometimes feel a profound sense of guilt at my hesitance to cook whole fish. I know I'm not alone out there though, so I devised these crispy pan-fried fish fillets, topped with a mix of both fresh and cooked scallions and cilantro—all in just one pan (my kitchen immaturity extends to washing dishes). Don't skip the fragrant Shaoxing wine (at the very least, substitute another rice wine or dry cooking sherry).

Serves 2 to 3

1 pound flaky white fish fillets (such as haddock or flounder)

2 teaspoons plus 1 tablespoon Shaoxing wine

¼ teaspoon fine sea salt

½ teaspoon white pepper powder

¼ cup cornstarch

¼ cup neutral oil

3 tablespoons hot water

1½ tablespoons light soy sauce

½ teaspoon sugar

2 scallions, white and green parts finely julienned

½ cup roughly chopped fresh cilantro leaves and stems

Pat the fish dry with a paper towel on both sides. Drizzle 2 teaspoons of the Shaoxing wine all over the fillets, using your hands to rub it on both sides of each fillet. Mix the salt and white pepper and rub it all over the fillets as well.

Add the cornstarch to a pie plate or other shallow rimmed dish. Dredge the fish thoroughly, pressing the cornstarch onto the fillets until they are completely coated.

Add the oil to a large nonstick skillet over high heat. (You could also use a well-seasoned cast-iron pan or a carbon-steel wok. Just be sure to heat it thoroughly before adding the oil to help create a nonstick surface— see page 23.) The oil is hot enough when a pinch of cornstarch dropped into the oil sizzles vigorously.

Gently lay the fish fillets in the oil. Fry for 2 minutes, then reduce the heat to medium-high and fry for an additional minute. (Don't touch it during these 3 minutes!) Flip the fillets over and fry for 3 to 4 minutes on the other side, until lightly golden.

In a small bowl, prepare the sauce. Combine the hot water with the light soy sauce, sugar, and remaining tablespoon Shaoxing wine.

Transfer the fish to a platter. Sprinkle half the scallions and cilantro over the fish. Add the other half of the scallions and cilantro to the pan of oil (that you cooked the fish in). With the heat still on medium-high, cook the herbs until they're just wilted, about 30 seconds. Lower the heat to medium and pour in the prepared sauce. Simmer for 5 seconds—just enough to deglaze the pan. You don't want the sauce to evaporate too much! Turn off the heat and pour the sauce over the fish. Serve immediately.

蒜蓉粉丝虾 suàn róng fěnsī xiā

Steamed Garlicky Shrimp
with Glass Noodles

Some of the best shrimp we've ever had was steamed with lots of garlic and served on a bed of glass noodles at our go-to neighborhood spot in Beijing. Fresh garlic is combined with a light mix of oyster and soy sauce to top the shrimp and delicate noodles (scallops also work wonderfully in this recipe). We'd venture to say that no amount of garlic is too much here. Just give yourself and your fellow diners some space after dinner—the garlic breath is real, but worth it.

Serves 2 to 3

1 bundle of mung bean glass noodles (50g/1.75 ounces dry weight)

½ cup warm water, plus more for soaking the noodles

12 ounces peeled and deveined jumbo or extra-jumbo shrimp, with the tails intact

2 teaspoons light soy sauce

1 teaspoon oyster sauce

½ teaspoon sugar

⅛ teaspoon fine sea salt

Pinch of white pepper powder

3 tablespoons neutral oil

2 tablespoons chopped garlic (from 5 to 6 cloves)

1 tablespoon chopped fresh cilantro or scallion

Place the glass noodles in a medium bowl and cover with warm water. Soak for 20 to 30 minutes, or until the noodles are softened.

Butterfly the shrimp by using a knife to slice them open from the back (without slicing all the way through) so they can sit on the plate with the tails pointing up vertically.

Drain the noodles in a colander and use kitchen shears to cut them into 3-inch lengths. Place the noodles evenly across the bottom of a shallow heatproof dish. Arrange the butterflied shrimp on top of the noodles with the tails pointing up.

For the sauce, mix the ½ cup warm water, light soy sauce, oyster sauce, sugar, salt, and white pepper in a small bowl.

Heat a large saucepan over low heat. Add the oil and garlic, and cook for 2 to 3 minutes, stirring occasionally, until the garlic turns slightly translucent. You want the garlic to cook slowly to soften it (rather than toasting or caramelizing) to help bring out its natural sweetness. Add the sauce mixture and increase the heat to medium. Bring the mixture to a simmer, then remove it from the heat to cool.

When the sauce is cool enough to touch (so it doesn't cook the shrimp on contact), pour it over the shrimp and noodles, taking care to spoon the garlic evenly over the shrimp.

Place a 2-inch-tall metal steaming rack in the bottom of a wok and fill the wok with enough water to come up to about 1 inch below the rack. Bring the water in the wok to a simmer over medium-high heat.

Place the dish on the steaming rack, cover, and steam for 4 to 5 minutes, until the shrimp just turns opaque (they should be opaque but not overcooked). Remove from the heat, top with the cilantro, and serve immediately.

Vegetables & Tofu

Growing up in China, vegetables were the staple of our diet. The livelihood of our village in Hubei, like most communities, was farming. In spring, my mother and I would venture out to look for wild vegetables like Shepherd's Purse, plucking them from roadsides and vegetable fields. Summer brought a small cache of loofah plants we cultivated in a patch of dirt behind our house. In fall, we ate pumpkin in soups, stir-fries, and braises, and we stashed potatoes away from the sun so they'd last through the cold winter months. Winter had us tying napa cabbages on strings and hanging them from our ceiling beams for storage, tiding us over until the spring shoots emerged once again. Believe it or not, even tofu was an indulgence, because someone had to get on a bicycle and ride twenty minutes to get it. In short, vegetables were the main event at mealtimes. So it was important to cook them well and make them as delicious and satisfying as we could! These vegetable and tofu dishes are some of our favorite recipes in this book. **JUDY**

鱼香茄子 yú xiāng qiézi
Eggplant with Garlic Sauce

Eggplant with garlic sauce is an indulgence at sit-down restaurants and tiny takeout spots alike. The tender eggplant, pork, and garlicky, sticky brown sauce make it positively addictive. Most restaurants deep-fry the eggplant for two reasons: to lock in the vibrant purple color, and to cook it until it's fall-apart tender in very little time. Our alternative method gets you tender eggplant with a little bit of char on the edges, using just enough oil to achieve that restaurant-quality look and taste. While we prefer Japanese or Chinese eggplants (the long, narrow, purple variety), regular globe eggplants will also work.

Serves 2 to 4

½ **cup hot water**

1 **tablespoon sugar**

1 **tablespoon cornstarch**

1½ **tablespoons oyster sauce** or vegetarian oyster sauce

1 **tablespoon rice vinegar**

1 **tablespoon Shaoxing wine**

1 **tablespoon light soy sauce**

1 **teaspoon toasted sesame oil**

½ **teaspoon dark soy sauce**

⅛ **teaspoon white pepper powder**

2 **tablespoons minced garlic** (from about 6 cloves)

1 **pound Japanese or Chinese eggplants** (2 to 3 long eggplants)

4½ **tablespoons neutral oil**

4 **ounces ground pork** or chicken (optional)

2 **teaspoons minced fresh ginger**

5 to 10 **dried red chilies,** seeded and sliced into small pieces

2 **scallions,** white and green parts finely chopped

In a small bowl, add the hot water and stir in the sugar to dissolve. Then add the cornstarch, oyster sauce, rice vinegar, Shaoxing wine, light soy sauce, sesame oil, dark soy sauce, and white pepper. Stir in half of the garlic (1 tablespoon). Set aside.

Trim the ends off the eggplants and cut them on an angle, rotating the eggplant with each cut, into triangular bite-size chunks. (Don't leave them out too long, or they will turn brown.)

Heat a wok over medium-high heat until it's smoking lightly, then pour 1½ tablespoons of the neutral oil around the perimeter of the wok to evenly coat it with oil. Spread the eggplant in a single layer, reduce the heat to medium, and cook for 3 to 4 minutes, flipping and stirring occasionally, until the eggplant is lightly browned. Spread another 1½ tablespoons of the oil around the perimeter of the wok. Continue cooking the eggplant (still in a single layer) for another 4 minutes, stirring occasionally, until evenly seared, soft, and slightly translucent. (You may want to do this in two batches.) Remove the eggplant from the wok and set on a plate.

Increase the heat to high and add the remaining 1½ tablespoons neutral oil to the wok. Add the ground pork (if using) and cook until opaque, breaking it up into small bits as you go. Add the ginger, dried chilies, and the remaining tablespoon of garlic. Cook for 1 to 2 minutes, stirring constantly, until the aromatics are toasted and fragrant.

Put the eggplant back into the wok and stir-fry until combined. Stir the sauce again to ensure the cornstarch is well combined with the liquid, then add it to the wok. Mix well and bring to a simmer, cooking until the sauce is just thick enough to coat a spoon. Stir in the scallions and serve.

蚝油青菜 háoyóu qīngcài
Blanched Greens
with Oyster Sauce

This dish offers something healthy and delicious to serve alongside just about anything else, prepared in mere minutes. All you do is blanch greens like Chinese broccoli (gai lan), choy sum, or even broccolini (a cross between regular broccoli and Chinese broccoli) with a dash of oil to give them a glossy sheen. You then simmer a few ingredients in a saucepan to make the delicious sauce, pour it over the blanched vegetables, and you're done!

Serves 4

1 pound Chinese broccoli, choy sum, or broccolini

2 tablespoons neutral oil

1 tablespoon oyster sauce or vegetarian oyster sauce

1 tablespoon light soy sauce

1 tablespoon water, plus more for blanching greens

½ teaspoon toasted sesame oil

¼ teaspoon sugar

⅛ teaspoon white pepper powder

Wash and trim the vegetables (see opposite). Bring a large pot of water to a boil.

Add 1 tablespoon of the neutral oil to a small saucepan over medium heat. Stir in the oyster sauce, light soy sauce, the 1 tablespoon water, the sesame oil, sugar, and white pepper. Bring the mixture to a simmer and let it bubble for 30 seconds. Turn off the heat.

When the water is boiling, add the remaining tablespoon oil. Add the greens and blanch until crisp-tender (90 seconds to 3 minutes, depending on the thickness of the stems).

Drain the greens thoroughly, then arrange on a dish. Pour the warm sauce over the greens, toss, and serve.

SQUEAKY-CLEAN GREENS

Leafy green vegetables must be cleaned properly before use. When it comes to culinary mishaps, there are few things worse than a bite of gritty sand ruining your wok hei buzz! Here is our tried-and-true method.

O Trim off any yellowing leaves or leaves with dark spots. If you can't easily puncture the woody end of stems with a fingernail, cut them off. For some vegetables with thicker stems, like Chinese broccoli, peel the tough outer layer around the base of the stem with a vegetable peeler, like you might do with asparagus. For veggies with many layers (like bok choy), peel apart the leaves or halve them lengthwise to open them up.

O Soak the vegetables in a very large bowl, basin, or clean sink of cold water. Agitate them with your hands to shake loose any dirt and sand, and let sit for 5 to 10 minutes. Then lift the vegetables out of the basin with your hands and transfer to a colander (don't pour the vegetables into the colander; any dirt will just go right back onto the greens). Discard the water (or use it to water plants) and rinse the basin thoroughly. Repeat this process at least one more time. We usually do a total of three rounds.

O If you're stir-frying the greens, drain them well and shake off as much excess water as possible after the last wash. A little moisture is okay, but overly wet vegetables are the enemy of wok hei.

O They're now ready for cooking!

干锅菜花 gān guō càihuā

Restaurant-Style Cauliflower Dry Pot

You can find this lip-smacking vegetable dish in restaurants across China. In Beijing, we ordered it far more often than any meat dish. It was usually served in a miniature chafing dish with a small flame underneath it to caramelize a bed of raw onions below the cauliflower. By the time you got to the bottom of the dish, you had incredibly delicious morsels of onion to polish off your rice with. Here, we mimic that experience by caramelizing onions in the wok and lining the serving plate with them before cooking the cauliflower. Look for Chinese cauliflower at your local Asian market. Also known as flowering cauliflower, the florets are less tight, with smaller buds on thinner, longer stems. If you can't find it, regular cauliflower also works.

Serves 4

3 tablespoons plus 1 teaspoon neutral oil

1 small red onion, thinly sliced

1 pound cauliflower, cut into bite-size florets

4 ounces boneless pork belly, thinly sliced into bite-size pieces (optional)

6 large garlic cloves, coarsely chopped

4 (⅛-inch-thick) slices fresh ginger

4 to 6 dried red chilies, seeded and sliced into small pieces

1 tablespoon spicy bean sauce

½ cup red bell pepper (in bite-size pieces)

2 tablespoons water

1 tablespoon oyster sauce or vegetarian oyster sauce

1 tablespoon Shaoxing wine

2 teaspoons light soy sauce

¼ teaspoon sugar

1 scallion, white and green parts chopped

Heat a wok over high heat until it begins to smoke lightly. Add 1 teaspoon of the oil and the red onion. Stir-fry for 30 to 60 seconds, until the onion is lightly browned and just beginning to wilt. Transfer to your serving plate.

Reduce the heat to medium and add 1 tablespoon of the oil to the wok. Add the cauliflower and stir-fry for about 5 minutes, until it is lightly browned at the edges, slightly translucent, and about 75 percent cooked. Remove to a plate.

With the wok still over medium heat, add the remaining 2 tablespoons oil, then add the pork belly (if using) and stir-fry for 1 to 2 minutes, until some fat renders out and the pork belly turns lightly golden brown around the edges.

Add the garlic, ginger, and chilies, and cook for 30 seconds. Add the spicy bean sauce and stir until the oil in the wok turns red.

Increase the heat to high and add the bell pepper and then the cauliflower. Stir-fry to combine, then add the water, oyster sauce, Shaoxing wine, light soy sauce, sugar, and scallion. Continue stir-frying for 2 minutes, until there is no visible pool of liquid at the bottom of the wok and the cauliflower is tender.

Scoop the cauliflower over the bed of onions in the serving dish and serve immediately.

炒青菜 chǎo qīngcài
Leafy Greens, Four Ways

There are a few things to keep in mind for achieving res-taurant-style leafy vegetables. First, use oil liberally—it brings out the vibrant color of the greens and makes them silky in texture. Delicate greens like spinach and pea tips will require about 25 percent more oil than a sturdier green like bok choy. Second, you have to be patient enough to preheat your wok until it just starts to smoke *before* adding the oil to achieve wok hei (see page 23). Third, salting the greens well is important, but so is adding a small pinch of sugar (especially for bitter greens like mustard greens). The sugar provides just enough contrast to bring out the flavor of the vege-tables. As for MSG, adding a pinch or two in addition to salt will get you even closer to that coveted restaurant taste. (Sampling the liquid that pools at the bottom of the wok is a good way to gauge salt levels.)

In this recipe, you'll find the basic process for cook-ing the greens along with four ways to take them in dif-ferent directions (you may be familiar with them if a waiter at a Chinese restaurant has ever asked you how you want your greens cooked). Assemble the ingredi-ents (each variation starts with 1 pound of greens) and cook some of the best-tasting vegetables you'll ever eat!

Serves 4

Plain (qīng chǎo, 清炒)
The word qīng means "clear" or "clean." The dominant flavor is wok hei with salt.

1 pound leafy greens (such as baby bok choy, choy sum, or pea tips)

3 tablespoons neutral oil

¼ teaspoon fine sea salt, or to taste

⅛ teaspoon sugar

⅛ teaspoon white pepper powder

(RECIPE CONTINUES)

Garlicky (suàn róng, 蒜蓉)

This is the most popular go-to. Depending on the vegetable, you can also include ginger to enhance flavor.

1 pound leafy greens (such as baby bok choy, choy sum, or pea tips)

3 tablespoons neutral oil

4 large garlic cloves, smashed and minced

¼ teaspoon fine sea salt, or to taste

⅛ teaspoon sugar

⅛ teaspoon white pepper powder

Spicy (qiàng chǎo, 炝炒)

The word qiàng means to "tickle the throat," from the spice of dried chilies and Sichuan peppercorns.

1 pound leafy greens (such as baby bok choy, choy sum, or pea tips)

4 tablespoons neutral oil

4 large garlic cloves, smashed and thinly sliced

4 dried red chilies, each cut into thirds, with seeds retained

1 teaspoon whole red or green Sichuan peppercorns (optional)

¼ teaspoon fine sea salt, or to taste

⅛ teaspoon sugar

⅛ teaspoon white pepper powder

With Fermented Bean Curd

(fǔrǔ, 腐乳)

This is one of our favorites. The white fermented bean curd melts down into a mellow umami flavor.

1 pound leafy greens (such as spinach, water spinach, or pea tips)

3 tablespoons neutral oil

2 (⅛-inch-thick) slices fresh ginger

3 large garlic cloves, smashed and roughly chopped

2 tablespoons white fermented bean curd, drained

1 tablespoon Shaoxing wine

⅛ teaspoon fine sea salt, or to taste (the fermented bean curd is salty)

¼ teaspoon sugar

⅛ teaspoon white pepper powder

Thoroughly wash the vegetables (see instructions on page 233) shake off the excess water, and cut or tear into bite-size pieces. The vegetables should be mostly dry (too much moisture will prevent wok hei). Heat a wok over high heat until it's just starting to smoke.

FOR PLAIN GREENS: Spread the oil around the surface of the wok.

FOR GARLICKY GREENS: Spread the oil around the surface of the wok and immediately add the garlic. Stir for 10 seconds.

FOR SPICY GREENS: Spread the oil around the surface of the wok and immediately add the garlic, dried chilies, and Sichuan peppercorns. Stir for 10 seconds.

FOR FERMENTED BEAN CURD GREENS: Spread the oil around the surface of the wok and immediately add the ginger. Cook for 15 seconds. Add the garlic and fermented bean curd, and break up the bean curd so you have a paste. Cook for another 15 seconds.

Add the greens and stir-fry, keeping them constantly moving to coat them in oil. If making the fermented bean curd version, pour the Shaoxing wine around the perimeter of the wok when the greens are half wilted.

Gather the greens in the center of the wok to allow the sides to heat up. Cook over high heat for 30 to 60 seconds, until the greens are tender. For tougher greens like broccoli and gai lan, cover with the wok lid during this stretch. Only cover once to cook or the vegetables may lose their vibrant green color.

Using a swirling motion, stir and spread the greens around the sides of the wok. Add the salt, sugar, and white pepper. Stir-fry, gathering the greens to the center again and swirling them around the wok if they are not yet tender. Serve immediately.

椒盐平菇 jiāoyán píng gū

Salt & Pepper Fried Oyster Mushrooms

Salt & Pepper Pork Chops (page 185) have always been a must-have at any Cantonese meal, but the salt and white pepper mixture is actually delicious on freshly fried *anything*—in this case, crispy oyster mushrooms. Sand ginger powder and ground Sichuan peppercorns complement the white pepper and add additional flavor. Sand ginger powder can be elusive to find even in well-stocked Asian groceries, but galangal powder or five-spice powder also work.

Serves 4

1 teaspoon white pepper powder

¾ teaspoon fine sea salt

½ teaspoon onion powder

¼ teaspoon garlic powder

¼ teaspoon sand ginger powder, galangal powder, or five-spice powder

¼ teaspoon ground Sichuan peppercorns

1 tablespoon Shaoxing wine

½ teaspoon toasted sesame oil

12 ounces fresh oyster mushrooms, torn into bite-size pieces (about 6 cups)

¼ cup potato starch

Neutral oil, for frying

6 large garlic cloves, roughly chopped

2 small shallots, thinly sliced

1 small long hot green pepper or Anaheim pepper, seeded and thinly sliced (optional)

MAKE THE SALT AND PEPPER SEASONINGS: In a small bowl, combine ¾ teaspoon of the white pepper, ½ teaspoon of the salt, the onion powder, garlic powder, sand ginger, and ground Sichuan peppercorns. In another small bowl, mix the remaining ¼ teaspoon white pepper and ¼ teaspoon salt.

PREPARE THE MUSHROOMS: Drizzle the Shaoxing wine and sesame oil over the mushrooms. Toss the mushrooms to distribute, then sprinkle the larger spice seasoning over the mushrooms, tossing again to distribute. Next, sprinkle the potato starch over the mushrooms and toss to coat.

CRISP THE GARLIC: Line a plate with a paper towel. Fill a small pot with 2 to 3 inches of neutral oil. Heat the oil over medium heat to 250°F, or until a piece of garlic added to the oil bubbles gently. Toss in the garlic and cook until it just begins to turn a very light golden color, turning the garlic with a fine-mesh strainer for 2 to 4 minutes (no longer or it may become bitter). Remove the garlic with the strainer and transfer to the lined plate.

DO THE FIRST FRY: Set a wire cooling rack over a sheet pan or line a plate with paper towels. Bring the oil to 335°F over medium-high heat. Fry the mushrooms in three batches for 1 to 2 minutes each, until lightly golden. If they stick together, use chopsticks to gently pry them apart. Transfer to the wire rack or plate and let the mushrooms sit for at least 3 minutes before the second fry.

DO THE SECOND FRY: Heat the oil once again to 335°F, and fry the mushrooms a second time for 1 minute per batch, until they turn a deeper golden color.

ASSEMBLE THE DISH: Heat a dry wok over high heat. When the wok is just smoking, reduce the heat to medium-high and add the shallots and hot pepper (if using). Stir-fry for 30 to 60 seconds, until the shallots and pepper lose their raw edge.

Add the crispy garlic and the smaller mixture of salt and white pepper. Stir-fry for 15 seconds. Toss in the mushrooms and serve.

干煸四季豆 gān biān sìjì dòu

Dry-Fried Green Beans

Walk into any Sichuan restaurant and you're likely to see these green beans on at least half the tables. The beans are blistered until tender on the inside and wrinkly on the outside. Technically speaking, "dry-fried" constitutes an absence of oil—we've done that version on the blog. However, most restaurant versions of this dish use oil for flavor and texture. The oil actually makes the outside of the green beans more wrinkly, making it much easier for them to cling to the little bits of ground pork in the dish. Serve these beans with our Mapo Tofu (page 250), and you have a Sichuan feast on your hands. The one special ingredient you'll need here is suì mǐ yá cài, a type of Sichuan preserved vegetable sold in small vacuum-sealed packages. It makes a world of difference as the salty punctuation for every bite of green bean.

Serves 4

¼ cup neutral oil

1 pound fresh green beans, ends trimmed

1 teaspoon minced fresh ginger

3 dried red chilies, seeded and sliced into small pieces (optional)

1 tablespoon minced garlic (from about 3 cloves)

3 tablespoons Sichuan preserved vegetables (suì mǐ yá cài, 碎米芽菜)

4 ounces ground pork or chicken (optional)

2 tablespoons Shaoxing wine

2 teaspoons light soy sauce

½ teaspoon salt

½ teaspoon Sichuan peppercorn powder

¼ teaspoon sugar

Heat the oil in a wok over medium-high heat. When the oil is hot enough to sizzle a string bean, shallow-fry the green beans in two batches. Toss them every minute or so while they fry so they cook evenly. They are done when wrinkled and very lightly scorched. Each batch takes 5 to 7 minutes, depending on the size of your green beans and how hot your stove gets. Remove the green beans from the wok and set on a plate, leaving behind any oil in the wok.

With the wok over medium-low heat, add the ginger, dried chilies, and garlic and cook for 30 seconds. Increase the heat to medium-high and add the Sichuan preserved vegetables. Cook for 1 minute.

Increase the heat to high and add the ground pork (if using). Stir-fry to break up the meat. When the pork is opaque, add the fried string beans, the Shaoxing wine, light soy sauce, salt, Sichuan peppercorn powder, and sugar. Toss everything well and continue stir-frying over high heat until any remaining liquid has cooked off. Serve immediately.

手撕包菜 shǒu sī bāo cài

Hand-Torn Cabbage Stir-Fry

This scrumptious cabbage stir-fry is one of our stand-bys. It's okay to be skeptical—it's not often that you hear the words "scrumptious" and "cabbage" in the same sentence. But we're here to reclaim some dignity for the lowly cabbage. They last forever in the back of the refrigerator, which is why we never leave the Chinese grocery store without one. Flat Taiwanese cabbage is ideal because it has a mild flavor with looser, more tender leaves. That said, if you can't find Taiwanese cabbage, green cabbage will do. Hand-tearing the cabbage leaves into pieces creates the rough edges that cling to more sauce!

Serves 4

1¼ pounds Taiwanese **cabbage** or green cabbage

2½ tablespoons **neutral oil**

4 ounces pork shoulder, thinly sliced (optional)

5 large garlic cloves, smashed

2 (⅛-inch-thick) slices fresh ginger

5 dried red chilies, seeded and sliced into small pieces (optional)

2 scallions, white and green parts separated and cut into 2-inch lengths

1 tablespoon oyster sauce or vegetarian oyster sauce

1 tablespoon Shaoxing wine

1 tablespoon light soy sauce

½ teaspoon sugar

¼ teaspoon white pepper powder, or to taste

½ teaspoon Chinese black vinegar

Fine sea salt

Wash the cabbage leaves clean and spin them in a salad spinner to get them thoroughly dry. Rip the cabbage leaves into 1½- to 2-inch pieces.

Heat your wok over high heat until it starts to smoke lightly. Add the oil and sear the pork (if using) for 1 to 2 minutes, until lightly brown around the edges. Add the garlic, ginger, chilies (if using), and the white parts of the scallions. Reduce the heat to medium and stir-fry for 1 minute, taking care not to burn the garlic.

Increase the heat to high and add the cabbage. Stir-fry for 2 minutes, until the cabbage begins to wilt. Then add the oyster sauce, Shaoxing wine, light soy sauce, sugar, and white pepper. Mix well and cook for 1 to 2 minutes using high heat to cook off the liquid. (If you like the cabbage soft, cover and cook for 2 minutes.)

Stir in the black vinegar, the green parts of the scallions, and salt to taste. Serve immediately.

Coming to (the Great) America(n)

JUDY

I SPENT MUCH of my childhood living with my paternal grandmother in Shanghai (see page 68). My maternal grandmother, on the other hand, I never knew was alive until she flew from America to visit us in the late 1970s, right after China reopened its doors to the world.

Fleeing a wealthy but unfaithful husband as a very young woman, my grandmother left China when her five children were still babies. She'd always felt a great deal of guilt over this, and it was 1983 when she helped all five of her children and their families immigrate to the United States. I was sixteen years old.

There was a lot of excitement, but also nervousness. The promise of America was too romantic to be true. We were told that in America, biàndì dōu shì jīn (遍地都是金), or "the ground is covered with gold," just waiting to be picked up. But as a teenager halfway through high school, I was scared of the change and the prospect of mastering a new language. Our destination was a small Chinese community in Monticello, New York.

I don't remember much about my first-ever plane ride to the United States, but I'll never forget the night we landed at JFK airport. It was one long stream of firsts: going through immigration, glimpsing the New York City skyline, and driving the seemingly endless Lincoln Tunnel to New Jersey before heading north to get to upstate New York. But the real shock came with the pitstop at a Great American Supermarket on the New York State Thruway, where I encountered the "land of plenty" for the first time.

It was late at night, and the Great American was near closing time, so there were few shoppers. My cousins and I stood in the produce section under the fluorescent lights, staring at piles of vegetables we'd never seen before. I was shocked and nearly paralyzed in place. Why was there no line? Shouldn't there have been someone *guarding* all this food? Everything about it was utterly unbelievable, even verging on unthinkable. That first trip to a supermarket is forever etched in my mind. The Great American was as miraculous as the Great Wall.

That fateful pitstop at the Great American marked the beginning of my brand-new life. And trust me, there were many more surprises to come, from being

berated by my high school classmates for not speaking a word of English, to looking forward to the chance to dine out, thanks to the 99-cent Burger King Whopper (some things transcend language barriers). As my English got better, I met Bill and got an inside look at Chinese American restaurant culture, waitressing and helping out at Sun Hing (see page 191). I eventually came around to cheese (when we first arrived in America, my cousins and I thought it was awful!) and learned that my favorite snack before bed was a slice of peanut butter toast with chocolate milk. Our lives since then have continued to bridge two cultures. Now I can proudly say that I can eat the smelliest blue cheese with the best of them, make American pop culture references in everyday conversation, and that my English is good enough to write this essay (with a little help from my daughters)! Looking back, what a journey it has been.

From top, left to right: My father, younger brother, mother, and me during our first winter in America; sitting down to dinner with my grandmother on her first return visit to Shanghai--my mother (center) couldn't be happier; with my cousins enjoying our first Thanksgiving meal (there was a burnt turkey on the table somewhere, because we had no idea how to cook one); trying to look cool during my college years while studying fashion design in New York; posing on Lombard Street in San Francisco while on a trip; with Bill perusing a Chinatown seafood market.

家常豆腐 jiācháng dòufu

Homestyle Tofu

On some Chinese menus, you may see the word jiācháng in front of several dishes. It translates to "homestyle" or "family-style." When you order one of these dishes, you're rolling the dice to try that particular chef's spin on what their interpretation of "home" tastes like. This tofu is saucy (all the better to soak into some rice), with a good garlicky flavor and an ample variety of textures from the wood ears and peppers. You might say it's the taste of home we crave.

Serves 4

FOR THE MUSHROOMS AND TOFU

⅔ cup dried wood ear mushrooms

1 pound firm tofu, drained

FOR THE SAUCE

½ cup water

1 tablespoon cornstarch

1 tablespoon oyster sauce or vegetarian oyster sauce

1 tablespoon light soy sauce

1 teaspoon dark soy sauce

½ teaspoon sugar

¼ teaspoon fine sea salt

FOR THE REST OF THE DISH

3 tablespoons neutral oil

2 (⅛-inch-thick) slices fresh ginger

1 star anise

2 scallions, white and green parts separated and cut on a diagonal into 2-inch lengths

2 teaspoons minced garlic (about 2 cloves)

½ red bell pepper, seeded and cut into 1-inch pieces

½ green bell pepper, seeded and cut into 1-inch pieces, or 2 long hot green peppers or Anaheim peppers

1 tablespoon water

1 tablespoon Shaoxing wine

PREPARE THE MUSHROOMS AND TOFU: In a medium bowl, cover the wood ear mushrooms with water and soak for 2 hours or until rehydrated. Rinse them to remove any grit or dirt. Drain and cut the wood ears in half into bite-size pieces.

Cut the block of tofu crosswise into ½-inch-thick rectangles. Cut each rectangle on a diagonal into 2 triangles.

MAKE THE SAUCE: In a small bowl, combine the water, cornstarch, oyster sauce, light soy sauce, dark soy sauce, sugar, and salt.

PAN-FRY THE TOFU: Heat a wok over medium-high heat until lightly smoking. (Preheating the wok before adding oil creates a nonstick surface.) Add 2 tablespoons of the oil and swirl it around the wok to coat the surface. Carefully add the tofu pieces in a single layer and pan-fry for 4 minutes on the first side, until golden brown. Use a thin spatula to carefully flip the tofu pieces and fry on the other side for another 4 minutes, until golden. Transfer the tofu to a plate.

ASSEMBLE THE DISH: Over medium heat, add the remaining tablespoon oil, along with the ginger and star anise. Cook for 20 seconds, until fragrant. Add the white parts of the scallions and cook for another 20 to 30 seconds.

Add the wood ears, garlic, peppers, and 1 tablespoon water. Stir-fry for 1 minute, until the peppers are tender but still have a fresh crunch. Increase the heat to medium-high and add the Shaoxing wine around the perimeter of the wok.

Re-stir the sauce to make sure the cornstarch is well incorporated into the liquid. Add the sauce to the wok and bring it to a simmer. Let the sauce thicken until it coats the back of a spoon. (If it's too thick, add a splash of water.) Stir in the tofu and add the green parts of the scallions. Mix until the tofu and vegetables are evenly coated in sauce and the scallions are wilted. Serve.

麻婆豆腐 má pó dòufu
Mapo Tofu
with Fermented Black Beans

With every bite of mapo tofu, the signature numbing sensation from the Sichuan peppercorn builds. This version is dotted with fermented black beans for an extra hit of flavor, and it uses velveted ground pork, which results in a silky, restaurant-like texture. Be sure to use high-quality Sichuan peppercorns. You should see only the red husks, with none of the bitter, black inner seeds. Also consider the freshness of those Sichuan peppercorns. (Choose those with a bright red color and avoid any that are dull or discolored. A bag that has been languishing on a grocery store shelf may not be as fragrant and numbing.) High-quality peppercorns will pack a wallop, so we offer a range of 1 teaspoon to 1 tablespoon—add as much or as little as you like. To make this dish vegetarian, substitute mushrooms for the velveted ground pork. (We have a vegan version on the blog.)

Serves 4

FOR THE PORK

6 ounces ground pork

2 teaspoons water

1 teaspoon Shaoxing wine

¾ teaspoon cornstarch

⅛ teaspoon baking soda

⅛ teaspoon white pepper powder

FOR THE REST OF THE DISH

¼ cup neutral oil

3 tablespoons finely minced fresh ginger (from a 2-inch piece)

3 tablespoons finely minced garlic (about 9 to 10 cloves)

1 teaspoon to 1 tablespoon ground Sichuan peppercorns (to taste)

1½ tablespoons spicy bean sauce

1½ tablespoons fermented black beans, rinsed twice in cold water and drained

⅔ cup plus ¼ cup water

1½ teaspoons cornstarch

¼ cup Ultimate Chili Oil (page 275; standing oil only; no flakes)

1 pound silken or soft tofu, cut into 1-inch cubes

¼ teaspoon sugar

¼ teaspoon toasted sesame oil

1 scallion, white and green parts finely chopped

MARINATE THE PORK: In a medium bowl, combine the ground pork, water, Shaoxing wine, cornstarch, baking soda, and white pepper.

ASSEMBLE THE DISH: Heat a wok over medium heat. Add the oil, followed by the ginger. Cook for about 1 minute, until the ginger turns lightly golden. Add the garlic and cook for 2 minutes. The garlic should become fragrant but not darken in color. (Ensure the garlic and ginger don't burn, or the dish will be bitter.)

Add the ground pork and break up the meat to mix it with the garlic and ginger. Increase the heat to medium-high and cook until the pork is just cooked through, about 1 minute. Add the ground Sichuan peppercorns, reserving ½ teaspoon to sprinkle over the finished dish. Then add the spicy bean sauce and fermented black beans. Stir and cook for 30 seconds. Stir in ⅔ cup water. Bring to a simmer and let the mixture bubble for 1 minute.

Combine the cornstarch with the remaining ¼ cup water to make a slurry, then stir it into the center of the wok. Simmer for another 1 to 2 minutes to thicken the sauce.

Stir in the chili oil, then gently slide the tofu into the wok. Use your spatula to gently toss the tofu in the sauce while keeping the cubes intact. Add the sugar and sesame oil. Simmer for 4 to 5 minutes, giving it a stir at the halfway point. Gently fold in the scallion, just until wilted. Serve with a final sprinkle of the remaining ground Sichuan peppercorns.

香煎芝麻豆腐 xiāngjiān zhīma dòufu

Sesame-Crusted Tofu
with Spicy Dipping Sauce

This recipe is for anyone who *still* isn't convinced of the wonders of tofu. With a crispy, pan-fried sesame-seed coating, anyone who insists tofu is bland and boring will think again. As with anything golden brown and crispy, you'll want something fresh or acidic to go with it. The herby, spicy, garlicky dipping sauce here fits the bill perfectly. Hot oil is poured over the minced garlic, chili flakes, and herbs to release and mellow their flavors before the other sauce ingredients are mixed in. This technique is common when making Chinese dipping sauces and dressings. The sauce would also be great with Poached "White Cut" Chicken (page 144), or as an alternative dressing for Fast Sizzled Cucumber Salad (page 73). Serve this tofu alongside some stir-fried greens (see page 236) and rice, and dinner is set.

Serves 4

1 (14- to 16-ounce) package firm tofu, drained

⅓ **cup untoasted sesame seeds**

¼ **cup cornstarch**

¾ **teaspoon fine sea salt**

¼ **teaspoon five-spice powder**

¼ **teaspoon white pepper powder**

¼ **cup chopped fresh cilantro leaves and stems**

2 scallions, white and green parts chopped

2 teaspoons minced garlic (about 2 cloves)

2 teaspoons Sichuan chili flakes

¼ **cup neutral oil**

2 tablespoons light soy sauce

2 tablespoons water

1 teaspoon sugar

½ **teaspoon rice vinegar**

Cut the block of tofu in half lengthwise, and then cut it into ½-inch-thick slices.

In a shallow bowl, combine the sesame seeds, cornstarch, salt, five-spice powder, and white pepper. Carefully coat the tofu slices in this mixture on both sides, taking care to press the mixture into the tofu slices evenly and thoroughly.

In the following order, add the cilantro, scallions, garlic, and chili flakes to a small heatproof bowl. (You will pour hot oil over it, and you will want the oil to mostly hit the garlic and chili flakes on top.)

Heat a large nonstick pan or cast-iron skillet over medium heat. Add 3 tablespoons of the neutral oil and spread it around the pan. When the oil is shimmering, add the tofu slices. Fry for 4 to 5 minutes per side, until golden brown and crispy. Transfer the tofu to a serving platter.

In the same pan, add the remaining tablespoon oil and heat until shimmering. Then, pour the hot oil over the garlic–chili flake mixture, using a rubber spatula to scrape every last drop! Stir in the light soy sauce, water, sugar, and rice vinegar to make a dipping sauce, and serve it with the crispy tofu.

Soups & Stocks

For many (especially if you are Cantonese, like me), a meal is just not complete without soup. Soups warm you in fall and winter and rehydrate your body even during the warmer months. In my experience, making soup often requires special attention to technique. Changing one simple step can make the difference between just okay and excellent. Simmering pork bones over low heat yields a clear broth, whereas seared bones over high heat results in a milky consistency. Stirring slow and steady when you "drop" the egg into your Egg Drop Soup (page 261) results in perfect threads and smooth tendrils—stir too fast and you get a cloudy mix. While these are just a couple of our favorite soup-making tricks, we hope you learn even more in this chapter. BILL

上海馄饨 shànghǎi húntún

Shanghai Street-Stall Wonton Soup

JUDY Growing up, I remember small hole-in-the wall wonton vendors and eager customers lining up with cook pots to carry their wonton soup home in for sharing with family. While these street stalls have all but disappeared, Shanghainese people still love wonton soup—an ideal breakfast, quick lunch, simple dinner, or midnight hangover preventative. The wrappers are usually paper-thin, and the wontons are made small to get the perfect ratio of wrapper to filling (look for the thinnest you can find, and keep in mind that wontons made from thicker skins will be bigger and take longer to cook). For the soup base, use our Chicken & Pork Stock (page 268) or Vegetable Stock (page 269). Both can be prepared ahead of time and frozen until you're ready to make soup. You can also add optional toppings, like egg ribbons, seaweed, and dried shrimp. If you were to have this soup in Shanghai, there would be jars of chili oil, rice vinegar, and white pepper powder on the table for you to customize your bowl. Feel free to do the same at home!

This is a big batch of wontons, so we assume you'll be freezing the majority of them for later. Determine how many servings of soup you want to cook in each sitting, and then multiply the soup ingredients as needed. Figure 12 wontons per serving. Wontons cook quickly, so make sure to have the broth on the stove and toppings ready *before* dropping them into the boiling water. Also feel free to halve the recipe if this quantity is too large.

Makes about 96 (8 dozen) wontons, enough for 8 servings of soup

FOR THE WONTONS

1 pound ground pork (80% lean)

8 ounces peeled and deveined shrimp (any size), roughly chopped

½ cup water

4 teaspoons Shaoxing wine

1 tablespoon light soy sauce

1 tablespoon oyster sauce

2 teaspoons finely minced fresh ginger

1 teaspoon cornstarch

1 teaspoon fine sea salt

1 teaspoon toasted sesame oil

½ teaspoon white pepper powder

2 (14-ounce) packages wonton wrappers (thinner Shanghai-style wrappers preferred, about 50 per package)

¼ cup cool water, plus more as needed

FOR EACH SERVING OF SOUP

1½ cups Chicken & Pork Stock (page 268) or Vegetable Stock (page 269)

Fine sea salt

White pepper powder

A few drops of sesame oil

1 tablespoon finely chopped scallion, white and green parts

1-inch square piece of dried laver/seaweed (optional)

1 teaspoon dried shrimp flakes (optional)

1 teaspoon pork lard (optional)

A few strands of egg ribbons (see page 258; optional)

PREPARE THE WONTON FILLING: In a large bowl, combine the pork, shrimp, water, Shaoxing wine, light soy sauce, oyster sauce, ginger, cornstarch, salt, sesame oil, and white pepper. Using a rubber spatula or a pair of chopsticks, whip the pork and shrimp mixture in one

(RECIPE CONTINUES)

direction for a good 10 minutes, until it resembles a cohesive, sticky paste that holds together. (You can also mix the filling in a stand mixer fitted with the paddle attachment on low speed for 5 minutes.)

ASSEMBLE THE WONTONS: Line a sheet pan with parchment paper. To assemble each wonton, take a wonton wrapper and put 1 tablespoon of the filling in the center. Gently squeeze the wrapper around the ball of filling to seal. (The stickiness of the filling will help it seal.) Place on the sheet pan ¼-inch apart and continue assembling the wontons until no filling remains. Once assembled, you must immediately cook or freeze your wontons (see Tip).

Bring a large pot of water to a boil to cook the wontons.

PREPARE THE SOUP BASE: Bring the stock to a simmer on the stove, lower the heat, and cover to keep warm. To each individual serving bowl, add the salt and white pepper to taste, the sesame oil, and scallions. Add the dried laver, dried shrimp flakes, lard, and egg ribbons (if using).

COOK THE WONTONS AND SERVE: By now, your pot of water should be boiling. Stir the boiling water in a circle to keep it moving slowly (this will prevent the wontons from sticking to the bottom of the pot). At the same time, add the wontons (don't cook more than 40 wontons at a time in a large pot of water, or they will become starchy; to cook more, boil more water in a separate pot).

Bring the water to a boil again, then add ¼ cup of the cool water to stop the boiling. Continue cooking like this until the wontons float to the surface, 2 to 3 minutes (anytime the water comes back up to a vigorous boil, add another ¼ cup of cold water; this cools down the pot and prevents the wrappers from overcooking before the filling inside is fully cooked). When the wontons begin to float, simmer them for a final 30 seconds. Meanwhile, move quickly to ladle about 1½ cups of the stock into each serving bowl. Stir the bowls to mix the stock and seasonings. Scoop the wontons out with a strainer and transfer to the bowls. Serve immediately.

TIP! HOW TO FREEZE WONTONS
Transfer any uncooked wontons to the freezer within 1 hour of assembly (any longer, and the wrappers may become soggy and tear open). Place the wontons on a sheet pan lined with parchment paper ¼-inch apart to avoid sticking, cover with plastic wrap (or use a clean plastic grocery bag), and freeze overnight. When frozen solid, transfer them to a resealable bag or container and store for up to 3 months.

HOW TO MAKE EGG RIBBONS
Egg ribbons add color, texture, and additional flavor to this wonton soup. Here's how to make them.

Heat a 10-inch nonstick pan over medium heat. In a small bowl, mix ½ teaspoon cornstarch with 2 teaspoons water until combined. Beat in 1 egg. When the pan is hot, add 1 tablespoon neutral oil and spread it around the pan to coat. Pour in the egg mixture and immediately swirl it around the pan to cover the surface. Cook just until the egg is set, then use two rubber spatulas to carefully flip it over. Cook for another 10 seconds or so to cook it through, then transfer to a cutting board. Fold the egg circle into a half-moon, and then in half again lengthwise. Slice into ⅛-inch-wide ribbons.

酸辣汤 suān là tāng

Hot & Sour Soup

When it comes to hot and sour soup, there's no room for moderation. The first spoonful should make your mouth pucker a little bit, followed by a burn in the back of your throat that tickles the sinuses. And when it comes to textures, the more the better—with two kinds of mushrooms, two kinds of tofu, dried lily flowers, and bamboo. People often mistakenly think the "hot" merely comes from chilies, but it's ample amounts of white pepper that make the difference.

Serves 6 to 8

FOR THE MEAT (OPTIONAL)

4 ounces boneless pork or chicken, partially frozen and finely julienned

1 tablespoon water

1 teaspoon cornstarch

2 teaspoons neutral oil

⅛ teaspoon fine sea salt

FOR THE SOUP

8 cups low-sodium chicken stock, Chicken & Pork Stock (page 268), or Vegetable Stock (page 269)

1 to 2 teaspoons freshly ground white pepper

1 tablespoon light soy sauce

2 teaspoons dark soy sauce

1 teaspoon toasted sesame oil

½ teaspoon fine sea salt

¼ teaspoon sugar

1 or 2 dried red chilies, seeded and sliced into small pieces (optional)

¼ teaspoon MSG (optional)

¼ cup dried lily flower, soaked in hot water for 2 hours, ends trimmed and cut in half

¼ cup dried wood ear mushrooms, soaked in hot water for 2 hours and roughly chopped

2 to 3 medium dried shiitake mushrooms, soaked in hot water for 2 hours and thinly sliced

¾ cup julienned bamboo shoots (about 4 ounces)

3 ounces spiced or plain pressed tofu (dòufu gān, 豆腐干), cut into 2-inch-long, ¼-inch-thick slices

4 ounces firm tofu, cut into 2-inch long, ¼-inch-thick slices

⅓ to ½ cup white vinegar

⅓ cup cornstarch

½ cup water

1 large egg, lightly beaten

1 scallion, white and green parts finely chopped

SEASON THE MEAT (IF USING): In a medium bowl, combine the pork with the water, cornstarch, neutral oil, and salt. Mix until the meat has absorbed the liquid in the marinade, and marinate for 20 minutes.

MAKE THE SOUP: In a nonreactive soup pot, bring the chicken stock to a boil over high heat. If the pork has clumped and stuck together, add another tablespoon water to loosen it. Stir the pork into the boiling stock, breaking up any clumps. Bring the soup to a simmer again and use a fine-mesh strainer to skim off any foam that floats to the top.

Use your fingers to sprinkle 1 teaspoon of the white pepper evenly over the soup (this prevents clumping), then add the light soy sauce, dark soy sauce, sesame oil, salt, sugar, dried chili (if using), and MSG (if using). Stir in the lily flowers, wood ears, shiitake mushrooms, and bamboo shoots. Bring the soup back up to a simmer, then stir in all the tofu and ⅓ cup of the vinegar.

Combine the cornstarch and water to make a slurry. With the soup simmering, use a ladle to stir the soup in a steady circular motion while drizzling in about three-fourths of the slurry. Check the consistency of the soup; it should be thick enough to coat the ladle. If it's too thick, add a little more stock or water; if it's too thin, add the remaining slurry. Taste and adjust the seasoning if necessary. Add more white pepper (up to 2 teaspoons total) for heat and more vinegar (up to ½ cup total) for tartness.

Keep the soup simmering (it should be bubbling before you add the egg, or the soup will turn cloudy). Use a ladle to stir it in a circular motion, and gradually pour the egg into the center of the soup (only the ladle moves while the egg is drizzled in at a slow and steady pace—see Egg Drop Soup on page 261 for more detail on this technique). The egg should immediately "flower" into cooked strands. Serve, garnished with the chopped scallion.

蛋花汤 dàn huā tāng
Egg Drop Soup

Everyone knows that game-time decision moment: egg drop, hot and sour, or wonton soup? Arguably the most popular and ubiquitous is egg drop soup. Ideally, you'll have a pleasant range of egg tendrils that bloom in the simmering broth (which is why the Chinese name for this soup translates to "egg flower soup"). If you lightly beat the eggs before pouring them in, you'll get egg flowers that are white or light yellow, with a superior mouthfeel and substantial taste.

Serves 2 to 4

4 cups low-sodium chicken stock, Chicken & Pork Stock (page 268), or Vegetable Stock (page 269)

¾ teaspoon fine sea salt

¾ teaspoon toasted sesame oil

⅛ teaspoon MSG (optional)

⅛ teaspoon sugar

⅛ teaspoon white pepper powder

⅛ teaspoon turmeric or 2 to 3 drops yellow food coloring (optional, but if you want "the look" . . .)

3½ tablespoons cornstarch

¼ cup water

2 large eggs, lightly beaten

1 scallion, white and green parts chopped (optional)

In a medium pot, bring the chicken stock to a simmer over medium-high heat. Stir in the salt, sesame oil, MSG (if using), sugar, white pepper (use your fingers to sprinkle it evenly over the soup to prevent clumping), and turmeric (if using). Taste the soup and adjust the seasoning, if needed.

Combine the cornstarch and water to make a cornstarch slurry, then gradually add it to the soup while stirring. Start with two-thirds of the mixture and simmer for 1 minute before checking the consistency. If you'd like it thicker, add the rest of the slurry. If it's too thick, add a splash of water or stock until you reach the desired consistency.

Now we're ready for the most exciting part: adding the egg. The soup should be at a low simmer so it's hot enough to cook the egg upon contact. (Note: This is where many people make the mistake of keeping the temperature too low, which results in a cloudy soup with insubstantial bits of egg.) If it's too hot—at a rolling boil—the egg may cook too quickly, resulting in large chunks of egg instead. The speed at which you stir the soup while adding the egg also determines whether you get large or small "egg flowers." The faster you stir, the smaller and more dispersed the egg will be. Stir slower and you'll get larger egg tendrils, as they have a chance to set in the hot broth). With the soup at a simmer, use a ladle to stir it in a circular motion, and gradually pour the egg in a thin stream into the center of the soup (only the ladle moves while the egg is drizzled in at a slow and steady pace).

Simmer the soup for 20 seconds more, then ladle it into serving bowls. Top with the chopped scallion (if using).

酸汤肥牛 suān tāng féi niú

Golden Soup
with Shaved Beef

This alluring golden soup is a popular Sichuan restaurant dish. Its beautiful color, achieved with a small amount of pumpkin puree, belies the pungent yet well-balanced sour and spicy flavors. The other key ingredient is store-bought Hainan yellow lantern chili sauce, which has a full-bodied heat and is mellowed just enough by thin slices of fatty, marbled beef and tender strands of enoki mushroom. For the chili sauce, we give a range of 1 to 2 tablespoons, so taste along the way to get the levels of chili and vinegar the way you like them. As for the beef, look in the freezer section of Chinese grocery stores for very thinly sliced, well-marbled beef for hot pot. That's the stuff to buy for this.

Serves 4 to 6

14 ounces fresh enoki mushrooms, roots trimmed, ripped into bite-size pieces

2 tablespoons Shaoxing wine

1 pound very thinly shaved fatty beef, slices separated

4 tablespoons neutral oil

3 (⅛-inch-thick) slices fresh ginger, julienned

6 large garlic cloves, finely chopped

1 to 2 tablespoons yellow lantern chili sauce

¼ cup fresh or canned unsweetened pumpkin puree

4 cups low-sodium chicken stock or Chicken & Pork Stock (page 268)

¼ cup white vinegar

¾ teaspoon sugar

Fine sea salt

2 long hot red or green peppers or Anaheim peppers, roughly chopped

1 scallion, white and green parts finely chopped

Fill a wok about halfway with water and bring to a boil over high heat. Add the enoki mushrooms and cook in the boiling water for 30 seconds. Scoop them out with a strainer and shake off excess water. Place the mushrooms in the bottom of a wide, deep, heatproof serving bowl.

Return the water in the wok to a full boil, then add 1 tablespoon of the Shaoxing wine and the beef slices. Cook just until the beef turns opaque, about 20 seconds. Remove using a strainer, and transfer to the serving bowl, placing the beef slices on top of the enoki mushrooms. Discard the cooking water and wash the wok.

Place the clean wok over medium-low heat and heat until any moisture has evaporated. Add 2 tablespoons of the oil, along with the ginger and two-thirds of the garlic. Cook for 1 minute, then add the yellow lantern chili sauce and pumpkin puree. Cook for 2 minutes.

Add the remaining tablespoon Shaoxing wine and the stock. Bring to a boil and then add the vinegar, sugar, and salt to taste. Simmer the broth for 3 more minutes.

Strain the soup through a fine-mesh strainer into the serving bowl, on top of the beef and enoki mushrooms. Discard any solids in the strainer. Top the beef with the chopped peppers, scallion, and remaining minced garlic.

Heat the remaining 2 tablespoons oil in a wok or small saucepan until shimmering, then pour it over the chilies and garlic. It will sizzle immediately and the fragrance of the aromatics will hit your nose! Serve.

广式例汤 guǎng shì lì tāng

Cantonese Lai Tong

JUDY — At some of our favorite Cantonese restaurants in Manhattan and Queens, the meal always starts with a tureen of lai tong (lì tāng, in Mandarin) or "daily soup," made with whatever ingredients they have on hand. Light, salty, savory, and slightly sweet, it's slow-simmered for hours to achieve nothing short of liquid gold. Having married into a Cantonese family, I sought to perfect this kind of soup years ago. Luckily, it wasn't hard. Just put all the ingredients in a pot, add water, and simmer away. This version uses classic Cantonese soup ingredients, including dried bok choy, dried figs, Chinese red dates, mandarin orange peel, and goji berries. You'll find them in well-stocked Chinese markets (likely in the same aisle). Make sure you're buying Chinese dried figs, as they are less sweet than figs sold for snacking and baking. If using pork ribs instead of neck bones, we call for an extra pound, as they're a bit less flavorful. This is a great soup to make in advance, because it tastes even better the next day.

Serves 8 to 10

2 ounces dried bok choy, soaked overnight

4 large dried shiitake mushrooms, soaked overnight

2 pounds meaty pork neck bones or 3 pounds pork ribs, soaked for 1 hour

13 cups water

2 to 3 large carrots, cut into large chunks (about 8 ounces)

3 (⅛-inch-thick) slices fresh ginger

2 dried Chinese red dates

6 Chinese dried figs

1 small piece (2g) dried mandarin orange peel

2 tablespoons (10g) dried Goji berries

1½ teaspoons fine sea salt, plus more to taste

Rinse the soaked bok choy clean and cut it into 1-inch pieces. If the soaking water looks clean and clear, that means the bok choy was thoroughly cleaned before it was dried and you can reserve the soaking water to use in the soup. If there's sediment, discard the water. In any event, reserve the mushroom-soaking water for the soup and let any sediment settle.

Add the soaked pork bones to a heavy-bottomed soup pot and add enough water to cover. Bring to a boil and boil the bones for 1 minute. Drain in a colander, rinse the pork, and wash out the pot. This step (along with the 1 hour of soaking) ensures a clear broth with a clean flavor.

Add the pork bones back to the pot, along with the bok choy, shiitake mushrooms, the 13 cups of water (including however much water you have from soaking the bok choy and the mushrooms), the carrots, ginger, dates, figs, orange peel, and goji berries. Cover and bring to a boil. Reduce the heat to the lowest setting and simmer for 4 hours. Do not stir or increase the heat; this keeps the broth clear.

Stir in the salt. Taste for seasoning and add more salt to taste just before serving.

SERVING TIP! While the prize of this soup is the broth itself, you can serve the pork bones with light soy sauce for dipping. It's a simple and delicious combination.

西湖牛肉羹 *xīhú niúròu gēng*

West Lake Soup

West Lake, famous for its swaying willows, towering pagodas, and natural beauty, is nestled in the city of Hangzhou, in Zhejiang Province. The steady hum of tourists who visit the lake's gardens and temples is as constant as the sound of the water lapping on its shores, punctuated only by the occasional tour guide's voice over a microphone, corralling their charges. This soup is named after the lake—perhaps owing to its origins in Zhejiang, or perhaps because the bright green cilantro suspended in the thickened broth brings to mind the lake's rippling water and aquatic plants, while the egg whites resemble clouds reflected on the lake's surface.

Given this soup's depth of flavor, you'll be surprised how quickly it comes together. Much of that flavor comes from ample amounts of chopped cilantro, which, we promise, is mellow and perfectly herbaceous. Last note: Take the time to finely chop the beef—it makes a world of difference. Ground beef, which some recipes call for, can sometimes result in a dry, mealy texture.

Serves 6 to 8

FOR THE BEEF

8 ounces boneless beef sirloin or flank steak, partially frozen

1 tablespoon water

1 teaspoon cornstarch

2 teaspoons light soy sauce

2 teaspoons Shaoxing wine

1 teaspoon neutral oil

¼ teaspoon baking soda

FOR THE SOUP

8 cups low-sodium chicken stock or Chicken & Pork Stock (page 268)

⅓ cup cornstarch

½ cup water

Fine sea salt

½ teaspoon white pepper powder

¼ teaspoon toasted sesame oil

3 large egg whites, lightly beaten

6 ounces soft tofu, cut into ¼-inch cubes

1½ cups finely chopped fresh cilantro leaves and stems

PREPARE THE BEEF: Finely dice the beef into ¼-inch pieces. (This is easier when the beef is partially frozen and still firm.) In a medium bowl, combine the beef with the water, cornstarch, light soy sauce, Shaoxing wine, neutral oil, and baking soda. Marinate for 30 minutes.

Bring a soup pot filled halfway with water to a boil over medium-high heat. Add the beef and blanch just until it turns opaque, about 30 seconds. Remove using a strainer or drain through a fine-mesh strainer, then set aside. Discard the beef-cooking water and clean out the pot.

MAKE THE SOUP: Place the pot back on the stove over medium-high heat, add the chicken stock, and bring to a simmer.

Combine the cornstarch and water to make a slurry, then gradually pour about three-fourths of it into the simmering broth, stirring constantly. Cook for 2 minutes, until thickened. If it's too thick, add a little more stock or water. If it's too thin, add the remaining slurry.

Season the soup with salt to taste, then use your fingers to sprinkle the white pepper evenly over the soup (this prevents the white pepper from clumping). Add the sesame oil.

Bring the soup back to a simmer, and use a ladle to stir the soup in one direction to create a whirlpool. Slowly stream in the egg whites while stirring continuously, until the egg whites "flower" into strands (see Egg Drop Soup on page 261 for more detail on this technique). Stir in the beef and add the tofu cubes, then simmer for 2 minutes to heat through. Finally, stir in the cilantro. Taste and adjust the seasoning once more. Serve immediately, while the cilantro is still bright green.

猪骨鸡骨高汤 zhū gǔ jī gǔ gāotāng
Chicken & Pork Stock

Unlike western stock or broth recipes that use an assortment of vegetables, herbs, and spices, Chinese cooking is all about making stocks in their purest possible form, not only so they can be used in a multitude of ways but also so the flavors of the chicken or pork really shine. In this case, it's the combination of both that makes this stock so good, yielding a savory, clear broth that's more than the sum of its parts. Use this stock for recipes like Crossing the Bridge Noodles (page 116) and Shanghai Street-Stall Wonton Soup (page 257), when the stock is just as important as what's in the soup. You can also use it in stir-fries and braises that call for stock.

Makes about 4 quarts

2¼ pounds chicken parts and bones (ideal to have some meat on the bones; economical options include chicken backs, necks, drumsticks, and/or a stewing chicken)

2¼ pounds pork neck bones or 3¼ pounds pork ribs

4 quarts water

4 (⅛-inch-thick) slices fresh ginger

3 scallions, trimmed

Soak the chicken and pork bones in a large bowl of cold water for 1 hour. It's best to change the water one or two times during this process. (This step is important, as it helps ensure you get a clear, pure-tasting stock.)

Drain the chicken and pork, then transfer to a large, heavy-bottomed stockpot (the thick bottom helps to ensure minimal amounts of stock will evaporate). Add the 4 quarts of water, the ginger, and scallions.

Bring to a boil over high heat, then reduce the heat to low. Skim off any foam floating on top, then cover the pot and simmer for 5 to 6 hours. The stock should simmer slowly, with movement but no visible bubbles. Do not stir it. The slow simmer will cook the stock and keep it clear at the same time.

When the stock is finished cooking, turn off the heat and let cool before straining. Skim off any grease (as desired) and store the stock for future use. It will keep for 4 to 5 days in the refrigerator, or for 4 months in the freezer. If freezing, leave 1-inch clearance in your freezer-safe containers, as the stock will expand as it freezes.

Judy's Homemade Chicken Stock

TIP! After simmering for 5 to 6 hours, the chicken will be quite dry and can be discarded. The pork bones, however, can be enjoyed with light soy sauce for dipping! If pork is not part of your diet, scan the QR code to check out our recipe for plain chicken stock.

全素汤底 quán sù tāng dǐ

Vegetable Stock

If you make our Chicken & Pork Stock, you'll be shocked by how well this entirely plant-based version creates a similar depth of flavor. Thanks to the white fermented bean curd (adds tons of umami), shiitake mushrooms (more umami), and dried kelp (triple umami!), there's no sacrifice here. Use this stock as a soup base or drink it straight out of the pot. Either way, you'll be utterly amazed by its rich taste.

Makes about 4 quarts

½ **large napa cabbage** (about 1½ pounds)

2 **tablespoons neutral oil**

7 **(⅛-inch-thick) slices fresh ginger**

2 **large garlic cloves,** smashed

2 **tablespoons white fermented bean curd**

1 **large onion,** quartered

1 **pound carrots,** cut into large chunks

8 **scallions,** cut in half

8 **ounces daikon radish,** peeled and cut into large chunks

1 **(5-inch) piece dried kelp/kombu,** rinsed

16 **medium to large dried shiitake mushrooms,** rinsed thoroughly

4½ **quarts water**

Fine sea salt

Position an oven rack in the center of the oven, then preheat the oven to 375°F.

Cut the napa cabbage half in half again lengthwise. Place the cabbage on a sheet pan and drizzle lightly with 1 tablespoon of the oil. Roast for 25 minutes, until the cabbage is wilted and browned at the edges.

In a stockpot or other large, heavy-bottomed pot, heat the remaining tablespoon oil over medium heat. Add the ginger and garlic, and cook for 1 to 2 minutes, until fragrant but not browned. Add the fermented bean curd and cook for 1 minute. Then add the roasted cabbage, along with the onion, carrots, scallions, daikon, kelp, dried shiitake mushrooms, and water.

Bring the contents of the stockpot to a boil, reduce the heat to low, cover, and simmer for 4 hours.

Strain the stock and season with salt to taste. The stock will keep for 4 to 5 days in the refrigerator, or for 4 months in the freezer. If freezing, leave 1-inch clearance in your freezer-safe containers, as the stock will expand as it freezes.

A Food Blogger Who Can't Follow a Recipe

& Other Cosmic Jokes

KAITLIN

I CAN'T FOLLOW a recipe. Seriously.

Even when I *think* I've followed a recipe to the letter, Sarah will pipe up during mealtimes and say, "Did you add the [insert thing hiding in plain sight that I will kick myself about]?" My fork stops mid-air—"Oops." Sarah purses her lips in the way that only older sisters do, and we all laugh, once again reassured of the universe's grand design (or maybe grand neglect) that I am a food blogger who cannot follow a recipe for the life of me.

I don't know where this unfortunate proclivity—or rather, lack thereof—came from, though I suspect it has something to do with the fact that I duped the world into thinking I was a "smart kid."

In fourth grade, we moved to a different town, and I started in a new school. That's when my scam really began. Before I'd even settled in, I was expected to fall into line as "the smart Chinese kid." I somehow got into the "advanced" fifth-grade classes, and these kids just *assumed* I was great at math (HA!). They hadn't seen a flubbed "gifted" test from third grade, my altogether average attempts at long division, or the fact that my dad had to step in to save my pitiful floundering butt at the first-grade science fair. Didn't they know I was just another eleven-year-old doofus? But out of a sense of survival, I latched on to being one of the smart kids. And so I became *smart* overnight.

After a while, fortunately or unfortunately, I clung to my identity as "the smart Chinese girl." Through some sheer force of will, and a "healthy" younger-sibling complex (Sarah's reputation always preceded me), I kept at it and found myself a high school valedictorian. I don't say all this to brag but rather to make it unequivocally clear that my inner B student is absolutely *bursting* to get out of her cage whenever the chance arises.

Clockwise from top left: This was snapped right after a retelling of an embarrassing childhood story—let's just say it involves duck fat; eating ramen noodles on a camping trip in Yosemite; Sarah and I in the Forbidden City on our first trip to China; pretending to be a waiter serving my parents a dinner that Sarah and I cooked—I may not have been the most diligent in the kitchen, but I was always enthusiastic!

Exhibit A: cooking. When your guard is down in your kitchen, it's all too easy to forget to marinate the chicken until the last minute, or to accidentally double the garlic, or to realize that you don't have country ribs like you thought and that the vaguely porky frost-covered thing in the freezer is actually pork belly, and now you need to completely change your dinner plans. From missed ingredients and overlooked steps to a persistent delusion and optimism that, no, the heat's not too high (it is)—if you can think it up, I've botched it.

But it has also occasionally ended in some pretty quality results. After all, when you're not busy following a recipe, you can spend your energy looking at how the fish is coming along, or add some extra ginger or fermented tofu to the wok because that's just how you like it. Some of our favorite recipes, like spicy lo mein noodles (dubbed "Kaitlin's Special Noodles," an early blog recipe) came from my lack of structure in the kitchen.

The secret to being a great home cook is often just about perseverance: If you mess something up, so what? Trust me; more often than not, you can salvage the situation, and as long as the end result still tastes good, you're golden. My mother always says that cooking a meal for someone is hard work, but the most important thing is simply that you care. What happens in between is open to interpretation. You know what you want your food to taste like, regardless of what *we* say. Sometimes, when judgment comes with those first few bites, and the writing's on the wall—yes, you did flub the soup—you dust yourself off and try again. Being a great cook is more about practice than about precision. Techniques that once seemed daunting become second nature, and recipes come to you from memory. I'll never have Sarah's focus in the kitchen, but at some point one comes to realize that you *can* make that substitution, and everything will be okay. (It's neither here nor there whether it was fully, uh, intentional . . .) You can even cook the noodles while you have one eye on whatever you're binge-watching at the moment, because this is YOUR domain.

So anyway, I've got some nerve writing recipes and asking people to follow them when, meanwhile, I'm hovering over my own screen—with my own mother's braised pork belly recipe no less—blatantly and unknowingly mixing up the measurements for light soy sauce . . . Er, wait, was it supposed to be dark soy sauce?

Sauces

I operate on two levels: can't follow a recipe or obsessively sleuthing out details to get the perfect results. The latter devotion is how we've gotten some of our best go-to chili oils and sauces over the years. (It's the fortunate loophole in my struggle to follow recipes, much to everyone's relief.) That said, I encourage you to channel a little bit of that alternative energy when making these sauces. Cook by your own sight, taste, and smell—while using these recipes as a guide—to create sauces that are perfect for your own palate. While you can let your creativity loose and add any sauce to anything your heart desires, there's also a benefit to knowing which sauce is truly best with what kind of dish. We wouldn't have you dip a dumpling into ginger-scallion oil, but a bowl of noodle soup just isn't as good without a generous drizzle of our Ultimate Chili Oil (page 275). **KAITLIN**

香辣红油 xiāng là hóng yóu
Ultimate Chili Oil

This chili oil changed our lives, giving us a boost for everyday dumplings and the confidence to conquer the realm of spicy Sichuan cooking. The key is to infuse the oil with a complex mixture of spices and aromatics, and heat it to the right temperature to get the perfect sizzle (and nutty aroma), while pouring it over the Sichuan chili flakes. When you stir the oil and flakes, you get the perfect drizzle for noodles and dumplings, but if you let the flakes settle, you have a pourable, pure chili oil for dishes like Mapo Tofu (page 250).

Makes 1½ cups

1½ cups neutral oil (such as peanut oil, canola oil, or vegetable oil)

1 Chinese cassia cinnamon stick, about 3 inches long

4 star anise

3 tablespoons whole Sichuan peppercorns

2 large dried bay leaves

1 teaspoon whole cloves

1 black cardamom pod

3 pieces dried sand ginger (about ½ tablespoon)

2 large garlic cloves, lightly crushed

1 medium shallot, halved

¾ cup Sichuan chili flakes

½ teaspoon fine sea salt, or to taste (optional)

Add the oil, cinnamon stick, star anise, Sichuan peppercorns, bay leaves, cloves, black cardamom, dried sand ginger, garlic, and shallot to a small pot or deep saucepan with at least 2 inches of clearance between the top of the oil and the rim of the pot.

Set the pot over medium heat to start, then gradually reduce the heat to medium-low or low as the oil heats up to between 225° and 250°F. The heat will cause tiny bubbles to slowly rise from the spices, and it will gently fry the garlic and shallot. If you notice the spices sizzling more vigorously than that or turning dark too quickly, reduce the heat or remove the pot from the heat entirely. Hovering closer to 225°F is the safest way to

prevent burning. Infuse the oil with the spices for at least 30 minutes or up to 1 hour for the best results, removing the garlic and shallot when they are a uniformly deep golden color. The spices should be dark, but not black or burned.

Place the Sichuan chili flakes in a heatproof medium bowl.

Use a slotted spoon to remove most of the spices from the oil; discard the spices. Increase the heat slightly to raise the temperature of the oil a bit. The right temperature will depend on how roasted the chili flakes are and how you prefer your chili oil. If you have very roasted, dried flakes, keep the oil between 250°F and 275°F. If you like a darker color, or if the flakes are a bright red and not as roasted and dried, bring the oil to between 275°F and 300°F. If you have chili flakes that are very fresh with a higher moisture content (they will feel more tacky than bone dry and will be a very bright red), the oil may need to be as hot as between 325°F and 350°F to achieve the correct sizzling effect. Your best bet is to test the oil temperature on a small amount of chili flakes—but do it quickly as the oil will cool as it sits.

Carefully pour the hot oil through a fine-mesh strainer onto the chili flakes. The flakes should sizzle, but not burn, and you'll smell a popcorn-like aroma. Stir to evenly distribute the heat of the oil.

At this point, stir in the salt (if using; or choose to keep your chili oil unsalted for use in other recipes, such as our Shortcut Dan Dan Noodles on page 97).

Allow the chili oil to cool, then store it in airtight containers in the refrigerator. Always use a clean utensil when dipping into it to prevent spoilage. The chili oil can last for up to 6 months if handled in this way, but we're pretty sure you won't have it that long.

蘸汁 zhàn zhī

Ultimate Dipping Sauce

This dipping sauce is reminiscent of the zingy table-side concoctions we had at hole-in-the-wall dumpling and bao houses in Beijing—heavy on raw garlic and the white, onion-y part of the scallion. Serve this with dumplings, buns, and scallion pancakes.

Makes about ¼ cup

1 teaspoon sugar

1 tablespoon hot water

1 tablespoon light soy sauce

1 teaspoon minced garlic

1 teaspoon rice vinegar

½ teaspoon toasted sesame oil

1 scallion, white part only, finely chopped

Ultimate Chili Oil (page 275; optional)

In a small bowl, dissolve the sugar in the hot water. Add the light soy sauce, garlic, rice vinegar, sesame oil, and scallion. Mix in a little chili oil (if using) to taste.

广式姜葱茸 (生)

guǎng shì jiāng cōng rōng (shēng)

Raw Ginger-Scallion Oil

There are two types of ginger-scallion oil: raw and cooked. The raw version preserves the spicy zing of the ginger and the bright oniony flavor of scallions, perfectly balanced with the oil. The salt doesn't just offer support, but also a flavor all its own, as the granules are suspended in the oil rather than dissolved, giving a salty bite to everything it's added to. This raw ginger-scallion oil is the traditional dipping sauce for Poached "White Cut" Chicken (page 144) but is also fantastic on rice with a fried egg. It can even be dolloped into a pan of hot oil to sauté leafy green vegetables when you're too lazy to cut fresh ginger.

Makes about ½ cup

2 scallions, white and green parts, trimmed, patted dry, and finely minced

3 tablespoons finely minced fresh ginger (from a 2-inch piece, peeled)

⅓ **cup neutral oil**

½ **teaspoon fine sea salt,** or to taste

Combine the scallions, ginger, oil, and salt in a small bowl. Mix thoroughly and serve!

广式姜葱茸 (熟) guǎng shì jiāng cōng róng (shú)

Cooked Ginger-Scallion Oil

At Hong Kong BBQ meat shops and restaurants, the recipe for cooked ginger-scallion oil is a closely guarded secret. For *years*, we'd go to our local roast-meat hookup—I'm talkin' about combo plates of char siu (see page 173), siu yuk (see page 180), and roast duck (page 153)—but we were never able to figure out what made their ginger-scallion oil so delicious. The secret? Vital flavor amplifiers of fish sauce, clear rice wine, and sand ginger powder, in that order of importance. If you think you hate fish sauce, trust us—a few drops in this oil make a big difference without adding fishiness (though it is optional if you'd like to keep this vegetarian). This sauce is a life-affirming hit of salty concentrated ginger flavor that's absolutely incredible with Cantonese roast meats.

Heat the oil in a small saucepan over medium heat until it just starts to shimmer. Stir in the scallions, coating them in the oil. After about 20 seconds, stir in the fresh ginger.

Reduce the heat slightly and cook for 7 to 8 minutes. The ginger should turn a duller yellow color and lose its raw bite.

Clear a space in the center of the saucepan and add the sand ginger powder, fish sauce (if using), and rice wine. Let the fish sauce and rice wine sizzle for a few seconds before stirring to combine.

Season with salt and serve.

Makes about ½ cup

7 tablespoons neutral oil

3 scallions, white and green parts, trimmed, patted dry, and finely chopped

½ cup roughly grated fresh ginger (from a 6-inch piece, peeled)

⅛ teaspoon sand ginger powder

⅛ teaspoon fish sauce (optional)

⅛ teaspoon clear rice wine

¾ teaspoon fine sea salt, or to taste

XO 醬 xo jiàng

XO Sauce

XO sauce is a luxurious condiment originating in Hong Kong, combining golden dried scallops, dried shrimp, and cured ham. To make it is more time-consuming than buying it, of course, but every time you add a scoop of the homemade stuff to enrich rice, noodles, or a big wok of leafy greens, you'll be glad you took the time. If you can, splurge on the slightly bigger, deep golden dried scallops, which have a richer flavor. For the shrimp, most sizes will work; just avoid the really miniscule feathery dried shrimp flakes (xiāpí, 虾皮). At every step of this recipe, be mindful of cooking temperatures and times. Invest in an instant-read thermometer; the ingredients are expensive, and you don't want to accidentally burn a batch! Also, be aware that preparation involves cooking in two woks (or a wok and a skillet) at the same time.

Makes about 2¾ cups

2¾ ounces dried shrimp (about ¾ cup)

2¾ ounces dried scallops (about ⅔ cup)

6 teaspoons Shaoxing wine

4 cups boiling water

1 (2½-ounce) piece Chinese cured ham or other dry-cured ham (about the size of half a deck of cards)

½ cup low-sodium chicken stock

1½ teaspoons light or dark brown sugar

1¾ cups neutral oil

1 to 3 fresh Thai bird's-eye chilies, finely diced (optional)

¾ cup finely minced shallots (from 4 to 5 medium)

1½ teaspoons dark soy sauce

¼ cup finely minced garlic (from about 10 large cloves)

1 tablespoon oyster sauce or fish sauce

2 tablespoons Sichuan chili flakes (optional)

SOAK THE DRIED SEAFOOD: Place the dried shrimp and dried scallops into two separate medium bowls. Add 1 teaspoon of Shaoxing wine to each bowl, along with enough boiling water to submerge the seafood (about 2 cups water for each bowl). Soak the shrimp for 1 hour. Soak the scallops for at least 2 hours (or up to 6 hours). Drain the shrimp and scallops, saving the soaking water for future stocks and soups, if desired.

STEAM THE SCALLOPS AND HAM: Place the soaked scallops in a shallow heatproof bowl, then add the ham in one piece. Place a metal steaming rack in a wok and fill the wok with enough water to come up to about 1 inch below the rack. (Or if your shallow bowl can fit into it, use a bamboo steamer and fill the wok with enough water to come ½ inch up the bottom rim of the steamer. Note that you may have to add more boiling water during steaming to maintain this water level.) Bring the water in the wok to a simmer over medium-high heat. Place the bowl of scallops and ham on the rack or in the bamboo steamer, cover, and steam over medium-high heat for 15 minutes. Remove the bowl from the steamer and let cool. Strain off and reserve any liquid that was in the steaming bowl.

MINCE AND STIR-FRY THE SEAFOOD-HAM MIXTURE (WOK #1): Mince the ham. Add the scallops to a food processor and pulse 6 or 7 times, until they resemble short, fine threads, then transfer to a bowl. Next, pulse the shrimp 7 or 8 times, until they resemble coarse breadcrumbs.

Place the liquid from steaming the scallops and ham in a medium bowl, then mix in the chicken stock and brown sugar. Set this seasoning mixture aside.

In a wok, deep pot, or Dutch oven, heat the oil to 225°F over medium-high heat. A piece of scallop added to the oil should bubble lightly without darkening.

(RECIPE CONTINUES)

Add the scallops and fry for 5 minutes, stirring periodically, until lightly golden. Next, stir in the shrimp and fry for 10 to 15 minutes, until the scallops and shrimp are both a deep golden color. (The shrimp will be slightly lighter in color than the scallops; the consistency of the scallops should be fried but soft, not crunchy.)

Next, add the ham to the wok and cook for an additional 3 minutes, until just crisped around the edges. Reduce the heat to medium-low to avoid burning the ham. The mixture will be foamy from the moisture in the seafood and ham; keep stirring to encourage this moisture to cook off. When the ham is a deep golden pink, add the chilies (if using) and cook for 1 minute.

Turn off the heat. Using a fine-mesh strainer, scoop out the seafood and ham mixture, letting the oil drain off so most of it is left behind in the wok. Transfer the seafood and ham mixture to a second wok or large skillet.

STIR-FRY THE SHALLOTS IN WOK #1: Heat the oil remaining in the first wok over medium-low heat. Add the shallots and let the oil slowly come back up to 225°F. Fry the shallots for 10 minutes, adjusting the heat as needed to maintain 225°F, until the shallots are slightly golden but not crispy.

SIMMER THE SEAFOOD-HAM MIXTURE IN WOK #2: Place the second wok or skillet containing the seafood and ham mixture over medium-high heat. Add the remaining 4 teaspoons Shaoxing wine, the reserved seasoning mixture, and the dark soy sauce. Stir to combine and bring to a simmer, letting the liquid cook off. It should be bubbling gently; reduce the heat if necessary.

SAUTÉ THE GARLIC IN WOK #1: Add the garlic to the shallots in the first wok and cook for 10 to 12 minutes, until the garlic is light golden and slightly crisped. (But also keep an eye on wok #2 and periodically stir the seafood/ham mixture.) As you cook the garlic, take care to not let it darken, or it will taste bitter. Reduce the heat if needed. The mixture will be very foamy again during this process. Stir to cook off the moisture. The shallots should end up a deeper golden color than the garlic.

COMBINE THE WOK MIXTURES IN WOK #1: When the liquid has cooked off in wok #2 and the shallot-garlic mixture is golden, carefully pour the seafood mixture into wok #1. Turn off the heat. Add the oyster sauce and chili flakes (if using). Stir to combine. Transfer the completed sauce to clean, sterile containers and let cool at room temperature before refrigerating. The sauce should last in the refrigerator for up to 3 months, or can be frozen in a freezer-safe airtight container for up to 6 months. Always use clean utensils when handling.

Desserts & Sweet Things

Chinese diners aren't known for having sweet tooths. As a kid, it didn't take long for me to notice this, when instead of a cookie or ice cream, most dinners ended with a freebie plate of orange wedges or cubed melon served with toothpicks. In spite of the occasional dessert disappointment, my sister and I did find plenty to look forward to. Visits to Chinatown brought enormous bakery boxes filled with all manner of sweet buns, and our time in Asia led to the discovery of new sweet treats, like Pineapple Cakes (page 289) and crispy Fried & Steamed Mantou with Condensed Milk (page 294). This chapter is an ode to those rare sweet endings to a big Chinese meal. I've also made good on a dream to reinvent the Chinese Bakery Cream & Fruit Cake (page 301)—a mainstay at any China-town birthday party—to blend our Chinese and American dessert sensibilities. **SARAH**

牛奶面包 niúnǎi miànbāo

Milk Bread

We're starting this chapter with the recipe we undoubtedly make most often: Chinese milk bread. This recipe makes two loaves or pull-apart buns in round cake pans, which are extra delicious with a cup of coffee in the morning or tea in the afternoon. You can also turn the dough into Red Bean Pineapple Buns (page 287), Mini Char Siu Bao (page 29), or even donuts (see page 293). While many Asian milk bread recipes call for a tangzhong (a paste of cooked flour and milk/water), we've found that we get better results with this much easier method. Make sure the ingredients are at room temperature before you start.

Makes 2 loaves or 16 buns

⅔ **cup heavy cream,** at room temperature

1 cup whole milk, at room temperature

1 large egg, at room temperature

⅓ **cup (70g) sugar**

4 cups (560g) all-purpose flour, plus more as needed

1 tablespoon (11g) active dry yeast or instant yeast

1½ teaspoons fine sea salt

Unsalted butter, at room temperature, for greasing the pans

Egg wash: 1 egg beaten with **1 tablespoon water**

Sugar water: 2 teaspoons sugar dissolved in **2 teaspoons hot water**

PREPARE THE DOUGH: In the bowl of a stand mixer fitted with the dough hook, add the ingredients in the following order: heavy cream, milk, egg, sugar, 4 cups flour, the yeast, and salt.

Turn the mixer on to the lowest setting to bring the dough together and continue to knead at low speed for 15 minutes, stopping the mixer to push the dough together if needed, until the dough is smooth and elastic. The dough should be somewhat tacky and stick to the bottom of the bowl. If it sticks to the sides, add flour 1 tablespoon at a time until the dough pulls away from the sides of the bowl. Otherwise, avoid adding additional flour. (If you don't have a stand mixer, stir all the dough ingredients together with a wooden spoon in a large bowl, and then knead in the bowl by hand for 20 minutes, until smooth and elastic.)

DO THE FIRST PROOF: Shape the dough into a ball and cover the bowl with an overturned plate or damp towel. Place the bowl a warm spot to proof until the dough has doubled in size, 1 to 2 hours, depending on the humidity and temperature in your kitchen. (Our trick is putting the dough in our closed microwave, with a large mug of hot boiled water next to it.)

SHAPE THE DOUGH: Knead the dough in the bowl for 5 minutes to punch out the air. Lightly grease two 9 by 5-inch loaf pans with butter (or two 9-inch round cake pans, if making buns).

Transfer the dough to a lightly floured surface and cut it into 6 equal pieces (about 180g each) for loaves or 16 equal pieces (65g to 70g each) for buns. For loaves, use a rolling pin to roll each piece into a 4 by 8-inch rectangle. With the short side of the rectangle facing you, roll the dough tightly into a 4-inch-long cigar. Place the cigar seam side down across the width of the pan. Roll out 2 more pieces of dough to fill the pan and repeat with the remaining pan and remaining 3 pieces of dough. If making buns, knead each piece into a round ball and arrange 8 balls, spaced evenly apart, in each cake pan.

DO THE SECOND PROOF: Cover the pans with a clean kitchen towel, and proof for 1 hour at room temperature.

BAKE: Position a rack in the middle of the oven, then preheat the oven to 350°F. Brush the risen dough with the egg wash. Bake for 22 to 24 minutes (same baking time, whether you used loaf pans or round pans), until golden brown.

COOL AND SERVE: After removing them from the oven, immediately brush the loaves or rolls with the sugar water. This will add shine and additional sweetness. Turn the loaves or buns out onto a wire rack to cool.

This bread is great warm, but you can store the loaves or buns in an airtight container at room temperature for 2 to 3 days, or in the refrigerator for 4 to 5 days.

IS YOUR YEAST ACTIVE?

This recipe does not require you to bloom the yeast before adding it to the other ingredients. However, if you are unsure about the freshness of your yeast, you can bloom it beforehand to make sure it's still active. Heat ⅓ cup of the 1 cup milk in the recipe to lukewarm. Measure out the ⅓ cup sugar called for in the recipe and add 2 teaspoons of it to the milk along with the yeast. Mix well and let stand at room temperature for about 10 minutes, until foamy. If the yeast doesn't foam, it is no good! If it does, simply add the foamy mixture to the bowl with the rest of the ingredients, including the remaining ⅔ cup milk and the rest of your ⅓ cup sugar.

红豆菠萝包 *hóngdòu bōluó bāo*

Red Bean Pineapple Buns

On every trip to Chinatown, we stop at a bakery and make a beeline for the plastic trays and tongs to pick out an assortment of buns to take home. Getting two or three of everything isn't out of the question if we're feeding a crowd (or feeling extra hungry). These buns are a mash-up of two favorites: the pineapple bun, which got its name from its distinctive cracked topping (there's actually no pineapple in it), and the red bean bun, filled with sweet red bean paste. We highly recommend making your red bean paste from scratch, as it is less sweet and has a better texture than store-bought.

Makes 16 buns

FOR THE RED BEAN PASTE

¾ cup (170g) dried adzuki beans (also known as red beans)

1½ cups water, plus more as needed

½ cup (100g) sugar

5 tablespoons (70g) salted butter

Neutral oil, for rolling the paste into balls

FOR THE BUN DOUGH

Milk Bread dough (page 284), ingredients mixed, ready for first proofing

FOR THE PINEAPPLE TOPPING

1 large egg yolk, at room temperature

½ cup (1 stick/115g) salted butter, at room temperature

¼ teaspoon vanilla extract

1 cup (120g) confectioners' sugar

1¼ cups (175g) all-purpose flour, plus more for kneading and shaping

¼ cup (30g) dry milk powder

¾ teaspoon baking soda

¼ teaspoon baking powder

Egg wash: 1 egg beaten with 1 tablespoon water

2 large egg yolks, lightly beaten

MAKE THE RED BEAN PASTE: In a medium bowl, cover the beans with at least 2 inches of water and soak overnight. Drain the beans in a colander and transfer to a medium (6- to 8-inch, 3- to 4-quart) pot, along with the 1½ cups water. The water should cover the beans by ¼ to ½ inch.

Bring the water to a boil, cover, and reduce the heat to medium-low. Simmer the beans gently for 40 to 60 minutes, until the beans smash easily when squished with a spoon, stirring occasionally and adding more water, ¼ cup at a time, if needed. (The cooking time and the amount of water needed may vary depending on the age and quality of the beans. Very old beans or beans that have been improperly stored may never soften, so check the sell-by date on the package.)

Uncover the pot and continue cooking the beans over low heat until the water has evaporated, stirring often. When all the liquid has cooked off and the beans have the texture of chunky mashed potatoes, turn off the heat. If you like perfectly smooth red bean paste, transfer the beans to a food processor and process until the mixture is totally smooth. If you like your paste a little chunky, just mash the beans with a potato masher until they reach your desired consistency.

Transfer the mashed beans to a large nonstick skillet set over medium-low heat. While stirring constantly with a rubber spatula, add the sugar in three batches, stirring until the sugar dissolves into the paste before adding the next batch. The color of the paste will darken and become shinier.

(RECIPE CONTINUES)

Add the butter in two batches, stirring the first batch until completely melted before adding the second. At this point, the bean paste should have the consistency of runny mashed potatoes. Increase the heat to medium and cook for an additional 20 minutes, until the paste is thick, a couple shades darker, and holds its shape. Stir continuously throughout the process, scraping the bottom and sides of the pot with a rubber spatula to prevent burning or crusting.

Transfer the bean paste to a bowl and let cool slightly. When the paste is warm but not hot, cover with an overturned plate and let cool for at least another hour. (Or put the paste in an airtight container just big enough to accommodate it and refrigerate for up to 3 days or freeze for up to 3 months.)

PROOF THE DOUGH: After following the instructions on page 284 to assemble the Milk Bread dough, proof for 1 to 2 hours, until it doubles in size.

PORTION OUT THE RED BEAN PASTE: Oil your hands lightly with neutral oil and separate the red bean paste into 16 roughly equal portions. (Alternatively, weigh the paste and divide that number by 16 to get precisely equal weights; each should weigh 25g to 30g.) Use your hands to roll each portion of paste into a smooth ball. Place the balls in a covered container and refrigerate until ready to assemble the buns.

FILL THE BUNS, THEN PROOF AGAIN: Line two baking sheets with parchment paper. With clean hands, knead the dough for 5 minutes to punch out the air. Transfer the dough to a lightly floured surface. Shape it into a ball, cut it into 4 pieces, and cut each piece into 4 pieces again to get 16 equal pieces of dough. (We use a digital scale to ensure each is the same weight, between 65g and 70g.) Cover the dough pieces with a clean kitchen towel to prevent drying.

Knead a piece of dough, shaping it into a smooth ball, then use a rolling pin to roll it into a circle about 4 inches in diameter, rolling the outer edges thinner than the middle. Place a ball of red bean paste in the center and fold the dough over the filling, pinching it closed. Place seam side down on the baking sheets, 8 buns per sheet. Repeat until all 16 buns are filled. Cover the buns with kitchen towels and proof for 1 hour.

MAKE THE TOPPING: In a medium bowl, use a rubber spatula to combine the egg yolk, butter, and vanilla. Stir in the confectioners' sugar. In another medium bowl, whisk together the flour, milk powder, baking soda, and baking powder. Fold these dry ingredients into the wet ingredients, then mix with your fingers just until the ingredients combine into a dough. Do not overmix, or the topping will be tough. Cover tightly and set aside at room temperature until your buns are finished proofing, or for at least 15 minutes. (If it's hot in your kitchen, chill the topping in the refrigerator for 15 minutes.)

TOP THE BUNS AND BAKE: Position a rack in the middle of the oven, then preheat the oven to 350°F. Brush the buns with the egg wash.

Divide the topping dough into 16 equal pieces (about 25g each) and roll each into a ball. On a very lightly floured surface, use a lightly floured rolling pin to roll out each ball into a 3½-inch circle. Slide a thin metal spatula under a circle and place it on the top of a bun, gently pressing it down. Repeat with remaining topping pieces and buns.

Working with one baking sheet of buns at a time, brush the topping on each bun with the beaten egg yolks. Bake in the center of the oven for 15 to 17 minutes, until the topping is cracked and golden. Repeat with the second tray, brushing the tops with the remaining beaten egg yolks before baking.

Enjoy these buns immediately, or cool and store in an airtight container at room temperature for up to 2 days (or refrigerate for up to 5 days). To reheat, microwave for 20 seconds.

凤梨酥 fènglí sū

Pineapple Cakes

These little golden cakes are a popular Taiwanese dessert—and unlike the aforementioned pineapple buns, these are actually made with pineapple! You may have seen the packaged version in Chinese grocery stores; more often than not, though, the filling is pineapple-flavored winter melon. Take our advice and make these yourself. They consist of pure, sweet pineapple filling baked in a tender, buttery crust. For the best results, weigh out the ingredients using a digital scale. If you don't want to buy the rectangular pineapple cake molds (which can be found online), use a standard or mini muffin pan. As it's fairly labor intensive, this recipe makes a large batch of 34 cakes. But the good news is, you can freeze them after baking to enjoy later! These are *so* good with tea.

Makes 34 cakes

FOR THE FILLING

6 cups (3 pounds, including any juice) finely diced fresh ripe pineapple (¼ inch or smaller, from 2 pineapples)

1½ tablespoons (20g) unsalted butter

⅓ to ½ cup (70g to 100g) granulated sugar

3 tablespoons (60g) maltose or 2 tablespoons (40g) honey

Neutral oil, for rolling the filling into balls

FOR THE CRUST

¾ cup (1½ sticks/170g) unsalted butter, at room temperature

6 tablespoons (50g) confectioners' sugar

3 large egg yolks

1½ cups (210g) cake flour, plus more for rolling

7 tablespoons (50g) dry milk powder

¼ cup (25g) almond flour

¼ teaspoon fine sea salt

PREPARE THE FILLING: Put the chopped pineapple, along with any juice, in a large (12-inch) nonstick pan over high heat. Cook for 20 to 25 minutes, until all the liquid has evaporated. Stir often with a rubber spatula to prevent sticking, burning, or crust formation along the edges of the pan.

Reduce the heat to medium, stir in the butter, and cook for 5 more minutes. Then add the granulated sugar in small batches until you reach your desired sweetness level. Cook for another 20 minutes to dry out the pineapple further, then add the maltose. Keep cooking and stirring for another 5 to 10 minutes (still over medium heat), until the pineapple develops a translucent appearance with an amber color and any remaining moisture has completely cooked off. The consistency should be dry enough for the filling to hold its shape as you fold it with the spatula. If the filling is too wet, the cakes will crack during baking. From start to finish, this process should take about 1 hour, and you'll end up with a little over 1½ cups of filling.

Transfer the filling to a heatproof container (with a lid, so you can chill the filling in the refrigerator) and let cool completely. Once cooled, cover and refrigerate for at least 8 hours or overnight (this can be done 1 to 2 days in advance).

MAKE THE CRUST: In the bowl of a stand mixer fitted with the paddle attachment (or in a large bowl with a hand mixer), beat the butter on low speed until fluffy. Gradually add the confectioners' sugar and continue beating until well combined. Then add the egg yolks one at a time, mixing until thoroughly incorporated with each addition and stopping the mixer to scrape down the sides and bottom of the bowl as needed.

In a medium bowl, whisk together the cake flour, milk powder, almond flour, and salt. Sift the flour mixture into the butter mixture, then use a rubber spatula to fold the dry ingredients into the wet ingredients.

(RECIPE CONTINUES)

With floured hands, gather and press all the loose pieces of dough together. It will feel very soft and pliable, like delicate pie dough. Do not overwork it. Cover with an overturned plate and refrigerate for 20 minutes to allow the dough to firm up.

DIVIDE THE FILLING AND CRUST DOUGH: Using a digital scale, divide the filling into 34 equal pieces (14g to 15g each). Lightly oil your hands with neutral oil, then roll the pieces into smooth balls. Place the balls on a plate and return them to the refrigerator to chill, uncovered.

With clean, dry hands, divide the dough into 34 equal pieces (about 16g each) and shape into balls. Place the dough balls on a plate, cover, and return them to the refrigerator to chill for at least 20 minutes more.

ASSEMBLE THE CAKES: Take out about 10 of the dough balls and 10 of the filling balls, leaving the remainder in the refrigerator to stay cold. (If the dough or filling gets too warm during assembly, chill it in the refrigerator for 15 to 20 minutes before continuing.)

Very lightly flour your work surface (too much flour may cause the delicate dough to crack) and a rolling pin (preferably a Chinese pin). Grab a bench scraper or thin spatula.

Roll out a ball of dough into a 2½-inch circle, applying light, even pressure to ensure that the dough is an even thickness. Slide the bench scraper beneath the circle to release it from the work surface. Holding the circle in your hand, place a ball of filling in the center and carefully close the edges of the dough around the filling, pinching it closed. (If the dough cracks during this process, don't worry. The dough is very pliable. Gently squeeze any cracks back together.) Roll the filled dough between your palms to form a smooth ball.

Place the ball in either a pineapple cake mold or a nonstick standard or mini muffin tin (no need to grease beforehand; if using the molds, you'll place them on an ungreased baking sheet). The combined weight of the dough and filling should be no more than about 32g, or it will overflow a standard pineapple cake mold during baking (each mold measures 2 by 1½ inches, with a ⅔-inch depth). Use either the flattening tool that comes with the pineapple cake molds or the flat end of your Chinese rolling pin to gently flatten the dough to fill the mold. You can lightly flour the flattening tool, if needed. Place the filled mold on the baking sheet (unless you're using a muffin pan) and repeat these steps until you've filled your first baking sheet or muffin pan. You can fit about 30 pineapple cake molds on a baking sheet spaced ½-inch apart, but our set only has 20 molds, so we bake these in two batches. You'll also make two batches if using a 24-cup mini muffin pan, or three batches if using a 12-cup standard muffin pan.

After assembling the first batch, return any remaining dough (covered) and filling (uncovered) to the refrigerator until you're ready to make the next batch.

BAKE AND SERVE: When you're about 20 minutes from completing the assembly of your first batch of cakes, position a rack in the middle of the oven, then preheat the oven to 300°F. Bake each batch of cakes for 17 to 20 minutes, until the tops are a very pale, even golden color. Watch them closely, as ovens vary and you don't want to accidentally burn the bottoms.

If the tops of the cakes have small cracks after baking, lightly press down on them with the bottom of a spoon while they're still hot; the crack will reseal as it cools. Let the cakes cool completely in the molds or pans, then gently push the cakes out of the molds or use a butter knife to ease them out. Repeat with subsequent batches.

The baked cakes will keep in an airtight container at room temperature for up to 2 days or can be stored in the refrigerator for up to 1 week. They can also be frozen in an airtight container for up to 2 months; simply thaw at room temperature before enjoying.

沙糖甜甜圈 shā táng tián tián quān

Chinese Sugar Donuts

KAITLIN / There are few items truly *unique* to a Chinese buffet, but the one thing you'd be hard-pressed to find outside this beautiful, Chinese American institution is the Chinese sugar donut. In our younger years, a visit to a Chinese buffet was a rare treat. Sarah and I would walk along the rows of warming trays heaped with lo mein and fried rice, filling our plates yet leaving *just enough* room for the little fried crab balls, french fries, and onion rings from what we liked to call the "deep-fried zone." At the end of that deep-fried rainbow were the *donuts*—tossed in sugar and glowing under the halo of a heat lamp. I could never resist grabbing one to round out the rest of my highly strategized dessert: a few squares of red Jell-O, a little metal bowl of chocolate pudding, and a plate of fruit because, duh, I care about my health. This recipe uses half a batch of our Milk Bread dough. You can either divide the ingredients by half or make the full recipe and bake a loaf of milk bread with the remaining half.

Makes about 20 donuts

½ batch Milk Bread dough (page 284), ingredients mixed, ready for first proofing

Neutral oil, for frying

½ to 1 cup white granulated sugar, for tossing the donuts

Proof the dough for 1 to 2 hours, until doubled in size. Punch the dough down and knead for 5 minutes, then transfer to a clean, unfloured surface.

Line a sheet pan with parchment paper. Shape the dough into a smooth ball and roll it out to a ½-inch thickness. Using a 2½-inch round biscuit cutter, stamp out the circles of dough as close together as possible to minimize scraps, repeating until there is no more dough left. (You can roll the final scraps into a ball to make one last rough donut.)

Set the dough circles on the sheet pan and use your index finger to make a dimple in the center of each circle to keep it from expanding too much during frying. Cover with a clean kitchen towel and let proof for 15 minutes.

While the donuts are proofing, fill a deep medium pot about halfway with the oil. Heat the oil to 300°F, and then reduce the heat to medium-low to maintain the temperature. Set a wire cooling rack on a sheet pan.

Carefully add a few donuts to the hot oil, frying in batches of 3 or 4 at a time. When each donut hits the oil, there should be only a small handful of bubbles around the edges. If it seems like the heat's too low, you're probably doing it right. The oil should stay between 285 and 300°F. You may need to reduce the heat to maintain the temperature; keep an eye on it.

Fry each batch of donuts for 10 to 12 minutes, flipping them halfway through, until they're a light golden brown. Use a slotted spoon to transfer the donuts to the rack on the sheet pan to drain and cool for 10 minutes. Continue frying the remaining donuts.

When the donuts have cooled for 10 minutes, place the sugar in a medium bowl and toss each donut in the sugar, one at a time, to coat. (The donuts will still be warm enough for the sugar to stick to them, but not so hot that the sugar starts to melt on contact.) Return the donuts to the wire rack. This works well if you sugar the first batch while a second batch is cooling and a third batch is frying.

Enjoy these donuts while they're still warm.

炸奶香馒头 zhà nǎi xiāng mántou
Fried & Steamed Mantou
with
Condensed Milk

Mantou are humble plain steamed buns made from wheat flour, usually eaten alongside savory dishes just like rice or noodles. In the case of this recipe, they easily transition from dinnertime to dessert when dipped in sweetened condensed milk. It's a favorite sweet treat in China for both its comfort factor and simplicity. The texture of mantou varies greatly, from dense and chewy to soft and fluffy. This recipe has a slightly higher hydration for pillowy, dessert-like mantou. We are presenting this recipe like most restaurants in China—half steamed and half fried. They must be steamed before frying (the steamed mantou can also be frozen, re-steamed, and then fried later). Feel free to also serve these mantou with other savory dishes in this book!

Makes 16 mantou

1 teaspoon active dry yeast

2 tablespoons (25g) sugar

Scant ¾ cup (170g) lukewarm water

2 cups (280g) all-purpose flour, plus more for rolling

1 teaspoon baking powder

¼ teaspoon fine sea salt

Neutral oil, for frying

¼ to ½ cup sweetened condensed milk

(RECIPE CONTINUES)

294

PREPARE THE DOUGH: Dissolve the yeast and 1 tablespoon of the sugar in the lukewarm water. Let sit for 15 minutes until foamy.

In the bowl of a stand mixer fitted with the dough hook (or a large bowl), add the flour, baking powder, the remaining tablespoon of sugar, and the salt. Stir on low speed (or by hand using a rubber spatula) to combine, and then gradually add the yeast mixture.

When the dough comes together, knead on low speed for 20 minutes, periodically stopping the mixer and pressing the dough together if needed (or knead by hand for the same amount of time). The dough should be smooth and elastic, and not sticky or tacky. If it is sticking to the bowl, mix in up to 2 tablespoons of additional flour a little at a time until the dough forms a smooth ball.

SHAPE THE MANTOU: Transfer the dough to a lightly floured surface. Knead by hand until smooth. Then, roll the dough into a 16-inch rope with even thickness.

Trim about 1 inch off each end of the rope. Divide the dough in half crosswise, divide each half in half again, and then divide each quarter into 4 equal pieces for a total of 16 pieces. If you need to, gently reshape the mantou so the cut corners don't stick out. The pieces should be smooth on the cut sides, with minimal air bubbles. Lastly, combine the two end pieces (that you trimmed off earlier) into a spare mantou.

PROOF THE MANTOU: Line two bamboo steamer racks with perforated parchment paper and place the dough pieces in the steamers about 1½ inches apart. (Alternatively, cut individual 2- by 3-inch parchment paper rectangles to place the buns on.) Cover and allow the buns to proof in a warm spot for 30 minutes.

STEAM THE MANTOU: Fill a wok with enough water to submerge the bottom rim of your bamboo steamer by ½ inch. Bring the water to a simmer over medium-high heat. Place the covered bamboo steamer racks in the wok, and steam for 8 minutes. Then turn off the heat and let the buns rest in the steamer with the lid on for another 5 minutes. Do not uncover the lid at any point during this steaming and resting process.

After 5 minutes, remove half the buns for frying and let them cool, uncovered, for 5 to 10 minutes at room temperature while you prepare the frying oil. (The other half of the mantou should be kept in the covered steamer to keep them from drying out.)

FRY THE MANTOU AND SERVE: Set a wire cooling rack over a sheet pan or line a plate with paper towels. Fill a small pot with 2 to 3 inches of the oil. Place the pot over medium-high heat and heat the oil until it reaches 350°F on an instant-read thermometer, then reduce the heat to medium to maintain the temperature.

Fry the mantou in batches of 2 to 3 at a time, for 5 to 7 minutes, until they're an even golden brown. Keep frying, letting the temperature gradually return to 350°F and turning the mantou often. If the mantou crust darkens quickly and becomes bubbly, the oil is too hot.

Transfer the fried mantou to the wire rack or plate to drain. Repeat with the remaining mantou.

Let the fried mantou cool slightly. Serve the mantou (steamed and fried) with the condensed milk for dipping, as desired, and enjoy!

八宝饭 bābǎofàn

Eight Treasures Sticky Rice

JUDY — This auspicious, traditional dessert of sweetened sticky rice filled with red bean paste and decorated with your choice of dried fruits and nuts is often served at Chinese New Year, weddings, and birthday parties. Be sure to select at least six kinds of "treasures" for the topping, since the sticky rice and red bean paste count for two. We've provided a list of toppings here—along with their associated symbolism—to help you nail a dessert jam-packed with joyful symbolic meanings. When I was growing up, we made bābǎofàn with lard, which gives the rice a glistening appearance. These days, I prefer using coconut oil. Not only is it readily available, it adds an another dimension of flavor to the rice and complements the fruit and nuts.

This is a sweet dessert served in small portions; the recipe yields enough for 3 standard Chinese rice bowls serving 2 to 3 people each, or 2 larger soup bowls (as shown on page 299) serving 3 to 4 people each. We like to make a couple small bowls to keep in the freezer—no special occasion necessary! Just steam to reheat, and you'll have a delicious dessert ready at a moment's notice.

Serves 6 to 8

2 cups uncooked short-grain glutinous rice (also called sweet rice or sticky rice)

1 cup water, plus more for soaking the rice

4 to 5 tablespoons (50g to 60g) sugar

2 tablespoons coconut oil, plus more for greasing the bowls and oiling your hands

6 types of fruits, nuts, and seeds, for decoration, (see suggestions)

1½ to 2 cups sweet red bean paste (store-bought or homemade; see page 287)

Decorative fruits, nuts, and seeds & their symbolic meanings:

- Lotus seeds: *harmony, fertility*
- Walnuts: *family unity and harmony*
- Peanuts (raw, unseasoned, shelled): *growth and fertility*
- Seeds (e.g., pumpkin, sunflower): *longevity and purity*
- Fresh longan ("dragon eye" fruit): *family unity and having many sons*
- Kumquats (fresh or candied): *prosperity*
- Dried Chinese red dates: *wealth and prosperity*
- Other dried fruits (such as raisins, apricots, prunes): *sweetness and success*
- Red colors (dried goji berries, jarred red cherries): *blessings and good fortune*
- Green colors (e.g., pumpkin seeds, green candied cherries): *longevity and purity*

SOAK AND COOK THE RICE: Add the glutinous rice to a large bowl and cover with 2 inches of water. Soak for at least 6 hours (ideally overnight), then drain.

Add the soaked rice to a shallow heatproof bowl, along with the 1 cup water. Place a 2-inch-tall metal steaming rack in the bottom of a wok (or any pot with a lid that will accommodate the bowl of rice and water) and add enough water to come up to about 1 inch below the rack.

Bring the water in the wok to a simmer over high heat, and place the bowl on the steamer rack. Cover and steam for 30 minutes.

Remove the rice from the steamer and use a rubber spatula to immediately mix in 4 tablespoons of the sugar and the 2 tablespoons coconut oil while the rice is still hot. Taste the rice and adjust the sweetness to your liking.

(RECIPE CONTINUES)

PREPARE YOUR SELECTED FRUIT AND NUTS: If using fresh, dried, or candied fruits, no preparation is needed. Lotus seeds or raw peanuts should be simmered in water over low heat for 10 to 15 minutes, until softened. Other nuts and seeds can be roasted in a 350°F oven for 5 to 7 minutes, until fragrant.

ASSEMBLE THE BOWLS: Choose three heatproof individual rice bowls or two larger soup bowls in which to assemble the desserts. Generously grease the bowls with coconut oil. At the bottom of each bowl, arrange your choice of dried fruits and nuts in whatever design or pattern appeals to you—be creative! Keep in mind that the items you place in the bottom of the bowl will be on the top of the final dessert, when the bowl is flipped over after steaming.

Grease your hands with a little bit of the coconut oil. Without disturbing your fruit and nut design, arrange the rice in the bowl, covering the fruit and nuts with a thin layer of the rice while leaving an indentation in the center where the red bean paste will go. Press the rice down firmly so there are no air pockets.

Add a large scoop of red bean paste to the center of the bowl (you can adjust the quantity to your liking). Then top the red bean paste with additional rice, so the rice reaches the rim of the bowl. Level out the top with your palms and press down with a rubber spatula to ensure the red bean paste is totally covered. Cover the bowl with an overturned plate until ready to steam.

STEAM THE EIGHT TREASURES: Set up your wok with a metal steaming rack as before. Bring the water to a simmer. You can either steam each bowl one at a time (cover the bowls to keep them warm while subsequent batches are steaming) or place multiple bowls on a heatproof pan or plate before placing on the rack to steam them all at once. Cover the wok and steam over medium heat for 15 minutes. Carefully remove the bowl(s) from the steamer using a clean dry towel or oven mitts. Place a flat serving dish on top of each bowl and flip the bowl upside down onto the dish. While the rice is still hot, use a kitchen towel or oven mitts to carefully lift the bowl up to reveal your design. Serve hot.

MAKE AHEAD
To make the Eight Treasures in advance and freeze, begin with freezer-safe bowls. Instead of brushing the bowls with the coconut oil, line them with plastic wrap or cheesecloth. When the bowls are assembled, cover the tops tightly with plastic wrap and freeze overnight. The next day, lift off the plastic wrap and use the liner wrap to lift the domes of sticky rice out of the bowls, then transfer to a reusable bag or container to store in the freezer for up to 3 months. To reheat, steam the rice already inverted on a heatproof serving dish for 25 to 30 minutes. There is no need to thaw the rice beforehand; brush the tops with a thin layer of coconut oil to give them a nice sheen right before serving.

水果奶油蛋糕 shuǐguǒ nǎiyóu dàngāo

Chinese Bakery Cream & Fruit Cake
Reinvented

SARAH Every Chinese American kid who's been to a birthday party in Chinatown knows the feeling. You get a glimpse of the colorful cake from the Chinese bakery down the street, covered in whipped cream, with red gel icing and syrup-lacquered fruit. But in your little kid heart, you feel no joy in seeing it. Because you know what awaits you is a particularly sponge-y, not-very-sweet cake when all you want is a grocery-store sheet cake with frosting flowers and balloons. With this recipe, I've fulfilled those childhood wishes. It blends the best of Chinese and American baking, hitting the familiar, nostalgic notes of airy whipped cream and fruit together with a moist, tender cake that has enough sweetness for little ones, and the lightness our elders crave.

Serves 12

FOR THE CAKE

3 tablespoons (45g) unsalted butter, at room temperature, plus more for greasing the pans

2½ cups (340g) cake flour, plus more for flouring the pans

1⅔ cups (330g) granulated sugar

⅓ cup (65g) vegetable oil

2 large eggs, at room temperature

2 large egg yolks, at room temperature

¼ cup (60g) sour cream, at room temperature

1 tablespoon vanilla extract

1 tablespoon baking powder

1 teaspoon fine sea salt

1¼ cups (300g) buttermilk, at room temperature

FOR THE WHIPPED CREAM

4 ounces (115g) cream cheese, at room temperature

¼ teaspoon vanilla extract

½ cup (60g) confectioners' sugar

2 cups (480g) heavy cream

FOR THE FRUIT AND GLAZE

8 ounces (225g) strawberries, washed, hulled, and thoroughly patted dry

3 ripe kiwifruit

1 cup canned sliced peaches, drained, or fresh ripe peaches, in season

2 tablespoons apricot jam

2 teaspoons water

MAKE THE CAKE LAYERS: Grease and flour three 9-inch round cake pans and line the bottoms with 9-inch parchment paper rounds. (Set the cake pan on a sheet of parchment, trace a circle around it with a pencil, then cut out the circle.) Position two racks in the upper and lower thirds of the oven, then preheat the oven to 350°F.

In the bowl of a stand mixer fitted with the paddle attachment (or in a large bowl with a hand mixer), combine the 3 tablespoons butter, granulated sugar, and oil. Cream the ingredients at medium speed for 1 minute.

Adjust the mixer to low, then add the eggs, one at a time, beating each until well incorporated. Add the egg yolks, also one at a time. Scrape down the sides and bottom of the bowl, then add the sour cream and vanilla. Beat until well combined, 2 to 3 minutes.

In a medium bowl, whisk together the 2½ cups of cake flour, the baking powder, and salt.

(RECIPE CONTINUES)

With the mixer on low speed, add the dry ingredients in three additions, alternating with the buttermilk, starting and ending with the dry mixture. With each addition, mix until just combined. Turn off the mixer and scrape down the sides of the bowl. Gently fold the batter with a rubber spatula until there are no more streaks of flour.

Divide the batter equally among the three baking pans. (For accuracy, weigh the batter for each pan using a digital kitchen scale, until they're all equal. We highly recommend this step to ensure even layers and an even bake across all of them.)

Gently tap the cake pans on the counter to surface any air bubbles. Bake for 15 to 18 minutes, until the edges of the layers are just beginning to brown and a toothpick inserted in the center of the cakes comes out clean. Let cool for 1 hour.

MAKE THE WHIPPED CREAM: In the bowl of a stand mixer fitted with the whisk attachment (or in a large bowl with a hand mixer), beat the very soft cream cheese and vanilla at medium-low speed until smooth, about 1 minute. Sift in the confectioners' sugar and beat on low speed until incorporated into the cream cheese. Scrape down the sides and bottom of the bowl and beat until very smooth.

Increase the speed to medium and gradually add 1 cup of the heavy cream in a slow stream. Turn off the mixer and scrape down the sides and bottom of the bowl. Turn the mixer back on at medium speed and slowly add the remaining cup cream. Continue whipping just until the cream transitions from soft peaks to firm peaks. Cover and refrigerate until ready to use.

Our Chinese cream and fruit birthday cakes over the years. Kaitlin and I preferred ice cream cakes back in the day, so sometimes we had the treat of two cakes: The Chinese bakery cake for the grandparents and an ice cream cake for us!

PREPARE THE FRUIT: Reserve 8 or 9 of your prettiest strawberries to decorate the top of the cake and slice the remaining berries from top to bottom, about ¼ inch thick. Peel and slice the kiwi into rounds about the same thickness as the strawberries. Dice the peaches into small cubes.

ASSEMBLE THE CAKE AND DECORATE: Place your first cake layer on a cake stand or flat plate. Using an offset spatula or butter knife, spread a very thin layer of whipped cream on the cake, just enough to be able to barely see the cake through it. Add a small circle of diced peaches in the middle and form a circle of kiwi slices around it. Then add the strawberries in a circle around the kiwi, leaving a ½-inch border around the edges of the cake. Spread another layer of whipped cream on top of the fruit, until mostly covered, making the surface as even as possible.

Stack the next cake layer and repeat with another thin layer of whipped cream, the fruit, and the cream layer to cover, evening it out again. Add the top cake layer and cover the entire cake with the remaining whipped cream. Decorate with the remaining strawberries, peaches, and kiwi.

Add the apricot jam to a small bowl along with the water. Heat in the microwave for 20 seconds. Stir the jam and strain, if desired, for a very smooth glaze. Brush the fruit on top of the cake with this glaze to give it extra shine.

Refrigerate the cake until ready to serve. This cake is best when eaten as fresh as possible. Enjoy within 2 days of assembling.

Building Out Your Chinese Pantry & Fridge

This is by no means an exhaustive list of Chinese ingredients, but if the item is used in this book, it's here! For a more comprehensive exploration of Chinese ingredients, or more detailed information on a particular item, scan the QR code to go to our Chinese Ingredients Glossary on the blog.

Sauces, Wines, Vinegars & Oils

HOISIN SAUCE (hǎixiān jiàng, 海鲜酱): A thick, dark condiment made with fermented yellow soybeans, sugar, garlic, and sesame, with a sweet, salty flavor. Choose a Chinese brand like Koon Chun or Lee Kum Kee.

CHEE HOU SAUCE (zhù hóu jiàng, 柱侯酱): A fermented soybean sauce similar to hoisin (less sweet, with a more complex fermented soybean flavor), used primarily in Cantonese braised dishes and roast meats.

GROUND BEAN SAUCE (mó shì jiàng, 磨豉酱): A fermented soybean paste, used in stewed dishes and Cantonese barbecue sauces. Not to be confused with sweet bean sauce (see next), which may also be called "sweet flour sauce," as it's (confusingly) made with fermented wheat flour rather than fermented soybeans.

SWEET BEAN SAUCE (tiánmiànjiàng, 甜面酱): Has a misleading name because its main ingredient is not fermented soybeans but, rather, fermented wheat flour. The result is a dark, sweet sauce that is nonetheless similar to a soybean paste or hoisin sauce.

SPICY BEAN SAUCE (là dòubàn jiàng, 辣豆瓣酱): A chunky paste made from fermented broad beans and chilies, used primarily in Sichuan cooking. You may also see it referred to as "spicy bean paste," "spicy broad bean paste," "broad bean chili sauce," or simply "doubanjiang." Look for "Pixian" on the label, a town in Sichuan famous for this paste.

YELLOW LANTERN CHILI SAUCE (huáng dēnglóng làjiāo jiàng, 黄灯笼辣椒酱): A very spicy, bright yellow chili sauce made with Hainan yellow lantern chilies, which have a heat level similar to habaneros.

Chinese Ingredients Glossary

CHILI GARLIC SAUCE (suàn róng làjiāo jiàng, 蒜蓉辣椒酱): A tangy, spicy condiment (and dim sum MVP) made with chilies, garlic, vinegar, and other seasonings. The most ubiquitous brand is Huy Fong.

FISH SAUCE (yú lù, 鱼露): Made by salting and fermenting anchovies or krill, and pressing out the mixture to get a salty, umami-laden sauce, featured mostly in Southeast Asian cooking (and occasionally, our cooking!).

CLEAR RICE WINE (mǐjiǔ, 米酒): Used less often than Shaoxing wine (see page 21) in our kitchen, with a purer flavor. Better for delicate steamed dishes and seafood.

RICE VINEGAR (mǐ cù, 米醋): Also known as rice wine vinegar, used to add acidity to sauces, stir-fries, dressings, and dipping sauces. If the label says "seasoned," it contains added sugar and salt. You may also see Shanghai rice vinegar, which is darker in color with a milder flavor.

CHINESE BLACK VINEGAR (zhènjiāng xiāngcù, 镇江香醋): Black in color with a full-bodied, complex flavor. Used in sauces and dressings, as a dipping sauce for dumplings, and in braised dishes. We use Chinkiang or Zhenjiang vinegar, which is widely available in Chinese groceries.

CHINESE RED VINEGAR (dà hóng zhè cù, 大红浙醋): Made from red yeast rice (which gets its color from a type of red mold used in fermentation), with half the acidity of regular white vinegar. Used primarily as a garnish for seafood soups, and in roasted and fried poultry dishes.

SESAME PASTE (zhīmajiàng, 芝麻酱): A richly flavored, thick paste made from toasted sesame seeds and used in sauces for dipping, noodles, hot pot, and more. Different from tahini, which is made with raw rather than toasted sesame seeds.

MALTOSE (mài yá táng, 麦芽糖): A natural sweetener produced from fermented grains with an extremely viscous, almost solid consistency. You can microwave it to soften it and make measuring easier. Used in Chinese desserts and for marinating/basting roast meats.

Spices & Seasonings

LUMP ROCK SUGAR AND BROWN ROCK SUGAR (bīngtáng, 冰糖): Lump rock sugar is made from refined crystallized sugarcane, ranging in color from pale gold to white, and comes in lumps of irregular size. Brown rock sugar still contains the molasses usually removed during the refining process and comes in more uniform wafer-like blocks. Both can be used interchangeably whenever rock sugar is called for.

SICHUAN PEPPERCORNS (huā jiāo, 花椒): An essential ingredient in Sichuan cooking, with a floral, citrus flavor and numbing effect on the tongue. Only the outer husk is used (the bitter black center is removed). Red Sichuan peppercorns are most common (if we call for them in this book, we mean red Sichuan peppercorns unless otherwise noted), though there is a green variety with stronger citrus-y notes and an even greater numbing effect. Can be used whole or ground into a powder (find it ground at Chinese groceries, or grind it yourself in a mortar and pestle or spice grinder).

SICHUAN CHILI FLAKES (làjiāo fěn, 辣椒粉): Used in chili oil, sauces, and a variety of Sichuan dishes. It can be made from several different types of red chili, with generally milder spice than regular red pepper flakes. Some are dry ground, and others are fried/roasted before grinding, with a higher moisture content.

DRIED RED CHILI PEPPERS (gàn làjiāo, 干辣椒): Vary in size, flavor, and heat level, including the popular medium-hot èr jīngtiáo (二荆条) and cháotiān jiāo (朝天椒) chilies from Sichuan and Guizhou provinces. Break the chilies open for added heat that comes from the loosened seeds, or use them whole for added fragrance with less heat.

STAR ANISE (bājiǎo, 八角): Resembling small wooden flowers, this spice has a powerful licorice flavor and is used as an aromatic in braised dishes, broths, and even stir-fries.

CHINESE CASSIA CINNAMON (guì pí, 桂皮): The most common type of cinnamon sold in both North America and East Asia, though in Chinese cooking it is usually used in its bark form as a spice for savory dishes.

BLACK CARDAMOM (cǎoguǒ, 草果): Also called tsaoko, it's a dried fruit pod with a wrinkled outer appearance, mild menthol flavor, and a smoky edge that comes from the drying process. Used to infuse oil for stir-fries, chili oils, and sauces, as well as in soups, broths, and braises.

WHITE CARDAMOM (bái dòu kòu, 白豆蔻): Creamy white seed pods that resemble small chickpeas with a mild floral aroma. Usually used as a layer of flavor in spice sachets for soups and braised meats.

SAND GINGER (shā jiāng, 沙姜): A close relative of galangal, sold as a powder for spice rubs and as whole dried pieces or slices for use in spice sachets for soup broths and braises.

GALANGAL (gāoliáng jiāng, 高良姜): Used most often in Southeast Asian cuisine, it resembles ginger root but has a much tougher, woodier texture, with a tart, spicy flavor. While we don't use it often in Chinese cooking, it's a reasonable substitute for sand ginger, particularly in powdered form.

CHINESE LICORICE ROOT (gāncǎo piàn, 甘草片): Usually sold as thin slices, with a pale yellow appearance and a complex flavor reminiscent of anise and fennel. Another aromatic ingredient for soups, broths, and braises.

DRIED MANDARIN ORANGE PEEL (chénpí, 陳皮): Harvested from sour oranges that are primarily grown for their peel and sun-dried to achieve a pungent and slightly bitter flavor that compliments beef, poultry, and fish. Should be dark in color and can actually improve with age.

FIVE-SPICE POWDER (wǔxiāng fěn, 五香粉): Most commonly a mix of Chinese cassia cinnamon, cloves, fennel, star anise, and Sichuan peppercorns. Gives many Cantonese roast meats their signature fragrance.

CURRY POWDER (gālí fěn, 咖喱粉): A spice mix including turmeric, coriander, chili, and cumin, it originated in India and was sold to the British as a ready-made ingredient that imitated the flavor of Indian curries. We use it in Hong Kong–style curry sauces. We prefer Madras curry powder, which is generally a spicier blend.

CHICKEN POWDER (jījīng, 鸡精): Dehydrated chicken stock similar to a bouillon cube, but in powdered form. Many brands contain MSG. While not used often in our kitchen, it can provide a shot of added flavor to a recipe.

MUSHROOM POWDER (mógū jīng, 蘑菇精): Comes in various grades from expensive dried porcini powders and organic shiitake mushroom powders to utilitarian bulk brands. Also called "umami powder," mushroom powder can add extra umami to any dish.

Dried, Salted, Cured & Fermented Things

DRIED SHIITAKE MUSHROOMS (gàn xiānggū, 干香菇): Also called black mushrooms, they come in varying sizes and levels of quality. Those with thick, closed caps and a cracked appearance (also called "flower mushrooms" or huā gū, 花菇) tend to be more expensive, but cheaper grades of black mushrooms can be easier to cook (they're less meaty, which also means they can be less rubbery in texture). Both will work in most applications. To reconstitute, soak overnight in room-temperature water or for about 2 hours in hot water (total time depends on size). To keep them submerged, you can weight them down with a small bowl or plate. Many recipes call for the reserved soaking liquid, which is full of flavor; just avoid any sediment that may have collected at the bottom of the liquid.

DRIED WOOD EAR MUSHROOMS (mù'ěr, 木耳): Also called black fungus, they're usually sold dried in loose form or tightly packed into small bricks. They rehydrate quickly in warm water, usually in under an hour. Some have thick woody ends that may need to be trimmed; also rinse off any dirt or grit before using.

DRIED LILY FLOWERS (jīnzhēn, 金针): The dried, unopened flowers of the daylily plant have an earthy, vaguely tart flavor. Also called lily buds, they're often used in steamed dishes, soups, and some stir-fries. Soak to reconstitute and trim any woody ends before using.

DRIED CHINESE RED DATES (hóng zǎo, 红枣): Also called dried jujubes, they're wrinkly, oblong dried fruits about the size of a large olive or kumquat. Used for decoration, sweetness, and flavor in desserts, soups, and beverages.

DRIED GOJI BERRIES (gǒuqǐ, 枸杞): Also called wolfberries and used mostly in soups and drinks. They look like small, narrow, bright red raisins.

CHINESE DRIED FIGS (wúhuāguǒ gān, 无花果干): Small dried white figs that are pale in color and less sweet than the dried figs you may eat as a snack or use in desserts. Used primarily in soups and herbal tonics in Chinese cuisine.

DRIED LOTUS SEEDS (liánzǐ, 莲子): Harvested from the large seed heads of the lotus plant (the same plant that produces lotus roots). Look for skinless lotus seed halves, which have an off-white appearance and already have the bitter green center of the seed removed. Used to make lotus seed paste as a filling for buns and pastries, as well as soups and other desserts.

SPLIT MUNG BEANS (lǜdòu rén, 绿豆仁): Green mung beans with the outer husk removed and split in half. They're a light yellow color, with a creamy texture after cooking.

DRIED ADZUKI BEANS (hóngdòu, 红豆): Also simply called "red beans," these small brick-red beans are usually cooked and sweetened to make sweet soups, desserts, or a paste-like filling for pastries, steamed buns, and breads.

DRIED ZONGZI LEAVES (zòng yè, 粽叶): Long, dark green dried reed or bamboo leaves (4 to 5 inches wide) used to wrap zongzi (sticky rice dumplings made with

various sweet or savory fillings; see page 53). Must be soaked overnight before using.

DRIED LOTUS LEAVES (hé yè, 荷叶): The very large round leaves of the lotus plant, used to wrap sticky rice and other steamed dishes to add fragrance and keep the food inside moist.

DRIED KELP (hǎidài, 海带): Known as kombu in Japanese cooking, a thick, meaty seaweed that comes both shredded and in large pieces. It adds savory flavor to soups and stocks and can also be marinated and eaten as a cold tossed salad.

DRIED LAVER/SEAWEED (zǐcài, 紫菜): A more tender, mild-flavored dried seaweed usually sold in round cakes and used mostly in soups.

DRIED BOK CHOY (báicài gān, 白菜干): Dehydrated bok choy stems and leaves used primarily in Cantonese soups. Must be soaked and thoroughly cleaned before use.

DRIED SHRIMP (xiāmi, 虾米): The most common and widely used type of dried seafood in Chinese cooking. Look for relatively meaty dried shrimps with a pink-orange color. We also sometimes use very tiny, feathery shrimp called xiāpí (虾皮), which look more like thin flakes and are used in fillings, stir-fries, and soups.

DRIED SCALLOPS (gānbèi, 干贝): Sometimes called conpoy (Cantonese phonetic), these vary in size and quality. Larger scallops are more flavorful and expensive. They add an intense seafood umami to fried rice, sauces, soups, congee, stir-fries, and stews.

FERMENTED BLACK BEANS (dòu chǐ, 豆豉): Black soybeans that are fermented with salt to create a slightly soft, dry texture and an incredibly savory flavor. Used in sauces, stir-fries, and steamed dishes across various regional cuisines, including Cantonese, Sichuan, and Hunan cooking.

FERMENTED BEAN CURD (fǔrǔ, 腐乳): A type of preserved tofu made with salt and rice wine. There is a plain white version often added to stir-fried greens and a red version (hóngfǔrǔ, 紅腐乳) made with red yeast rice that is commonly used in meat marinades and braises.

SALTED DUCK EGG YOLKS (xián yādàn, 咸鸭蛋): Made by curing duck eggs in salt, these yolks have a deep orange, jewel-like appearance and can be purchased in vacuum-sealed packages.

CHINESE CURED PORK SAUSAGE (làcháng, 腊肠): The type we use most often comes from southern China (known as lap cheong in Cantonese). They are reddish preserved sweet pork sausages seasoned with sugar and wine, and used in a variety of stir-fries, rice dishes, steamed dishes, and buns.

CHINESE CURED DUCK LIVER SAUSAGE (gāncháng, 肝肠): Gon cheong in Cantonese, these are similar in flavor to Chinese cured pork sausages, but traditionally made with duck liver in addition to pork and pork fat. They're darker in color, with a slightly softer texture and richer flavor.

How to Make Chinese Cured Pork Belly

CHINESE CURED PORK BELLY (làròu, 腊肉): A Cantonese-style cured pork belly (lap yuk in Cantonese) often served steamed over rice or in stir-fries. This can be hard to find but is easier than you would think to make at home.

CHINESE CURED HAM (huǒtuǐ, 火腿): There are many types of ham from several notable regions in China, including Yunnan, Hunan, and Zhejiang. We like Jinhua ham from an area south of Shanghai, but Chinese cured ham can be substituted with any dry cured ham, like Serrano or the dry-cured country hams from the American South.

DRIED PRESERVED RADISH (luóbo gān, 萝卜干): Salted, preserved, and dried daikon radish, with a crunchy texture and very salty flavor. Look for whole preserved radish pieces or packets of chopped radish that have a dry appearance and light golden brown color. Not to be confused with preserved mustard stems (zhàcài, 榨菜), which can sometimes be mislabeled "preserved radish."

DRIED PRESERVED MUSTARD GREENS (méigān cài, 梅干菜): Fermented and dried vegetables (generally a mix of various mustard greens and cabbages, sometimes with added dried bamboo shoots) with a dark brown appearance, originating in Guangdong's Hakka cuisine (though it's also used in other regional Chinese cooking, such as that of Zhejiang Province). Used in steamed dishes and braises. Must be soaked before use.

PICKLED MUSTARD GREENS (xuě cài, 雪菜): Sometimes labeled "pickled potherb mustard," these are mustard greens that have been sun-dried, salted, and fermented. You'll find them in vacuum-sealed packages or cans.

SUI MI YA CAI/SICHUAN PRESERVED VEGETABLE (suì mǐ yá cài, 碎米芽菜): A salty, lightly sweet chopped pickled mustard green stem from Yibin in southeastern Sichuan Province. Usually sold in small 3.5 oz./ 100g vacuum-sealed packets and used for noodles, fried rice, and stir-fries.

Fresh Vegetables, Herbs & Fungi

BOK CHOY (bái cài, 白菜): Comes in several varieties, including Shanghai bok choy (small bulbous bunches with smooth light green stems and tender rounded leaves), dwarf bok choy (similar small size, white stems, curly dark green leaves), and large bok choy (large, thick white stems and dark green leaves). You can also find medium bok choy that are somewhere between the small and large varieties.

CHINESE BROCCOLI (jiè lán, 芥兰): A leafy green vegetable with dark blue-green leaves, thick, firm stalks similar to broccoli or asparagus, and sometimes small flower buds. Can be blanched or stir-fried and comes in both large and baby varieties.

CHOY SUM/YU CHOY (cài xīn, 菜心 or yóu cài, 油菜): Tender, long, light green stalks and large, rounded dark green leaves. Can buy larger varieties as well as more tender, young greens. Mild sweet flavor, great for stir-frying or blanching.

WATER SPINACH (kōng xīn cài, 空心菜): Also known as ong choy in Cantonese or kangkung in parts of Southeast Asia, this is a long leafy green with hollow stems that grows in water or damp soil. Comes in two varieties: green stem (narrow, vibrantly green leaves, thin stems) and white stem (wider hollow stems, lighter green color, arrow-shaped leaves). Use soon after buying, as they don't last long in the fridge.

PEA TIPS (dòu miáo, 豆苗): Also called pea leaves or pea shoots, these are the tender young leaves and stems picked from the ends of a snow pea plant. They have a sweet, grassy flavor.

NAPA CABBAGE (dà báicài, 大白菜): A large, heavy oblong cabbage with creamy white stems and pale green, curly leaves. An incredibly versatile vegetable for soups, stir-fries, fillings, braises, steamed dishes, or pickles.

TAIWANESE FLAT CABBAGE (táiwān yuánbáicài, 台湾圆白菜): Looks similar to a green cabbage, but flatter and more oblong in shape, with looser leaves that are crispier, milder tasting, and less tough than regular green cabbage.

CHINESE CELERY (qíncài, 芹菜): Also known as leaf celery, Chinese celery has longer, thinner stalks, with a stronger celery flavor than regular celery and a more fibrous texture.

CHINESE CHIVES (jiǔcài, 韭菜): Also called garlic chives, these are flatter and wider than standard chives, with a strong garlicky (rather than oniony) flavor. Often paired with scrambled eggs and used in dumpling fillings, these chives are used as a vegetable rather than an herb or garnish. You can also buy garlic chive stems (jiǔcài tái, 韭菜苔), which are the meatier flowering stems of the garlic chive plant (rather than the flat leaves) with unopened flower buds at the top. The white flowers are very fragrant and also edible.

YELLOW CHINESE CHIVES (jiǔhuáng, 韭黄): Garlic chives that have been grown without light, resulting in a pale yellow color. They are generally more tender than the dark green chives, with a more subtle flavor.

THAI BASIL (tàiguó luólè, 泰国罗勒): A fragrant basil native to Southeast Asia, with pointed deep green leaves, purple stems, and flavor notes of anise and cinnamon.

THAI BIRD'S-EYE CHILI (tàiguó xiǎo làjiāo, 泰国小辣椒): A small chili used extensively in Southeast Asian cuisine, with a heat level just under a habanero. Comes in colors ranging from yellowish green to red.

LONG HOT PEPPERS (niújiǎo jiāo, 牛角椒): In China, long, thin-skinned, spicy (usually green, but sometimes red) peppers are common in stir-fries. Here in the United States, the most accessible equivalent is the Italian long hot pepper, also confusingly known as Italian long sweet pepper. These are a bit of a mixed bag—some can taste quite mild, but others can pack quite the punch! These can be found in many Chinese grocery stores, as well as some supermarkets. Can be substituted with Anaheim or even cubanelle peppers if you prefer a milder flavor.

BAMBOO SHOOTS (sǔn, 笋): The tender shoots of the bamboo plant. Fresh shoots must be boiled before using, though they are most commonly purchased in cans, vacuum-sealed packages, or frozen. There are two main types: spring bamboo (春笋, chūnsǔn), which are slender and segmented, and winter bamboo (冬笋, dōngsǔn), which are thick, meaty, and stubby. Sliced or julienned canned bamboo shoots are made from winter shoots.

BEAN SPROUTS (dòuyá, 豆芽): There are two types of bean sprouts: mung bean sprouts (绿豆芽, lǜ dòuyá) and soybean sprouts (黄豆芽, huáng dòuyá). Both are bright white and crunchy, with a yellow head (the bean) and tail. Soybean sprouts have a more fibrous, large bean at the top. We use soybean sprouts in cold appetizer dishes or as a fresh counterpoint for spicy dishes.

EDAMAME (máodòu, 毛豆): Green immature soybeans, often sold frozen either shelled or still in the pod. We usually buy shelled, frozen edamame.

CHINESE AND JAPANESE EGGPLANT (qiézi, 茄子): These long and narrow eggplants have fewer seeds and are more tender than standard globe eggplants. Choose between the lighter purple Chinese variety or the darker, almost black-skinned Japanese type.

DAIKON RADISH (luóbo, 萝卜): Long white radish used in pickles, stir-fries, braises, and soups. Look for heavy, firm radishes that are 9 to 12 inches long with bright white skin. If the radish still has its fresh green stem attached, it's very fresh. Similar to daikon is the Korean radish, which is fatter and stubbier, with a faded light green color close to the stem. These can be milder and sweeter than daikon.

LOTUS ROOT (lián'ǒu, 莲藕): The crunchy, fibrous rhizome of the lotus plant, which grows in the mud of the ponds where these plants live. They have hollow tubes running through the middle, making them look like pinwheels after slicing. Trim the ends and peel the outer skin before slicing or chopping. They can be steamed, stir-fried, added to soups, braised, or deep-fried.

TARO (yùtou, 芋头): A starchy vegetable with brown, hairy skin ranging in size from small potato-size specimens to large football-size ones. We use the starchier large taro more often than the small taro, which can have an almost slimy, waxy texture after cooking.

WATER CHESTNUTS (bíjì, 荸荠 or mǎtí, 马蹄): Usually available canned, water chestnuts come from an aquatic grasslike plant. They are crunchy, starchy, and often added to dumpling fillings and stir-fries, particularly in Chinese American takeout dishes.

SHIITAKE MUSHROOMS (xiānggū, 香菇): Also called black mushrooms, they add meaty umami to any dish. Look for fresh mushrooms with meaty closed caps, which are generally higher quality and more flavorful than those with thin open caps.

OYSTER MUSHROOMS (píng gū, 平菇): Distinct from king oyster mushrooms, these mushrooms have white gills and brown/gray fan-like caps, with a vaguely seafood-y umami flavor.

KING OYSTER MUSHROOMS (xìng bào gū, 杏鲍菇): Sometimes called king trumpet mushrooms, these meaty, cylindrical mushrooms consist of a thick white stem and a small light brown cap.

ENOKI MUSHROOMS (jīnzhēngū, 金针菇): Long, thin needle-like mushrooms with very small caps and a crunchy texture. Commercially grown varieties are off-white owing to limited light exposure. These mushrooms are used in a variety of stir-fries, soups, fillings, and cold appetizers. Closely related to enoki mushrooms are those labeled, "seafood mushrooms," which also come in clusters, have thicker stems and caps, and do actually have a subtle shellfish flavor.

Tofu, Bean Curd & Wheat Gluten/Seitan

FIRM TOFU (lǎo dòufu, 老豆腐): One of the most versatile, common types of tofu available, made from coagulated soy milk and pressed to remove moisture until firm. You can find even more specific types, such as medium firm and extra firm, but we usually buy those labeled simply "firm tofu."

SOFT AND SILKEN TOFU (nèn dòufu, 嫩豆腐): Has a higher moisture content, making it more delicate, with a smooth custard-like texture. Some say that "soft" tofu is the Chinese equivalent of Japanese "silken" tofu. We've found that tofu products labeled "soft" are less delicate than silken, but they can be used interchangeably in most cases.

PRESSED TOFU (dòufu gān, 豆腐干): A very firm, dry type of tofu with a dark brown outside and off-white inside. Comes in ½- to ¾-inch-thick squares or rectangles, with plain or five-spice varieties that can be used interchangeably.

DRIED BEAN CURD STICKS (fǔzhú, 腐竹): Also called dried bean threads, Japanese yuba, or foo jook in Cantonese. Made from the skin that forms on top of cooked soy milk. The film is lifted off the soy milk, rolled into tubes, and dried. They must be soaked before use, and have a chewy, slippery texture after soaking.

TOFU SKIN (dòu pí, 豆皮): This term can be used to describe two products: flat sheets of bean curd skin made from the skin that forms on top of cooked soy milk (use these for Crossing the Bridge Noodles on page 116), similar to dried bean curd sticks (see previous), or thicker sheets of compressed tofu, often with a finely dotted texture, used in stir-fries and soups, or tied into thick knots for braises. Both can be cut into thin strips or stuffed with fillings.

WHEAT GLUTEN (miànjīn, 面筋): Made from a process in which wheat flour is "washed" to remove starch and to isolate the gluten in the flour. Sold fresh, frozen, or dried and also known as seitan. Some gluten products are deep-fried before they're packaged.

Rice, Noodles, Grains, Flours & Starches

JASMINE RICE (tàiguó xiāngmǐ, 泰国香米): Originating in Southeast Asia, with tender grains that remain distinct and intact when cooked properly and have a fragrant scent (reminiscent of popcorn) when cooking. Our choice for an everyday long-grain white rice. Look for premium brands from Thailand.

GLUTINOUS RICE (nuòmǐ, 糯米): Also known as sweet rice or sticky rice, with opaque grains. Although there are short and long-grain varieties, short-grain glutinous rice is more common in Chinese cooking. Should be soaked for at least 6 hours before steaming.

WHEAT NOODLES (miàntiáo, 面条): Basic noodles made from wheat flour and water. Can be sold fresh or dried, in varying thicknesses and shapes for noodle soups, stir-fries, and tossed noodle dishes.

LO MEIN NOODLES (lāo miàn, 捞面 or yóu miàn, 油面): There are generally two types of lo mein yóu noodles: cooked and uncooked. The cooked versions are usually called yóu miàn, or "oil noodles," and only need to be rinsed in warm water to loosen them before cooking. Uncooked lo mein noodles, however, need to be boiled in water and then rinsed of excess starch before cooking.

HONG KONG–STYLE EGG NOODLES FOR PAN-FRYING (gǎng shì chǎomiàn, 港式炒面): Sold fresh or dried, these thin, yellow egg noodles are sometimes labeled "pan-fried noodles." They're first boiled and then pan-fried until crispy and golden brown. They can then be stir-fried or topped with saucy stir-fries of meat and vegetables. Don't confuse them with wonton noodles, which also often say "Hong Kong" on the label but are a darker yellow color and used in soup.

RICE VERMICELLI (mǐfěn, 米粉): Sometimes labeled "rice stick," "mai fun," or "mei fun," they are very thin dried white rice noodles that are great in either soups or stir-fries, like our Homestyle Mushroom Mei Fun (page 119). Must be soaked before stir-frying.

WIDE RICE NOODLES (hé fěn, 河粉): These can be purchased either fresh or dried. The fresh noodles are sold in sheets that have been steamed, oiled, and folded. The dried noodles are easier to find and must be boiled or soaked before adding to soups or stir-fries (prep instructions on the package can sometimes be inaccurate, so check them while cooking to cook them just until al dente).

MIXIAN (mǐxiàn, 米线): Rice noodles that have a thickness more like spaghetti, popular in Yunnan Province. While you probably won't be able to find noodles specifically from Yunnan, Vietnamese brands make similar noodles for Bun Bo Hue (a spicy Vietnamese noodle soup). We've generally found that dried mixian has the best texture, though you can also get fresh mixian in the refrigerated section of some large Chinese markets.

RICE CAKES (niángāo, 年糕): Almost like a Chinese version of gnocchi but made with rice. They have a chewy texture, like a thick noodle, and come in either small flat oval shapes or small logs. The logs are more common in Korean cooking. We use the ovals in soups and stir-fries.

MUNG BEAN GLASS NOODLES (fěnsī, 粉丝): These translucent, very thin vermicelli noodles usually come in small 1.75 ounce/50g bundles and can be used in soups and some stir-fries. They're very absorbent when cooked and can quickly soak up sauces or soups.

WONTON WRAPPERS (húntún pí, 馄饨皮): These square wrappers can be found in the refrigerated section of most grocery stores. The white wrappers are more common (we like those labeled "Shanghai Style"), while the yellow ones (sometimes labeled "Hong Kong Style") can be very thin and used to make some Cantonese-style wontons. If purchasing them in a non-Chinese grocery store, you may not have the benefit of choice. Anything you can find will work in a pinch, but avoid the thin Hong Kong–style wrappers for wontons that are destined for the fryer or to be tossed in sauce, as they are too delicate.

DUMPLING WRAPPERS (jiǎozi pí, 饺子皮): These are round wrappers. We like white Shanghai-style dumpling wrappers of moderate thickness for most dumplings. For recipes like siu mai, we use the thinner yellow dumpling wrappers, sometimes labeled "Hong Kong Style."

SPRING ROLL WRAPPERS (chūnjuǎn pí, 春卷皮): Find these delicate, thin square wrappers in the refrigerated or frozen section of the Chinese grocery store, sometimes labeled "Spring Roll Pastry." Don't confuse them with Vietnamese rice paper wrappers, which are translucent circular wrappers that are sold dried.

RICE FLOUR (zhān mǐfěn, 粘米粉): Made from grinding long-grain rice into a very fine powder. Not to be confused with glutinous rice flour.

GLUTINOUS RICE FLOUR (nuòmǐ fěn, 糯米粉): Flour milled from glutinous (sticky) rice to make various desserts, pastries, and dim sum dishes.

WHEAT STARCH (chéng fěn, 澄粉): The pure starch extracted from wheat flour, with the gluten removed. Most commonly used as a binding agent and in conjunction with other types of starch to make translucent dumpling wrappers.

TAPIOCA STARCH (líng fěn, 菱粉): A starch made from tapioca root. Can be used as a thickening agent, or in things like dumpling wrappers or noodles.

POTATO STARCH (tǔdòu diànfěn, 土豆淀粉): Another root starch made from potatoes. Particularly useful in making crispy coatings for fried foods.

Acknowledgments

We still can't believe we had the opportunity to write this cookbook together. It is the result of much love, sweat, tears, and care—the unspoken ingredients in every recipe from *The Woks of Life*. Thumbing through old photo albums, revisiting childhood stories, and pouring so many hours into this book has reminded us that we couldn't have done this without each other.

We are so grateful to our blog readers, many of whom have been cooking with our family for almost a decade. Your encouraging comments have made us laugh, cry, and push ourselves to continue to improve what we do. Thank you for sharing our passion and joining us on this culinary journey to preserve family food traditions. You keep us going.

A special thanks goes out to the readers, close friends, and family members who generously volunteered their time (and ingredients!) to test recipes to make this book the best it could be: Gretchen Brown, Ken Casebier, Alex Ciepley, Justin Cohen, Dennis Ferrer, Janis Frey, Taylor Horton, Daniel Lawless, Kate Lee, Wenqi Li, Laura Liao, Deborah Martinez, Laura McCarthy, Jane Ng, Kat Ng, Sandy Ng, Judy Orpin-Geringer, Thomas Ruan, Jessica Safirstein, Dominick Sciusco, Jocelyn Siegel, David Sweedler, Elena Tackett, Lisa Tom, Helen Wang, Carol Yang, Ed Yau, and Leor Yoffe.

We also want to thank our agent, Judy Linden, for being in our corner with pep talks always at the ready, and Alison Fargis, for offering us support in the home stretch. Thanks to our editor, Raquel Pelzel, for believing in our vision to make a cookbook that is part family album, and Jen Wang, for taking on the difficult task of designing a book that feels both modern and nostalgic—and making everything look amazing. Thanks to Aaron Wehner, Francis Lam, and to the rest of the Potter team for all the hard work it takes to transform our words and pictures into something tangible and beautiful. Christine Han and Alex Medina—thank you for the photos of our family, which we will always treasure, and for three fun days of cooking, eating, and traipsing around New York City's Chinatown in search of roast meats and tofu pudding. Heidi Zhang, we appreciate you being another set of eyes for all the translations throughout the book, as well as your meticulous attention to detail!

To mama and yeye and popo and gonggong, and all the generations that came before us, we thank you for keeping recipes and traditions alive in us. For those who have passed on, we know that there would have been so much more they could teach us.

We're immensely grateful to our friends and family for sharing memories, digging through old photos, regularly asking us how the book is going, and keeping us sane through it all. Justin, our newest fifth family member, thank you for helping shoulder the caloric load of blogging days, trying recipes and helping us do better, and washing mountains of dishes.

And finally, thank you dear reader, for picking up this book and inviting us into your kitchen.

Index

Published in the United States by Clarkson
Potter/Publishers, an imprint of Random
House, a division of Penguin Random
House LLC, New York.
ClarksonPotter.com
RandomHouseBooks.com

CLARKSON POTTER is a trademark and
POTTER with colophon is a registered
trademark of Penguin Random House LLC.

Library of Congress
Cataloging-in-Publication Data
is available upon request.

ISBN: 978-0-593-23389-4
Ebook ISBN: 978-0-593-23390-0

Printed in Malaysia

10 9 8 7 6 5 4 3 2 1

Photographers: Sarah Leung (food),
Christine Han (lifestyle)
Photography Assistants:
Kaitlin Leung, Alexis Medina

Recipe Developers: Bill Leung, Judy Leung,
Sarah Leung, and Kaitlin Leung
Food Stylists: Judy Leung and
Kaitlin Leung

Editor: Raquel Pelzel
Editorial Assistant: Bianca Cruz

Designer: Jen Wang
Production Editor: Terry Deal
Production Manager: Kelli Tokos
Compositor: Merri Ann Morrell and Dix
Copy Editor: Carole Berglie
Indexer: Elizabeth Parson

Marketer: Stephanie Davis
Publicists: Kristin Casemore
and Leilani Zee